DATE DUE			
Oct 29 '82			

Simulation:
Principles and Methods

WINTHROP COMPUTER SYSTEMS SERIES

Gerald M. Weinberg, *editor*

WAYNE T. GRAYBEAL

United States Air Force Academy

UDO W. POOCH

Texas A&M University

Simulation:
Principles and Methods

LITTLE, BROWN AND COMPANY
Boston   Toronto

Library of Congress Cataloging in Publication Data

Graybeal, Wayne T
  Simulation, principles and methods.

  Includes bibliographies and index.
  1. Digital computer simulation.   I. Pooch, U. W.,
joint author.   II. Title.
T57.62.G7   001.4′24′02854   79-19479
ISBN 0–316–325813

Library of Congress Catalog Card No. 79–19479

ISBN 0–316–325813

9 8 7 6 5 4 3

BP
Published simultaneously in Canada
by Little, Brown & Company (Canada) Limited

Printed in the United States of America

To Dennis Goehring—
and Dennis knows why

U.W.P.

Contents

5 *Introduction to queueing theory*   99

6 *Discrete system simulation*   127

Contents

ILLUSTRATIONS AND TABLES

ILLUSTRATIONS AND TABLES

Foreword

Of the thousands of ways computers have been misused, *simulation* tops the list. The reasons for this widespread abuse are not hard to find:

1. Every simulation simulates *something*, but there's no particular reason it should simulate what the simulator had in mind.

2. Computer outputs are readily mistaken for gospel, especially by people who are working in the dark and seeking any sort of beacon.

3. Simulation languages have succeeded in making it easier to achieve impressive simulations, without making it easier to achieve valid simulations.

4. There are no established curricula based on extensive practical experience. Thus, everyone is an "expert" after writing one simulation, of anything, in any language, with any sort of result.

5. The promise of simulation is so great that it's easy to confuse hope with achievement.

Underlying all these reasons is lack of knowledge. Can a single book hope to remedy this kind of deficiency all by itself? Unfortunately, the answer is, and always will be, "no." The problem is too big, and books by themselves never do anything. *People* do things — sometimes with the help of good books — but books themselves are entirely passive, no matter how good they might be.

Simulation: Principles and Methods is a highly worthwhile book. Properly used, it can make a contribution to the restoration of confidence in simulation as a tool of systems thinking. That's why we've included it in our Computer Systems Series. Having put it in the Series, however, I feel obligated to say something about what I mean by "properly used."

One of the great advantages that Graybeal and Pooch have over many other authors of simulation books is their *objectivity*. Up until now, most of the important simulation books have been written by advocates of some particular language or approach. Such books are as much political as educational — as is quite appropriate for a subject in its infancy. But we've now matured past the point where we simulate in language X or use method Y merely because we don't know anything about language A or method B. In Graybeal and Pooch, the student of simulation can obtain a balanced picture of what options are available to solve problems, rather than a treatise on "why my method is the best method of solving problems and the only method you should know."

When I refer to a "student" of simulation, I introduce another of the significant features that Graybeal and Pooch have brought to their subject — the clarity of presentation. Up until now, most people have learned about simulation through self-study. When they had a problem, they asked a friend and got a book on simulation. Because they had a problem, they were motivated to work through the book, regardless of any extraneous difficulties laid down by the author.

Today, however, there is an increasing audience of "students" who will be studying simulation in a formal class with the aid of an experienced teacher. For these students, a different type of book is needed, and *Simulation* addresses that need. The writing is clear, but doesn't go into more detail than a student wants when surveying a subject for the first time. There are many examples, well chosen for their pedagogic value. There are exercises with which the student can test understanding while progressing through the book. In short, *Simulation* is a "textbook," not a simulation manual, and that's just what we demand today.

Not that *Simulation* shouldn't be used by anyone who's using simulation for the first time without benefit of a classroom. On the contrary. I can think of nothing better for the eager professional than to curb the impulse to plunge into some language manual, and to first read *Simulation* instead. The presentation is good enough that a well-motivated reader can readily glean the book's many lessons, and thus prepare for more intelligent reading which leads to the eventual manual.

Alas, I can't require eager people to slow down and read the books they ought to read. If I could, then perhaps I could legislate some of simulation's worst abuses out of existence. Lacking legislative power, I can only offer good books such as this in our Series, hoping that instructors will adopt them as texts and readers will use them to evade the next generation of simulation tragedies and comedies.

GERALD M. WEINBERG

Series Editor

Preface

The objective of this text is to acquaint potential researchers with the principles behind one of the most widely used tools presently available — simulation using the digital computer. The simulation of the operation of a system, whether it be in economics, management sciences, or one of the engineering disciplines, has rapidly become one of the most useful and common applications of digital computers. There are many reasons for this, among them the fact that simulation allows the assessment of the potential performance *before* a newly designed system is operable. Moreover, simulation permits the comparison of various operating strategies of a present system without affecting the day–to–day performance of the system. Finally, simulation allows time compression or expansion of the system's operation. That is, it is possible to simulate months or years of activity by a system in a few minutes of computer time.

Along with the widespread use of simulation has come a great deal of misuse. A simulator is only as sound as the techniques used in constructing it, and the validity of the results gained from a simulation experiment is influenced by such factors as the techniques used in the collection of data and the analysis techniques used in summarizing the data. Further, prior to its use, a simulator must be validated, or shown to actually model the system being studied. In this text, a broad body of theory requisite for the proper development and operation of a system simulator will be presented.

This book is suitable as a general text in a course on system simulation at the undergraduate or first-year graduate level. The slant of the examples and applications is toward the engineering disciplines and computer science; however an effort has been made to moderate the mathematical formalism and theoretical details to enhance its usefulness in other disciplines such as economics, management sciences, and business administration. The text is nearly self-contained in that the background necessary to understand and use the developed theory is minimal. The ability to program in some high-level language (preferably FORTRAN) is essential, since most of the examples and exercises involve writing programs. An introductory course in differential/integral calculus is necessary to provide the link between, for example, the probability density function and cumulative distribution function for some random variable. A standard introductory course in probability and statistics would prove helpful, although the pertinent subjects in that area are covered in some detail in this text.

This text evolved from lecture notes used in a one-semester graduate level course at Texas A&M University. A particular effort has been made to present a balanced treatment of the basic aspects of simulation. These aspects include modeling fundamentals, probability and statistical concepts, queueing fundamentals, random number generation, programming languages, the design of experiments and verification/validation of a completed model. The sections on verification/validation as well as some discussion of the pitfalls of data collection should provide the practitioner with information seldom mentioned or emphasized in simulation texts.

Chapter 1 of the text is introductory in nature and can reasonably be assigned as an advanced reading assignment prior to actually commencing the course. In it, the concept of a system is discussed, system methodology is introduced, and some of the terminology of simulation is presented.

Chapters 2 and 3 present fundamental concepts of probability and statistics, at the level normally presented in an introductory probability/statistics course. The concept of a distribution as well as discussion of some of the common distributions encountered in simulation are discussed in Chapter 2, while estimation and hypothesis testing are presented in Chapter 3. Those readers with a sound background in these concepts can exclude these two chapters, or at the most skim them briefly.

Chapter 4 concerns the generation of random numbers. It includes a survey of some of the more commonly used generation techniques as well as a discussion of some common tests employed to assess the randomness of a generated sequence.

Chapter 5 comprises an introductory look at queueing systems. Queueing systems are among the most common types being simulated. A brief treatment of the analytic modeling of such systems is presented to aid in developing and validating simulation models of these systems.

Chapters 6, 7, and 8 are concerned directly with the construction of simulation models, and as such comprise the main thrust of the text. Discrete system simulation is discussed in Chapter 6, while Chapter 8 deals with continuous system simulation. Chapter 7 compares and contrasts the general-purpose languages such as FORTRAN with the simulation languages GPSS, SIMSCRIPT, and GASP IV. Specifically discussed are the motivation behind the development of the simulation languages and the features each provides to support the development of simulation models.

Chapter 9 concerns the design of simulation experiments. Three common statistical designs are presented. This chapter also surveys techniques for optimization of response surfaces — a problem encountered in many simulation studies.

In preparing this text, we have attempted to establish a methodology useful in developing and applying simulation. This methodology includes probability and distribution theory, statistical estimation and inference, the generation of random variates, systems theory, time management methods, verification and validation techniques, experimental design and programming language considerations. Without doubt, there are operating simulators which were developed using few of the techniques discussed, and which yield "good" results. There are also "bad" simulators which were developed using the techniques discussed. However, we feel that these instances are isolated exceptions rather than the rule. Some will disagree — we respect their prerogative.

WAYNE T. GRAYBEAL
UDO W. POOCH

Simulation:
Principles and Methods

1

Basic concepts and terminology

The concept of modeling, on which simulation is based, has been in use for many years. Some examples of historical models are Newton's second law, $\mathbf{F} = \overline{m}\mathbf{a}$, relating the force exerted on a body to its acceleration; Kepler's model of the universe in which he postulated that the sun rather than the earth was the center of the universe; and Einstein's theory of relativity. Since the concept of modeling is so old, what has happened to heighten interest in this problem-solving method in recent years? The answer is that the electronic computer was invented. With the advent of the computer, simulation has been applied to nearly every field of human endeavor. Problems in fields as diverse as business, politics, law enforcement, and nuclear engineering have been successfully solved with the use of simulation.

Simulation has been defined by Shannon (1.4) as "the process of designing a computerized model of a system (or process) and conducting experiments with this model for the purpose either of understanding the behavior of the system or of evaluating various strategies for the operation of the system." Though the literature gives many definitions for simulation, this definition seems to encompass the more important aspects of this problem-solving process. Of particular importance is the linking of simulation with the traditional model-building approach to problem solving. More will be said about this later. Suffice it to say at this point that the main impact of computers on the model-building approach is that the form of the model has changed.

Concept of a system

1.1   Central to any simulation study is the idea of a system. To model a system, one must first understand what a system is. The term *system* is defined in *Funk and Wagnall's Standard Dictionary* as "an orderly collection of logically related principles, facts or objects." When used in the context of a simulation study, the term *system* generally refers to a collection of objects with a well-defined set of interactions among them. An example is the solar system. The planets and the sun form the collection of objects; gravitational force is one of the interactions among the objects (elements) of the system. This definition of a system is general enough to allow its application to many problems.

Systems can be defined more broadly than simply as a collection of objects and interactions. For example, one could include in the consideration all external factors capable of causing a change in the system. These external factors form the *system environment*. The state of a system is the minimal collection of information with which its future behavior can be uniquely predicted in the absence of chance events. Since the inclusion of time in the consideration of a system implies that the state of a system changes, there must be some process or event that prompts this change. Such a process or event is called an *activity*. The system state may change in response to activities internal to the system or to activities external to the system. Activities external to the system are referred to as *exogenous*, while activities internal to the system are referred to as *endogenous*. Although it is convenient to distinguish between exogenous and endogenous activities, it is not always possible to do so. When one is defining a given system, it is not always apparent which factors are internal to the system and which are external. Furthermore, with a given system definition an exogenous activity may prompt a series of endogenous activities. The resulting system state may in turn trigger another exogenous activity. Thus in many cases very little distinction can be made between endogenous and exogenous activities; instead it is the change in the system state induced by an activity that is of primary interest.

There are a number of ways of classifying systems. An obvious classification distinguishes between systems that are natural and those that are man-made. The solar system is a natural system, while the automobile is a man-made system. Other classifications that can be used include continuous versus discrete, deterministic versus stochastic, and open versus closed.

Continuous versus discrete systems

1.1.1 The terms continuous and discrete applied to a system refer to the nature or behavior of changes with respect to time in the system state. A system whose changes in state occur continuously over time are *continuous* systems; systems whose changes occur in finite quanta, or jumps, are *discrete*. Some systems possess the properties of both continuous and discrete systems. Some of the system state variables may vary continuously in response to events while others may vary discretely. Such systems can validly be labeled *hybrid* systems.

> *Example 1.1* Consider a system comprising the automobiles on a given five-mile stretch of a busy freeway. One state variable of interest might be the number of cars. This variable varies discretely with time. If this is the only variable of interest, the system can be considered a discrete system. On the other hand, suppose that the variable of interest is the average distance between automobiles. Since this quantity varies continuously over time (and one assumes that it is possible to measure the distance with infinite accuracy), this state variable is continuous. If it is the only state variable of interest, the system can be classified as continuous. Of course, since both variables are contained within a state description of this system, the system can also be called a hybrid system.

Stochastic versus deterministic systems

1.1.2 A *deterministic* system is a system in which the new state of the system is completely determined by the previous state and by the activity. Considered in another way, a given system evolves in a completely deterministic manner from one state to another in response to a given activity. This type of system is depicted in figure 1.1, where S_0 refers to the state of the system before activity A and S_n refers to the system state after the occurrence of the activity.

A *stochastic* system contains a certain amount of randomness in its transitions from one state to another. In some cases it might not be possible to assign a probability to the state that the system will assume after a given state and activity. In other cases these probabilities are known or can be determined. A stochastic system is depicted in figure 1.2, where

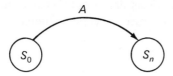

Figure 1.1
A deterministic system

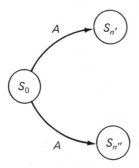

Figure 1.2
A stochastic system

$S_{n'}$ and $S_{n''}$ are two possible states that the system can enter after the state S_0 in response to activity A. Thus a stochastic system is nondeterministic in the sense that the next state cannot be unequivocally predicted if the present state and the stimulus (activity) is known.

    Example 1.2   Consider a system made up of a single-bay service station in which customers are serviced immediately if the server is idle or join a waiting line (queue) if the server is busy. If the time required to serve a customer varies randomly, the system is stochastic. The state variable of interest, an arriving customer's waiting time, cannot be deterministically calculated from the information that there are X customers in the system before the activity "customer Y arrives."

Open versus closed systems

1.1.3   A *closed* system is a system in which all state changes are prompted by endogenous activities. In contrast, *open* systems are systems whose states change in response to both exogenous and endogenous activities. It is sometimes difficult to distinguish between endogenous and exogenous activities, and even if the distinction can be made, they are handled in the same way in most simulation studies. It is also difficult to distinguish between open and closed systems. This distinction is mentioned only for completeness, and it is doubtful that we will need to refer to it again.

System methodology

1.2   Simulation is based on a problem-solving method that has been in use for many years, sometimes referred to as the model-building method or more commonly the scientific method. Thus when system simulation is used to solve a problem, the following time-tested steps, or stages, are applied.

1. Observation of the system
2. Formulation of hypotheses or theories that account for the observed behavior
3. Prediction of the future behavior of the system based on the assumption that the hypotheses are correct
4. Comparison of the predicted behavior with the actual behavior

The system being studied may impose constraints on certain steps of this scientific method. Consider the simulation of a system that does not yet exist. Obviously the observation of such a system is not possible, but the simulation of such a system may still be possible if the analysis is carefully conducted and if the ultimate system requirements are known. The scientific method's requirement for prior observation of the system has resulted in the development of a slightly different approach to problem solving, called *system methodology*. This methodology consists of four phases: planning, modeling, validation, and application. The correspondence between the four phases of the system methodology and the appropriate steps of the scientific method should be obvious.

Planning

1.2.1   The initial phase of this problem-solving process is planning. The planning, or premodeling, phase includes the initial encounter with the system, the problem to be solved, and the factors pertaining to the system and its environment that are likely to affect the solution of the problem. This definition of the planning phase assumes that the problem has been adequately defined. Obviously the more accurate and precise the problem statement is, the more smoothly the solution process can proceed.

Once the problem has been clearly defined, an estimate of the resources required to collect data and analyze the problem (system) can be made. Resources such as time, money, personnel, and special equipment should be considered. If crucial resources are not available, solution of the problem can be judged infeasible before a significant amount of time or money is spent. The alternative to discontinuing the project is to modify the definition of the problem. The problem can be restated so that it can be successfully solved with available resources. In some cases this constraint may mean solving a less ambitious problem. The importance of this initial resource estimate cannot be overemphasized; it is clearly more desirable to modify objectives at an early stage than to fall short because crucial resources are unavailable.

The second major task in the planning phase is to analyze the system. In this phase the analyst attempts to become familiar with all relevant aspects of the problem being studied. A thorough literature search to discover previous approaches to similar problems may prove valuable in choosing possible courses of action. Consultation with other qualified persons may provide insight into aspects of the problem that the primary researcher has overlooked or misunderstood. The importance of this initial problem analysis should not be underestimated. The analyst must be willing to spend the time and the effort necessary to fully understand the system or problem under study. Many projects have failed or incurred overruns in cost or time because of an inadequate understanding of the project.

Modeling

1.2.2   The second phase of the problem-solving process is the modeling phase. In this phase the analyst constructs a system model, which is a representation of the real system. The characteristics of this model should be representative of the characteristics of the real system. Note the use of the term *representative* rather than identical. Many real systems are so complex that a model with characteristics identical to those of the real system would be equally complex and thus unmanageable or prohibitively expensive. One of the goals of this phase, then, is to select some minimal set of the system's characteristics so that the model approximates the real system yet remains cost-effective and manageable. The model includes these characteristics and a well-defined set of relations among these characteristics.

There are many types of models, including descriptive models, physical models, mathematical models, flowcharts, schematics, and computer programs. *Descriptive models* are simply verbalizations of the system's composition and its response to a given stimulus. *Physical models* are scaled facsimiles of the system being analyzed; examples are models used to evaluate aircraft designs in wind tunnel experiments and mock-ups of landscaping and buildings in architectural design studies. *Mathematical models* are abstract expressions of the relationships among system variables; examples of these models are Newton's laws of motion and the description of the stress factors of a dam as it is filled with water. The advantage of mathematical models is that they can be manipulated with paper and pencil. With these models it is not necessary to construct an expensive mock-up of the system to study its behavior. Their disadvantage is that the accurate description of a given system may require an expression so complex that it would make even the most facile mathematician shudder. *Flowcharts* and *schematics* display the basic logical interactions between system components and may be as detailed as desired. When used as a prelude to computer program models, flowchart models are valuable aids to programming and program documentation.

If the system being studied is so complex that no representative model can be used, then the well-known problem reduction technique, or subsystem modeling, is an alternate approach. In this approach the system is divided into a collection of less complex subsystems. Each of these subsystems is modeled, and an overall system model is constructed by linking the subsystem models appropriately. This approach of course requires that subsystems may be readily modeled, identified, and isolated.

Three general approaches have been used in defining or identifying subsystems. The first method, called the *flow approach,* has been used to analyze systems characterized by the flow of physical or information items through the system. If the system to be modeled is an automobile assembly plant, the flow approach would appear to be a feasible way of breaking this system into subsystems. In the flow approach subsystems are identified by grouping aspects of the system that produce a particular physical or information change in the flow entity.

A second technique used in identifying subsystems is the *functional approach.* This technique is useful when there are no directly observable "flowing" entities in the system. Instead, a logical sequence of functions being performed must be identified. System characteristics that perform a given function are grouped to form a subsystem. This approach can be used in manufacturing processes that do not use assembly lines.

The third method for identifying or isolating subsystems is called the *state-change* approach. This procedure is useful in systems that are characterized by a large number of interdependent relationships and which must be examined at regular intervals to detect state changes. System characteristics that respond to the same stimulus or set of stimuli are then grouped to form a subsystem.

Once the subsystems have been identified and isolated, they must be modeled. Of course, the subsystems could in turn be subdivided into sub-subsystems, and so on, as far a necessary. The goal is to subdivide the total system in such a way that each subsystem is easily comprehensible and readily identified. If subsystems cannot be identified and isolated, the analyst has no choice but to model the entire system with a single model and hope that this large model will be manageable. If the subsystem approach has been used, the submodels must be linked into an overall system model. The logical interactions of the subsystems must be identified and implemented in a form compatible with the overall model.

If the model is a computer program, as is the case in a simulation model, the modeling phase also involves the selection of the language in which the program is to be written. A number of considerations determine the choice of a programming language, including the difficulty of translating the model and interrelationships into the language, the presence or absence of facilities in the language to support such routine activities as queue management, generation of random numbers, and output formatting, and the analyst's familiarity with the language. A crucial step in using a computer program to model a system is the construction of detailed system flowcharts. Although flowcharting has fallen into disfavor in recent years (some are even written after the program), flowcharts provide a visual representation of the program's logic and serve as program documentation after the logic has been translated into code. As a general rule, the better the formulation of the model when the flowchart is made, the easier it is to create a complete computer program model of the system.

Another task in the modeling (programming) phase of a simulation study is the estimation of the system variables and parameters. At this point real-world data are summarized into a manageable statistical description of the system's characteristics. This is commonly done by collecting data over some period of time and then computing a frequency distribution for the desired variables. A number of pitfalls await the unsuspecting researcher in the collection and interpretation of data. The cost in terms of time, money, and personnel can become prohibitive; the data may be incomplete or inaccurate; the data may contain unsuspected interdependencies, periodicities, or complexities; the method of collection may introduce an inadvertent bias into the data. Other than the inherent cost of collecting data, most of these pitfalls can be avoided through the use of experimental design procedures.

Validation

1.2.3   A model is validated by proving that the model is a correct representation of the real system. Validation should not be confused with verification. When a computer program is verified, for example, the program is checked to ensure that the logic does what it was intended to do. A verified computer program can in fact represent an invalid model. The program may do exactly what the programmer intended, yet it may not represent the operation of the real system.

Validation of computer simulation models is a difficult task. There is considerable disagreement about what constitutes validation. Despite this disagreement, there are techniques that have proven useful in this phase of the simulation process. One technique is to compare the results of the simulation model with results historically produced by the real system operating under the same conditions. A second technique is to use the simulator to predict results. The predictions are then compared with the results produced by the real system during some future period of time.

Whichever validation technique is used, the method of comparing the outputs of the real system and those of the simulated model is basically the same. Various statistical procedures can be used to determine whether the data produced by the simulator could have been produced by the real systems and vice versa. Two such methods are the chi-square goodness-of-fit test and the Kolmogorov-Smirnov test.

Validation of a simulation model is not easy, but it must be performed before the simulation model can be used. The lack of precision in the validation process is evidenced in the literature by statements such as "90% of the predicted values lie within 5% of the observed values." Whether this statement implies that the simulator is a good one or a bad one is left to the interpretation of the analyst. Such a statement does convey considerably more information than a statement such as "the results obtained were quite good."

Just as a good experimental design can aid in the data collection in the modeling phase, so can validation aid in correctness of the simulation model. Most standard experimental designs require that observations be taken on the system variables that can be controlled. The simulation model must operate under identical conditions. Only then can valid inferences be drawn about the relationship between the resulting output (observations) of the real system and the outputs of the simulation model. In most designs several factors can be varied simultaneously, and thus some information on interactive effects of those factors can be obtained. Several effects may be estimated from the same data. Careful design of the simulation experiment will prove beneficial in the long run.

Application

1.2.4 Once the model has been properly validated, it can be applied to solving the problem at hand. However, the development of the simulation model may still not be complete. Observation of the output from the model may reveal programming errors, the desirability of a change in the way the simulator has been implemented, or even the need to reformulate or modify the original problem statement. It has been said that no computer program is completely free of errors. This is especially true of simulation models. A simulator may work error-free for a long period of time until it encounters a new and perhaps unique combination of program parameters that generates the next error.

Advantages and disadvantages of simulation

1.3 Simulation has been applied to nearly every field of human activity in the past few years. One might then ask, If simulation is so good, why is any other type of modeling used? The answer is that simulation is not applicable in many cases, and even in some cases in which it does apply, there may be easier and cheaper ways of solving the problem. Phillips, Ravindran, and Solberg (1.2) state that simulation is one of the easiest tools of management science to use but probably one of the hardest to apply properly and perhaps the most difficult one from which to draw accurate conclusions. Whether one agrees with this statement or not, one should realize that there are distinct advantages and disadvantages to simulation.

Adkins and Pooch (1.1) list five advantages of simulation modeling.

1. It permits controlled experimentation. A simulation experiment can be run a number of times with varying input parameters to test the behavior of the system under a variety of situations and conditions.

2. It permits time compression. Operation of the system over extended periods of time can be simulated in only minutes with ultrafast computers.

3. It permits sensitivity analysis by manipulation of input variables.

4. It does not disturb the real system. This is a great advantage, since most managers would be reluctant to try experimental strategies on an on-line system.

5. It is an effective training tool.

They also list four disadvantages to using the simulation approach to problem solving.

1. A simulation model may become expensive in terms of manpower and computer time. This is not surprising if the magnitude of the problems being attempted is considered. For example, consider the simulation of messages through a large-scale (1000-node) communication network. Just the bookkeeping requirements for a problem of this magnitude are staggering. The cost of a simulation experiment can be minimized through in-depth understanding of the system being simulated *before* the model is developed and through careful design of the simulation experiment.

2. Extensive development time may be encountered. Most simulation models are quite large and, like any large programming project, take time. Strategies such as the chief programmer team, top-down design, and modular programming, which have been applied to other large programming projects, are likely to be useful in the development of system simulators and could reduce the development time.

3. Hidden critical assumptions may cause the model to diverge from reality. Ideally this phenomenon should be discovered in the validation phase of the simulation process, but it might go undetected, depending on the severity of the problem and the diligence with which the model is validated.

4. Model parameters may be difficult to initialize. These may require extensive time in collection, analysis, and interpretation.

Thus although simulation has proved an effective approach to problem solving, it has its drawbacks. The researcher should be aware of these drawbacks *before* becoming committed to this approach.

Simulation terminology

1.4 Since the use of simulation modeling has become so widespread, a terminology unique to the field has evolved. This terminology is by no means standard, but enough authors have used it that it has gained some acceptance. Some of the terms have been introduced in the course of this chapter; others will be used as the need arises.

1. About the model
   a. A real-world object is called an *entity*.
   b. Characteristics or properties of entities are called *attributes*.
   c. Any process that causes changes in a system is called an *activity*.

     d. A description of all the entities, attributes, and activities, as they exist at some point in time is called the *state of the system*.

  2. About the environment

     a. The objects and processes (entities and activities) surrounding the system are called the *system environment*.

     b. Activities that occur within the system are called *endogenous* activities.

     c. Activities in the environment that affect the system are called *exogenous* activities.

     d. The classification of all activities as either endogenous or exogenous establishes the *system boundary*.

     e. A system with no exogenous activities is called a *closed* system; otherwise the system is *open*.

  3. About the system

     a. *Continuous* systems include variables that can assume any real value in a prescribed set of intervals; these systems are characterized by smooth changes in the system state.

     b. *Discrete* systems include variables that can assume only particular values from among a finite set of alternatives; these systems are characterized by discontinuous changes in the system state.

     c. A system whose response is completely determined by its initial state and input is said to be *deterministic*.

     d. A system whose response may take a range of values given the initial system state and input is said to be *stochastic*.

  4. About the simulation

     a. *Validation* refers to the proof that the model is a correct representation of the real system.

     b. *Verification* refers to the proof that the simulation program is a faithful representation of the system model.

     c. *Experimental design* refers to a sequence of simulation runs in which parameters are varied, with both economy and sound statistical methodology considered in achieving some specified goal.

Summary

The use of the simulation approach to problem solving has become widespread since the development of the electronic computer. This chapter has surveyed the systems approach to problem solving, on which simulation is founded. The usual sequence of steps that occur before an attempt is made to solve the problem is to identify the problem, perform a systems analysis, and restate the problem within the context of the system definition. Once this has been done, according to Pritsker (1.3), there are four basic tasks that should be performed in a simulation project.

1. Determine that the problem requires simulation. The crucial factors are the cost, the feasibility of conducting real-world experiments, and the possibility of mathematical analysis.

2. Build a model to solve the problem.

3. Write a computer program that converts the model into an operating simulation program.

4. Use the computer simulation program as an experimental device to resolve the problem.

The next few chapters survey some of the fundamental methods used in simulation. Readers familiar with these subjects may want to merely skim those chapters before moving on to later chapters.

References

1.1   ADKINS, GERALD, and POOCH, UDO W. "Computer Simulation: A Tutorial." *Computer* 10, no. 4 (April 1977):12–17.

1.2   PHILLIPS, D. T., RAVINDRAN, A., and SOLBERG, J. J. *Operations Research Principles and Practice.* New York: John Wiley and Sons, 1976.

1.3   PRITSKER, A. A. B. *The GASP IV Simulation Language.* New York: John Wiley and Sons, 1974.

1.4   SHANNON, ROBERT E. "Simulation: A Survey with Research Suggestions." *AIIE Transactions* 7, no. 3 (September 1975): 289–301.

2

Probability and distribution theory

One of the problems commonly encountered while modeling real-world systems is that few systems exhibit constant, predictable behavior. Observations or measurements in a physical system often vary depending on, among other things, the time of the observation. These variations often appear to be random or chance variations. Despite this inherent unpredictability, some model or mathematical structure is required to describe the system. The system is generally described by a probability model that in most cases is developed through experimentation. Experiments are performed on the system, the outcomes of those experiments are noted, and a model is then postulated on the basis of these outcomes. Inferences based on this model are then made, and additional experiments are conducted in an attempt to validate the model. In general, the more experiments performed on the system, the more likely the model is to accurately reflect the true nature of the system.

Since the development of a probability model is so important in the simulation of any system, this chapter is devoted to probability and probability models.

Probability

2.1   To understand the development of a probability model and the importance of this model in describing physical systems, one must understand the concepts of probability. These concepts, many of which have their origins in gambling games, are simple and intuitive in most cases and can usually be grasped easily through an example.

Probability is a measure of uncertainty. This uncertainty is conveyed through phrases like "probably," "in all likelihood," "there is a good chance that." This definition, however, is not precise enough for our purposes, and a more precise definition will be given after an example.

Example 2.1   Consider the simple experiment of tossing a coin. If we assume that the coin is thin enough that the possibility of its landing on its edge can be ignored, then there are two possible outcomes to this experiment. Either it will land heads up, or it will land tails up. Can you predict with certainty which side it will land on if it is tossed? The answer, most probably, is no. The side on which it lands is unpredictable, or uncertain, because the outcome is influenced by the construction of the coin, the manner of tossing, the regularity of the surface on which it lands, and so on.

An experiment such as that in example 2.1, in which the outcome is uncertain or unpredictable, is called a *random experiment*. The outcomes of this random experiment are called *simple random events*. Thus one simple random event for the experiment of example 2.1 is the event "the coin lands heads up." The other is the event "the coin lands tails up." Each of these two events will have some measure of likelihood or certainty attached to it — the probability of its occurrence. This measure of likelihood is determined through experimentation. The experiment is conducted a number of times, and its outcomes are noted. The relative frequency of occurrence of a given outcome should stabilize, or tend to a limiting value. This limiting value is defined as the *probability* of the event.

Once all possible outcomes (events) of a random experiment are determined and a probability has been attached to each, a *probability (stochastic) model* is said to have been determined.

Example 2.2   Consider the example of tossing a die. The outcomes of this experiment are $\{\boxdot, \boxdot, \boxdot, \boxdot, \boxdot, \boxdot\}$. For convenience, represent these outcomes as 1, 2, 3, 4, 5, and 6 respectively. Suppose that experimentation has shown that the likelihood that a given face will appear is proportional to the number of spots on the face. Then the probability model for this experiment is

Event	1	2	3	4	5	6
Probability	1/21	2/21	3/21	4/21	5/21	6/21

In example 2.2 the probability of each of the events is different. This is generally the case; however, there are experiments in which the likelihood of each of the events is the same. In this case the events are said to be *equally likely* or *equiprobable.*

Example 2.3 Consider the well-known wheel of fortune, which is a circular disk with pegs placed around its perimeter, and a pointer (flapper) protruding into the slots between the pegs (figure 2.1). The disk is

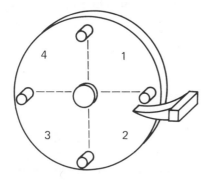

Figure 2.1
The wheel of fortune

pinned through its center to some fixed surface, and each slot is numbered. The experiment consists of spinning the wheel and noting which number is under the pointer when it stops. The outcomes (events) are thus {"1 is under the pointer," "2 is under the pointer," "3 is under the pointer," and "4 is under the pointer"}. Again, for convenience, denote these events as 1, 2, 3, and 4 respectively. Suppose that experimentation revealed these events to be equally likely. Then the probability model for this experiment is

Event	1	2	3	4
Probability	1/4	1/4	1/4	1/4

In the three examples given thus far the outcomes (events) were nonnumerical, although a numerical correspondence was evident. It is nearly alway advantageous to envision the outcomes of a random experiment as numerical. For this reason, the idea of a random variable is introduced. Simply stated, a *random variable* is a quantity whose value is determined by the outcome of a random experiment. More precisely, the random variable **X** is a function whose domain is the event space (set of all possible outcomes of a random experiment) and whose range is some subset of the real numbers. This definition is summarized by

$$\mathbf{X} : E \to R$$

Example 2.4   Consider the event space of the experiment described in example 2.2.

$$E = \{\, \boxed{⚀}\ \boxed{⚁}\ \boxed{⚂}\ \boxed{⚃}\ \boxed{⚄}\ \boxed{⚅}\,\}$$

A random variable $\mathbf{X}\colon E \to R$ can be defined by rules of the form

$$\boxed{⚀} \to 1 \qquad \boxed{⚃} \to 4$$
$$\boxed{⚁} \to 2 \qquad \boxed{⚄} \to 5$$
$$\boxed{⚂} \to 3 \qquad \boxed{⚅} \to 6$$

In fact, this is precisely what was used in the example.

Example 2.4 illustrates that there is nothing deep, dark, or mysterious about random variables. Nor is there anything highly significant about them. In most cases they are defined for convenience.

Set theory, compound events

2.2   As defined in the previous section, a simple random event is a single outcome of a given random experiment. In some cases we are less interested in individual events than in combinations of these events. This section reviews some of the fundamentals of set theory as they relate to combining simple random events into composite events (hereafter simply referred to as events).

DEFINITION 2.1   *An event is some subset of the event space of a random experiment.*

The event space for a random experiment, defined as the collection of all possible outcomes of the experiment, will be denoted by Ω.

Example 2.5 Consider the experiment of tossing two dice and noting the sum of the faces showing. The event space is

$$\Omega = \{2, 3, 4, 5, 6, 7, 8, 9, 10, 11, 12\}$$

and some events are

$E_1 = \{2\}$ ("snake eyes" appear)

$E_2 = \{3, 4, 5\}$ (the sum is 3, 4, or 5)

$E_3 = \{2, 4, 6, 8, 10, 12\}$ (an even number appears)

This definition of an event, then, includes all possible subsets of the event space — the simple events, compound events, and even the event space itself.

It is sometimes of interest to know the probability than an event E will not occur rather than that it will. This leads to the following definition.

DEFINITION 2.2   *The complement of an event E, denoted $\overline{E}$, is the set of elements that are in Ω but not in E.*

Example 2.6 The complements of the events defined in example 2.5 are

$\overline{E}_1 = \{3, 4, 5, 6, 7, 8, 9, 10, 11, 12\}$

$\overline{E}_2 = \{2, 6, 7, 8, 9, 10, 11, 12\}$

$\overline{E}_3 = \{3, 5, 7, 9, 11\}$

There are two basic ways of combining two events to form a third event: union and intersection.

DEFINITION 2.3   *The intersection of two events E_1 and E_2, denoted $E_1 \cdot E_2$, is defined as the outcomes that the events have in common. Two events that have no outcomes in common are said to be* mutually exclusive.

DEFINITION 2.4   *The union of two events E_1 and E_2, denoted $E_1 + E_2$, is defined as the outcomes in either E_1 or E_2 or both.*

Example 2.7 The union and intersection of the events defined in example 2.5 are

$$E_1 + E_2 = \{2, 3, 4, 5\} \qquad\qquad E_1 \cdot E_2 = \varnothing$$

$$E_1 + E_3 = \{2, 4, 6, 8, 10, 12\} \qquad\qquad E_1 \cdot E_3 = \{2\}$$

$$E_2 + E_3 = \{2, 3, 4, 5, 6, 8, 10, 12\} \qquad\qquad E_2 \cdot E_3 = \{4\}$$

Thus one can use these rules for combining events to construct a number of related events from any given initial set. For any event E note that $E + \overline{E} = \Omega$ and $E \cdot \overline{E} = \varnothing$ (null set).

It should be clear that the probability that *some* event in the event space will occur is 1 (certainty) whereas the probability that *no* event in the event space will occur is 0 (impossibility).

PROPERTY 2.1   *For any random experiment, it must be true that*

$$P(\Omega) = 1, \qquad P(\varnothing) = 0$$

If the outcomes of a random experiment are equally likely, calculation of the probability of some event composed of a number of different outcomes is straightforward.

DEFINITION 2.5   *Suppose that a random experiment has N equally likely outcomes. Further, suppose that some event E is composed of n outcomes. Then the probability of the event E, denoted P(E), is given by*

$$P(E) = n/N$$

The probability of the complement of E, $P(\overline{E})$, is given by

$$P(\overline{E}) = 1 - P(E) = (N - n)/N$$

Example 2.8   Consider the events defined in example 2.5. If the outcomes of the random experiment are equally likely (the probability of each is 1/11), the probabilities of E_1, E_2, and E_3 are

$$P(E_1) = 1/11 \qquad P(\overline{E}_1) = 10/11$$

$$P(E_2) = 3/11 \qquad P(\overline{E}_2) = 8/11$$

$$P(E_3) = 6/11 \qquad P(\overline{E}_3) = 5/11$$

A fundamental result relating the probability of the union and intersection of two events E_1 and E_2 has been derived.

PROPERTY 2.2   *If E_1 and E_2 are two events from a random experiment, then*

$$P(E_1 + E_2) = P(E_1) + P(E_2) - P(E_1 \cdot E_2)$$

Example 2.9   Suppose the outcomes of the experiment discussed in example 2.5 are equally likely. Consider the events defined in example 2.7. Then

$$P(E_1 + E_2) = P(E_1) + P(E_2) - P(E_1 \cdot E_2)$$
$$= 1/11 + 3/11 - 0 = 4/11$$
$$P(E_2 + E_3) = P(E_2) + P(E_3) - P(E_2 \cdot E_3)$$
$$= 3/11 + 6/11 - 1/11 = 8/11$$
$$P(E_1 + \overline{E_1}) = P(E_1) + P(\overline{E_1}) - P(E_1 \cdot \overline{E_1})$$
$$= 1/11 + 10/11 - 0 = 1$$

Note that in this special case (equally likely outcomes), these probabilities could be calculated without recourse to the formula of property 2.2 simply by enumerating the outcomes contained in each event and applying definition 2.5 directly. Property 2.2 is most useful for random experiments that do not have equally likely outcomes.

Conditional probability, independent events

2.3   At times one has certain prior knowledge concerning the outcome of a random experiment. This prior knowledge may make a given event either more or less likely. Of course, complete knowledge of the outcome is not possible, otherwise the probability of any event containing that outcome is 1, while the probability of any event not containing that outcome is 0. We wish to consider the case where there is partial knowledge beforehand. An example may help clarify this notion.

Example 2.10   Suppose that two dice are thrown. Before you learn the exact outcome, someone tells you that the sum is even. This knowledge obviously affects the probability that the exact sum is 2 or that the exact sum is 3. In fact, if the dice are fair (all outcomes are equally likely), the probability that the sum is 2 is 1/6 with the knowledge that the sum is even, 1/11 without this knowledge. The probability that the sum is 3 is 0 with the knowledge that the sum is even, 1/11 without this knowledge.

When advance knowledge affects the probability that a given event has occurred, this knowledge is said to have conditioned the probability of that event.

DEFINITION 2.6   *If E_1 and E_2 are two events from a random experiment, then the probability that event E_1 has occurred given that event E_2 has occurred is called the* conditional probability *of E_1 given E_2. This probability is denoted $P(E_1|E_2)$, and may be calculated as*

$$P(E_1|E_2) = P(E_1 \cdot E_2)/P(E_2)$$

This definition is quite intuitive when E_2 is viewed as having conditioned (reduced) the event space. That is, once it is known that event E_2 has occurred, only a reduced subset of the original event space is possible. The probability of E_1 must now be calculated from the reduced event space.

Example 2.11   Consider the random experiment of drawing a card from an ordinary, well-shuffled deck of 52 cards. Suppose that after the draw you are told that the card is red. What is the probability that it is the two of hearts?

Define event E_1 as the event that the card is the two of hearts, and event E_2 as the event that the card is red. Then $E_1 \cdot E_2$ is the event that the card is both red and the two of hearts, the event that the card is the two of hearts. Then

$$P(E_1|E_2) = \frac{P(E_1 \cdot E_2)}{P(E_2)} = \frac{1/52}{1/2}$$
$$= 4/52 = 1/26$$

In this example the knowledge that the card was red conditioned the event space so that it contained only 26 instead of 52 equally likely outcomes. The event that the two of hearts was drawn was then just one of these 26 equally likely simple random events.

Sometimes the knowledge that one event has occurred does not affect the probability that another event has occurred. In this case the events are said to be independent.

DEFINITION 2.7   *Two events E_1 and E_2 are said to be independent if*

$P(E_1|E_2) = P(E_1)$

Combining this definition with property 2.2 gives the following property.

PROPERTY 2.3   *If E_1 and E_2 are independent events, then*

$P(E_1 \cdot E_2) = P(E_1) \cdot P(E_2)$

Example 2.12   Suppose that a box contains eight black balls and two white balls. A random experiment is conducted in which two balls are drawn from the box. Define E_1 as the event that a black ball is drawn on the first draw and E_2 as the event that a black ball is drawn on the second draw.

If the first ball drawn is replaced before the second one is drawn, the two events are independent. The probability of drawing two consecutive black balls is then

$P(E_1 \cdot E_2) = P(E_1) \cdot P(E_2) = (8/10) \cdot (8/10) = 64/100$

If the first ball is not replaced before the second is drawn, the events are not independent. Hence the probability of drawing two consecutive black balls is

$$P(E_1 \cdot E_2) = P(E_2|E_1) \cdot P(E_1)$$
$$= (7/9) \cdot (8/10) = 56/90$$

Discrete distributions

2.4   As defined earlier, a random variable is a function that associates a numerical value with each simple random event (outcome) of a random experiment. The random variable is either discrete or continuous depending on the type of value assigned to the outcomes. If a random variable assumes a discrete number (finite or countably infinite) of values, it is called a discrete random variable. Otherwise it is called a continuous random variable.

Example 2.13   The value of the sum of two thrown dice varies discretely between 2 and 12. The random variable that assigns this sum to each outcome is a *discrete random variable.*

Example 2.14　The time t between failures of a particular electronic component varies continuously, $0 < t < \infty$. The random variable assigning this time to each failure is a *continuous random variable.*

When a frequency or probability function is associated with a discrete random variable, one is said to have defined a *discrete probability distribution.* This distribution tells how the outcomes of a random experiment (reflected in the values assumed by the random variable) are distributed.

Example 2.15　Consider the random experiment of tossing a single die. Define **X** as the random variable that "counts" the spots of the side facing up. Then **X** can assume the values 1, 2, 3, 4, 5, or 6. Assume that the die is loaded so that the probability that a given face lands up is proportional to the number of spots on the face. The discrete probability distribution for this random experiment is

x	1	2	3	4	5	6
$P(\mathbf{X} = x)$	1/21	2/21	3/21	4/21	5/21	6/21

This distribution can be depicted graphically as in figure 2.2. This example illustrates some properties that every discrete probability function must have.

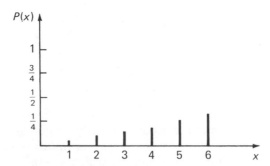

Figure 2.2
Probability function for the loaded die problem

PROPERTY 2.4　*Let **X** be a discrete random variable that takes the values $x_1, x_2, \ldots, x_n$, and let P be the probability function, with $P(x_i) = P(\mathbf{X} = x_i)$. Then*

1. $P(x_i) \geq 0$, for all x_i, $i = 1, 2, \ldots , n$.

2. $\displaystyle\sum_{i=1}^{n} P(x_i) = 1$

Another useful function is the *cumulative distribution function* (cdf). This function, normally denoted $F(x)$, measures the probability that the random variable **X** assumes a value less than or equal to x. That is, $F(x) = P(\mathbf{X} \leq x)$.

Example 2.16 Consider the experiment described in example 2.15. The cumulative distribution function is

x	1	2	3	4	5	6
$F(x)$	1/21	3/21	6/21	10/21	15/21	21/21

Depicted graphically, this function appears as in figure 2.3. This sketch points out some properties that any cumulative distribution function must have.

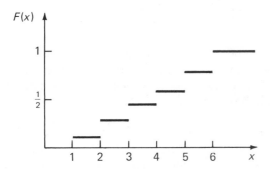

Figure 2.3
Distribution function for the loaded die problem

PROPERTY 2.5 Let **X** *be a discrete random variable, and let F be the associated cumulative distribution function, with* $F(x) = P(\mathbf{X} \leq x)$. *Then*

1. $0 \leq F(x) \leq 1$, $-\infty < x < \infty$
2. *If* $x_1 \leq x_2$, *then* $F(x_1) \leq F(x_2)$. *That is, F is nondecreasing.*
3. $\lim\limits_{x \to \infty} F(x) = F(\infty) = 1$, $\lim\limits_{x \to -\infty} F(x) = F(-\infty) = 0$.

Note that the probability function P is defined only for the values that **X** can assume, while F is defined for all values of x. The jumps in the step function F occur at values in the range of $\mathbf{X}$ that have nonzero probabilities.

One way of classifying a discrete probability distribution is by its *expectation*, or long-run average value.

DEFINITION 2.8   *Let* $\mathbf{X}$ *denote a discrete random variable that takes the values* $x_1, x_2, \ldots, x_n,$ *and let P denote the associated probability function. The expectation, or expected value, of the random variable, denoted* $E(\mathbf{X})$ *is given by*

$$E(\mathbf{X}) = x_1\, P(x_1) + x_2\, P(x_2) + \cdots + x_n\, P(x_n)$$

$$= \sum_{i=1}^{n} x_i\, P(x_i)$$

Example 2.17   Consider the experiment discussed in example 2.15. The expectation of the random variable $\mathbf{X}$ is

$$\begin{aligned}
E(\mathbf{X}) &= (1)(1/21) + (2)(2/21) + (3)(3/21) + (4)(4/21) \\
&\quad + (5)(5/21) + (6)(6/21) \\
&= 1/21 + 4/21 + 9/21 + 16/21 + 25/21 + 36/21 \\
&= 91/21 \doteq 4.33
\end{aligned}$$

One would expect the long-run average to be 4.33. Obviously the die would never show 4.33, but if the experiment is conducted a large number of times and the outcomes averaged, this computed average should approach the expectation.

Another way of classifying a discrete random variable is through specification of its variance. This quantity is a measure of dispersion; it indicates how the random variable is dispersed about its expected value.

DEFINITION 2.9   *Let* $\mathbf{X}$ *denote a discrete random variable that takes the values* $x_1, x_2, \ldots, x_n,$ *P the associated probability function, and E the expectation operator. The variance of* $\mathbf{X},$ *denoted* $V(\mathbf{X})$ *is given by*

$$\begin{aligned}
V(\mathbf{X}) &= (x_1 - E(\mathbf{X}))^2\, P(x_1) + \cdots + (x_n - E(\mathbf{X}))^2\, P(x_n) \\
&= \sum_{i=1}^{n} (x_i - E(\mathbf{X}))^2\, P(x_i) \\
&= E[(\mathbf{X} - E(\mathbf{X}))^2]
\end{aligned}$$

Example 2.18   Consider the experiment discussed in example 2.15. The expectation of the random variable $\mathbf{X}$ was calculated in example 2.17 as $E(\mathbf{x}) = 91/21$. The variance of $\mathbf{X}$ is

$$V(\mathbf{X}) = (1 - 91/21)^2 \, (1/21) + (2 - 91/21)^2 \, (2/21) + (3 - 91/21)^2 \, (3/21)$$
$$+ \, (4 - 91/21)^2 \, (4/21) + (5 - 91/21)^2 \, (5/21) + (6 - 91/21)^2 \, (6/21)$$
$$= (-70/21)^2 \, (1/21) + (-49/21)^2 \, (2/21) + (-28/21)^2 \, (3/21)$$
$$+ \, (-7/21)^2 \, (4/21) + (14/21)^2 \, (5/21) + (35/21)^2 \, (6/21)$$
$$\doteq 0.5291 + 0.5185 + 0.2540 + 0.0212 + 0.1058 + 0.7936$$
$$\doteq 2.2222.$$

The variance, simply stated, measures the average squared deviation from the mean (expected value). Along with the expectation, it provides a convenient way of summarizing the important aspects of a probability distribution.

As is apparent from the definition, the variance is in terms of squared units. Because this proves unwieldy in some instances, the standard deviation has been developed.

DEFINITION 2.10   *Let* **X** *denote a discrete random variable and* $V(\mathbf{X})$ *its variance. The standard deviation of* **X**, *denoted* $S(\mathbf{X})$ *is given by*

$$S(\mathbf{X}) = [V(\mathbf{X})]^{1/2}$$

The computation of $V(\mathbf{X})$ and hence of $S(\mathbf{X})$ is made somewhat simpler by using the linearity of the expectation operator E.

$$V(\mathbf{X}) = E[(\mathbf{X} - E(\mathbf{X}))^2]$$
$$= E[\mathbf{X}^2 - 2\mathbf{X}\,E(\mathbf{X}) + (E(\mathbf{X}))^2]$$
$$= E[\mathbf{X}^2] - 2E(\mathbf{X})\,E(\mathbf{X}) + (E(\mathbf{X}))^2$$
$$= E[\mathbf{X}^2] - (E(\mathbf{X}))^2$$

Example 2.19   The variance calculated in example 2.18 can be alternatively calculated as follows.

$$V(\mathbf{X}) = E(\mathbf{X}^2) - [E(\mathbf{X})]^2$$

$$= \sum_{i=1}^{6} x_i^2 \, P(x_i) - (E(\mathbf{X}))^2$$

$$= [(1)(1/21) + (4)(2/21) + (9)(3/21)$$
$$+ \, (16)(4/21) + (25)(5/21) + (36)(6/21)] - (91/21)^2$$

$$= \left[\frac{1 + 8 + 27 + 64 + 125 + 216}{21} \right] - \frac{8281}{441}$$

$$= \frac{441}{21} - \frac{8281}{441} = 21 - 18.7777$$

$$= 2.2222$$

The standard deviation of **X** is then

$$S(\mathbf{X}) = [V(\mathbf{X})]^{1/2} = [2.2222]^{1/2} = 1.4907$$

The expected value $E(\mathbf{X})$ is normally denoted by the Greek letter μ, while the standard deviation is normally denoted by the Greek letter σ. The importance of these summary measures in characterizing a distribution will become apparent later.

Continuous distributions

2.5   A continuous random variable is a random variable that assumes a continuum of values.

Example 2.20   A manufacturer of a given electronic component is trying to determine the length of the appropriate warranty to offer customers. The variable of interest is the time before failure of the component. Since this variable can theoretically assume any value greater than 0, it is a continuous random variable.

Since a continuous random variable can assume an uncountably infinite number of values, calculation of the probabilities by enumeration, as was done in the discrete case, is not possible. In fact, when working with continuous random variables, one encounters the seeming contradiction that the probability that the random variable assumes any particular value in its range is 0, while the probability that it assumes some value in its range is 1. Thus to gain any measure of probability, one must resort to the continuous analog of the cumulative distribution function, given by $F(x) = P(\mathbf{X} \leq x)$.

PROPERTY 2.6   *The cumulative distribution function (cdf) of a continuous random variable* **X** *has the following properties.*

1. $F(x)$ *is continuous.*
2. $F'(x)$ *exists except at most a finite number of points.*
3. $F'(x)$ *is continuous, at least piecewise.*

Without getting too deeply into the mathematical aspects of these properties, one can observe that they imply that the range of **X** consists of one or more intervals, that the cdf is a smooth curve over each interval, and that the derivative can be integrated over all intervals of interest.

DEFINITION 2.11 *The probability density function, denoted f(x), is the derivative of the cumulative distribution function.*

$$f(x) = \frac{d}{dx} F(x)$$

The term *density* refers to the analog of computing the mass in a physical sense. That is, the probability density function gives the distribution of the probability of **X** over its range. Note, however, that the probability density function *f* evaluated at a point does *not* give the probability that the random variable **X** will assume that value.

PROPERTY 2.7 *The probability density function f of a random variable* **X** *has the following properties.*

1. $f(x) = 0$ *if x is not in the range of* **X**.
2. $f(x) \geq 0$.
3. $\int_{-\infty}^{\infty} f(x)dx = 1$.
4. $F(x_1) = \int_{-\infty}^{x_1} f(x)dx$.

Example 2.21 Suppose that the lifetime in months of the electronic component referred to in example 2.20 was found to have the probability density function

$$f(x) = e^{-x}, \quad 0 \leq x < \infty$$
$$= 0, \quad \text{otherwise}$$

This function may be plotted graphically as in figure 2.4. The cor-

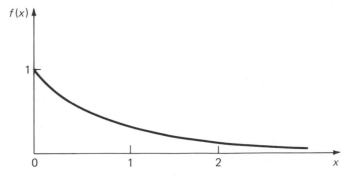

Figure 2.4
Density function for the component lifetime problem

responding cumulative distribution function appears graphically as in figure 2.5.

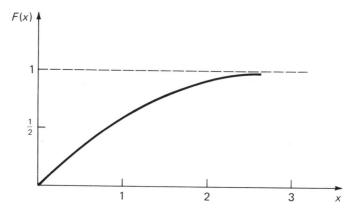

Figure 2.5
Distribution function for the component lifetime problem

One can compute the probability that the component will fail within ten months as follows.

$$P(\mathbf{X} \leq 10) = F(10) = \int_{-\infty}^{10} f(x)dx$$

$$= \int_{-\infty}^{0} 0 \, dx + \int_{0}^{10} e^{-x} \, dx$$

$$= -[e^{-x}]_{0}^{10} = -e^{-10} + 1$$

$$= 1 - 0.000045$$

$$= 0.99995$$

This corresponds to finding the area under the curve of $f(x)$ between 0 and 10.

Just as with discrete distributions, a continuous distribution can be summarized using the expectation (mean) and variance.

DEFINITION 2.12   *Let* $\mathbf{X}$ *be a continuous random variable, and let* $f(x)$ *denote its probability density function. The expectation of* $\mathbf{X}$, *denoted* $E(\mathbf{X})$, *is given by*

$$E(\mathbf{X}) = \int_{-\infty}^{\infty} xf(x) \, dx$$

Example 2.22 Consider the experiment described in examples 2.20 and 2.21. The expected life of the component is

$$E(\mathbf{X}) = \int_{-\infty}^{\infty} xf(x)dx$$

$$= \int_{-\infty}^{0} 0 \, dx + \int_{0}^{\infty} xe^{-x} \, dx$$

$$= -xe^{-x} \mid_0^\infty - \int_{0}^{\infty} (-e^{-x})dx$$

$$= e^{-x} \mid_0^\infty = 1$$

DEFINITION 2.13 *Let* **X** *be a continuous random variable, and let f(x) denote its probability density function. The variance of* **X**, *denoted V*(**X**), *is given by*

$$V(\mathbf{X}) = \int_{-\infty}^{\infty} (x - E(\mathbf{X}))^2 f(x)dx$$

$$= \int_{-\infty}^{\infty} x^2 f(x)dx - (E(\mathbf{X}))^2$$

The standard deviation *S*(**X**) is given by

$$S(\mathbf{X}) = [V(\mathbf{X})]^{1/2}$$

Example 2.23 Consider the experiment described in examples 2.20–2.22. The variance in lifetime for the electronic component can be computed by

$$V(\mathbf{X}) = \int_{-\infty}^{\infty} (x - E(\mathbf{X}))^2 f(x)dx$$

$$= \int_{-\infty}^{\infty} x^2 f(x)dx - (E(\mathbf{X}))^2$$

$$= \int_{0}^{\infty} x^2 e^{-x} \, dx - 1$$

$$= [-x^2 e^{-x} - 2xe^{-x} - 2e^{-x}]_0^\infty - 1$$

$$= 2 - 1 = 1$$

The standard deviation *S*(**X**) is given by

$$S(\mathbf{X}) = [V(\mathbf{X})]^{1/2} = 1^{1/2} = 1$$

It is not possible to achieve a continuous distribution in a real-world experiment, since all known measuring devices yield discrete values. However, when a discrete random variable is measured at enough points that it begins to take on the appearance of a continuous random variable, it is convenient to approximate the discrete distribution by a continuous one. In that way one can use the tools of calculus to calculate probabilities, means, and variances rather than tediously sum up a large number of fractional numbers.

Functions of a random variable

2.6   In many applications, once a random experiment is conducted and the distribution of the random variable determined, some related quantity must be examined. In such cases it is sometimes convenient to define a new random variable as a function of the original random variable.

Example 2.24   Suppose that a random experiment is conducted in which the quantity of interest is the temperature of a liquid. Let **X** denote the random variable that measures this temperature in degrees centigrade (Celsius), and assume that the distribution of **X** is known. Suppose now that we want to investigate the distribution of the temperature in degrees Fahrenheit. Rather than conduct the experiment again, we can simply modify the original observations using the relationship

$$Y = \frac{9}{5}X + 32$$

The new random variable **Y**, then, is a function of the original random variable **X**.

This example illustrates one of the simpler functions of random variables, a linear function.

DEFINITION 2.14   *Let **X** denote a random variable corresponding to the outcomes of some random experiment. Suppose the random variable **Y** is related to **X** by the relation **Y** = a**X** + b, where a and b are arbitrary constants. Then **Y** is said to be a* linear function *of **X**.*

If the distribution of **X** is known, it is quite straightforward to determine the distribution of **Y**. Each observation of **X** is multiplied by the constant a and then added to the constant b. The corresponding probabilities remain the same.

It is also quite easy to calculate the expected value and variance for simple linear functions of random variables. For example, suppose that **X** is a continuous random variable corresponding to the outcomes of a random experiment and that $\mathbf{Y} = a\mathbf{X} + b$. Then

$$E(\mathbf{Y}) = E(a\mathbf{X} + b)$$

$$= \int_{-\infty}^{\infty} (ax + b) f(x) dx$$

$$= a \int_{-\infty}^{\infty} xf(x)dx + b \int_{-\infty}^{\infty} f(x)dx$$

$$= aE(\mathbf{X}) + b$$

Similarly

$$V(\mathbf{Y}) = V(a\mathbf{X} + b)$$

$$= \int_{-\infty}^{\infty} (ax + b)^2 f(x)dx - (E(a\mathbf{X} + b))^2$$

$$= \int_{-\infty}^{\infty} a^2 x^2 f(x)dx + 2ab \int_{-\infty}^{\infty} xf(x)dx + b^2 \int_{-\infty}^{\infty} f(x)dx - (E(a\mathbf{X} + b))^2$$

$$= \int_{-\infty}^{\infty} a^2 x^2 f(x)dx + 2ab\, E(\mathbf{X}) + b^2 - (aE(\mathbf{X}) + b)^2$$

$$= a^2 \left[\int_{-\infty}^{\infty} x^2 f(x)dx - (E(\mathbf{X}))^2 \right]$$

$$= a^2 V(\mathbf{X})$$

These results may seem surprising, but they are really quite intuitive. For example, the additive constant b has no effect on the variance. This makes sense intuitively; the addition of a constant shifts all observations uniformly and thus does not affect their relative positions with respect to the mean. These results also hold for discrete random variables, with substitution of the summation sign Σ for the integral sign $\int$, and the probability function P for the density function f.

Example 2.25   Suppose that for the random experiment described in example 2.24, the random variable **X** was distributed with mean (expected value) equal to 30 degrees and variance equal to 64 degrees squared. Then

$$E(\mathbf{Y}) = \frac{9}{5} E(\mathbf{X}) + 32$$

$$= \frac{9}{5} \ (30) + 32$$

$$= 86 \ \text{degrees}$$

$$V(\mathbf{Y}) = \left(\frac{9}{5}\right)^2 V(\mathbf{X})$$

$$= (3.24)(64) = 207.36 \ \text{degrees squared}$$

The standard deviation of **Y** is then

$$S(\mathbf{Y}) = [207.36]^{1/2} = 14.4 \ \text{degrees}$$

Using the technique illustrated for a simple linear function, one can calculate the expected value of any arbitrary function of a random variable. If $\mathbf{Y} = g(\mathbf{X})$, then

$$E(\mathbf{Y}) \ = \ E(g(\mathbf{X})) \ = \ \sum_i g(x_i)P(x_i) \quad \text{in the discrete case}$$

or

$$E(\mathbf{Y}) = E(g(\mathbf{X})) = \int_{-\infty}^{\infty} g(x) f(x) dx \quad \text{in the continuous case}$$

and

$$V(\mathbf{Y}) = V(g(\mathbf{X})) = \sum_i (g(x_i) - E(g(x_i)))^2 P(x_i) \quad \text{in the discrete case}$$

or

$$V(\mathbf{Y}) = V(g(\mathbf{X})) = \int_{-\infty}^{\infty} (g(x) - E(g(x))^2 f(x) dx \quad \text{in the continuous case}$$

Moments

2.7   The previous section introduced the notion of a function of the random variable **X**. One simple function whose expectation is of interest is the power function $g(\mathbf{X}) = \mathbf{X}^r$, for $r = 1,2,3, \ldots$.

DEFINITION 2.15   *The expectation of the power function* $g(X) = X^r$, $r =$ *1,2,3, . . . , is called the* rth *moment of the random variable* X *taken about zero and is denoted* μ_r.

Applying the definition of expectation, one can calculate the rth moment of a random variable X taken about zero as

$$\mu_r = \sum_i x_i^r P(x_i) \quad \text{if } X \text{ is discrete}$$

or

$$\mu_r = \int_{-\infty}^{\infty} x^r f(x) dx \quad \text{if } X \text{ is continuous}$$

Moments can also be calculated about a point other than zero, say some constant c. The computational formula for moments about a constant c is

$$\mu'_r = \sum_i (x_i - c)^r P(x_i) \quad \text{if } X \text{ is discrete}$$

or

$$\mu'_r = \int_{-\infty}^{\infty} (x - c)^r f(x) dx \quad \text{if } X \text{ is continuous}$$

These quantities are called moments because of their obvious analogy to moments of inertia in physics. Some of these moments have significance in summarizing various characteristics of the distribution.

First moment. The first moment about zero simply gives the expected value or mean of the distribution. It is denoted by the Greek letter μ and serves as a measure of the central tendency or location of the distribution. It is computed as follows.

$$\mu = \sum_i x_i P(x_i) \quad \text{if } X \text{ is discrete}$$

or

$$\mu = \int_{-\infty}^{\infty} x f(x) dx \quad \text{if } X \text{ is continuous}$$

Second moment. The second moment about the mean gives the variance of the distribution. It is denoted by σ^2 and gives a measure of dispersion or the spread of the distribution. The square root of the variance is called the standard deviation (root mean square). The variance (moment of dispersion) is calculated as follows.

$$\sigma^2 = \sum_i (x_i - \mu)^2 \, P(x_i) \quad \text{if } \mathbf{X} \text{ is discrete}$$

or

$$\sigma^2 = \int_{-\infty}^{\infty} (x - \mu)^2 f(x) dx \quad \text{if } \mathbf{X} \text{ is continuous}$$

Third moment. The third moment about the mean is a measure of the symmetry of the distribution. If it is positive, the distribution is asymmetrical and positively skewed (the peak of the distribution is to the left of the mean). If it is zero, the distribution is symmetric. If it is negative, the distribution is asymmetric and negatively skewed. These three cases are depicted in figure 2.6. The third moment about the mean is calculated by

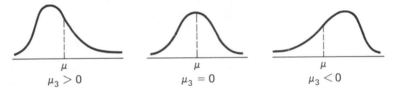

Figure 2.6
Illustration of the third moment about the mean

$$\mu'_3 = \sum_i (x_i - \mu)^3 \, P(x_i) \quad \text{if } \mathbf{X} \text{ is discrete}$$

or

$$\mu'_3 = \int_{-\infty}^{\infty} (x - \mu)^3 f(x) dx \quad \text{if } \mathbf{X} \text{ is continuous}$$

Fourth moment. The fourth moment about the mean is a measure of kurtosis or the flatness or peakedness of the distribution. It is calculated by

$$\mu'_4 = \sum_i (x_i - \mu)^4 \, P(x_i) \quad \text{if } \mathbf{X} \text{ is discrete}$$

or

$$\mu'_4 = \int_{-\infty}^{\infty} (x_i - \mu)^4 f(x) dx \quad \text{if } \mathbf{X} \text{ is continuous}$$

Generating functions

2.8   Another function of the random variable **X** which is of interest is the function $g(\mathbf{X}) = e^{\mathbf{X}\theta}$, where θ is some variable.

DEFINITION 2.16   *The function* $M(\theta) = E[e^{\mathbf{X}\theta}]$, *where E is the expectation operator, is termed (if it exists) the* moment-generating function *of the random variable* **X**.

Using the concept of expectation developed earlier, one can calculate the moment-generating function by

$$M(\theta) = E[e^{\mathbf{X}\theta}] = \sum_i e^{x_i\theta} P(x_i) \quad \text{if } \mathbf{X} \text{ is discrete}$$

or

$$M(\theta) = E[e^{\mathbf{X}\theta}] = \int_{-\infty}^{\infty} e^{x\theta} f(x)dx \quad \text{if } \mathbf{X} \text{ is continuous}$$

Example 2.26   Suppose **X** is a continuous random variable that has the probability density function $f(x) = e^{-x}$, $0 < x < \infty$, and 0 elsewhere (see example 2.21). Then the moment-generating function is

$$M(\theta) = E[e^{\mathbf{X}\theta}] = \int_0^{\infty} e^{x\theta} \cdot e^{-x}dx$$

$$= \int_0^{\infty} e^{-(1-\theta)x}dx = \frac{1}{1-\theta}, \quad \theta \neq 1$$

The function M is called the moment-generating function because all moments of **X** can be readily calculated from it.

In particular, $e^{\mathbf{X}\theta}$ can be expanded in an infinite series as

$$e^{\mathbf{X}\theta} = 1 + \mathbf{X}\theta + \frac{\mathbf{X}^2\theta^2}{2!} + \cdots + \frac{\mathbf{X}^n\theta^n}{n!} + \cdots$$

Then applying the expectation operator gives

$$M(\theta) = E[e^{\mathbf{X}\theta}] = 1 + E(\mathbf{X})\theta + \frac{E(\mathbf{X}^2)\theta^2}{2!} + \cdots + \frac{E(\mathbf{X}^n)\theta^n}{n!} + \cdots$$

$$= 1 + \mu_1\theta + \frac{\mu_2\theta^2}{2!} + \cdots + \frac{\mu_n\theta^n}{n!} + \cdots$$

Thus the moments of **X** can be calculated by expanding $M(\theta)$ in an infinite series and noting the coefficients of the powers of θ.

Example 2.27   Consider the distribution discussed in example 2.26.

$$M(\theta) = \frac{1}{1-\theta} = 1 + \theta + \theta^2 + \theta^3 + \cdots + \theta^n + \cdots$$

$$= 1 + (1)(\theta) + (2!)\frac{\theta^2}{2!} + \cdots + (n!)\frac{\theta^n}{n!} + \cdots$$

Then

$$\mu = \mu_1 = 1, \qquad \mu_2 = 2, \ldots, \mu_n = n!$$

Suppose that **X** is an integer-valued discrete random variable with probability function P. Then the moment-generating function can be simplified using the transformation $Z = e^\theta$. The resulting function, called the *probability generating function* or the Z-transform of **X**, is given by

$$\Psi(z) = E[\mathbf{Z}^x] = \sum_i z^i P(x_i)$$

This function is used to calculate the moments of a distribution and will be useful in developing the steady-state equations for a simple queueing system in chapter 5.

Multivariate distributions

2.9   Everything we have done thus far in this chapter has assumed that a simple random variable **X** was defined on the event space of some random experiment. In the simulation of real-world systems it is sometimes convenient or even necessary to define more than one random variable on the event space. We must then consider the joint distribution of the random variables. In this section we consider the special case of two random variables. Results are easily extended to the case in which more than two random variables are defined on the same event space.

If **X** and **Y** are two random variables defined on the same event space, then outcomes of the random experiment consist of ordered pairs (x,y) in two-dimensional space. Events then are formed by combining these two-dimensional outcomes.

Example 2.28   Consider the random variables **X** and **Y** defined on the same event space. If **X** can assume the values 0, 1, 2, 3, 4 and **Y** can assume the values 0 and 1, then the random variables can jointly assume the values

$$\Omega = \{(0,0), (0,1), (1,0), (1,1), (2,0), (2,1), (3,0), (3,1), (4,0), (4,1)\}$$

In the case of discrete random variables a probability function P_{XY} assigns the probability to some event E.

DEFINITION 2.17   *For any two discrete random variables* **X** *and* **Y** *the joint probability function* $P_{XY}(x,y)$ *is a function defined such that*

$$P_{XY}(x,y) = P(X = x \text{ and } Y = y)$$

That is, P_{XY} gives the probability that the random variable **X** assumes the value x at the same time that **Y** assumes the value y.

The joint cumulative distribution function for a pair of random variables can be analogously defined.

DEFINITION 2.18   *For any two random variables* **X** *and* **Y** *defined on the same event space, the joint distribution function* $F_{XY}(x,y)$ *is a function defined such that*

$$F_{XY}(x,y) = P(X \leq x \text{ and } Y \leq y)$$

Note that this function is defined for all values of x and y. Furthermore, this definition holds for continuous as well as discrete random variables.

The probability that a continuous random variable assumes any particular value in its range is 0. This observation carries over the multivariate distributions. If **X** and **Y** are continuous random variables defined over the same event space, then $P(X = x \text{ and } Y = y) = 0$ for any x, y. This leads to development of a joint density function.

DEFINITION 2.19   *Let* **X** *and* **Y** *be two continuous random variables defined on the same event space. The joint density function* $f_{XY}(x,y)$ *is a function defined by*

$$f_{XY}(x,y) = \frac{\partial^2 F_{XY}(x,y)}{\partial x \partial y}$$

whenever this derivative exists. This definition gives a means of calculating the cumulative distribution function at a particular point (x,y).

$$F_{XY}(x,y) = \int_{-\infty}^{x} \int_{-\infty}^{y} f(u,v) \, du \, dv$$

where u and v are dummy variables.

Although in most cases we are interested in the joint distribution of **X** and **Y**, it is also possible to consider the distribution of either random variable alone. This type of distribution is called the marginal distribution.

DEFINITION 2.20   *Let **X** and **Y** be continuous random variables defined on the same event space, with joint density function f_{XY}. The marginal density functions for **X** and **Y** are given by*

$$f_X(x) = \int_{-\infty}^{\infty} f(x,y)dy, \qquad f_Y(y) = \int_{-\infty}^{\infty} f(x,y)dx$$

*Similar formulas apply if **X** and **Y** are discrete random variables.*

This definition of the marginal distributions allows us to consider what it means for two jointly distributed random variables to be independent.

DEFINITION 2.21   *Let **X** and **Y** be two random variables defined on the same event space. The random variables are said to be independent if*

$$F_{XY}(x,y) = F_X(x) \, F_Y(y)$$

The marginal density functions for continuous random variables (probability functions for discrete random variables) allow calculation of the means and variances of the random variables.

DEFINITION 2.22   *Let **X** and **Y** be continuous random variables defined on the same event space. Then*

$$E(X) = \mu_X = \int_{-\infty}^{\infty} x f_X(x)dx, \qquad V(X) = \int_{-\infty}^{\infty} (x - \mu_X)^2 f_X(x)dx$$

*Similar formulas hold for **Y**, and when **X** and **Y** are discrete.*

The variance of a random variable **X** is a measure of dispersion. When we are dealing with joint random variables **X** and **Y**, another quantity of interest is the *covariance*.

DEFINITION 2.23   *Let* **X** *and* **Y** *be jointly continuous random variables with joint density function* $f_{XY}(x,y)$. *The covariance of* **X** *and* **Y**, *denoted* σ_{XY}, *is given by*

$$\sigma_{XY} = E[(\mathbf{X} - \mu_X)(\mathbf{Y} - \mu_Y)]$$

$$= \int_{-\infty}^{\infty} \int_{-\infty}^{\infty} (x - \mu_X)(y - \mu_Y) f_{XY}(x,y) \, dx \, dy$$

An analogous definition exists for discrete random variables.

The covariance is a measure of the linear association of the random variables **X** and **Y**. In particular, a quantity known as the correlation may be defined as

$$\rho_{XY} = \sigma_{XY}/\sigma_X \sigma_Y$$

A value of $\rho_{XY} = 0$ implies no correlation between **X** and **Y**, whereas a correlation of $+1$ or -1 implies perfect linear correlation.

Of particular importance in statistical analysis is the expectation and the variance of the sums of jointly distributed random variables.

DEFINITION 2.24   *Let* **X** *and* **Y** *be jointly distributed random variables, and define* $\mathbf{U} = a_1 \mathbf{X} + b_1 \mathbf{Y}$. *Then*

$$E[\mathbf{U}] = a_1 \mu_X + b_1 \mu_Y$$
$$V[\mathbf{U}] = a_1^2 \sigma_X^2 + b_1^2 \sigma_Y^2 + 2a_1 b_1 \sigma_{XY}$$

If $\sigma_{XY} = 0$ (**X** *and* **Y** *are uncorrelated), the latter expression simplifies somewhat.*

Note that independent random variables are uncorrelated. The converse of this is not true in general.

In this section we have briefly examined jointly distributed random variables. The treatment was necessarily brief. The importance of these concepts should become clear as we proceed.

Some common distributions

2.10   A number of common distributions have emerged from the study of real-world systems. Although in some cases the outcomes of experiments do not precisely follow these distributions, they are often used as first approximations to the real distribution. In this section we will explore in some detail these common distributions and attempt to indicate their utility in the study of real-world systems.

Bernoulli distribution

2.10.1   The Bernoulli distribution, a discrete distribution, is one of the simplest and is useful in experiments having only two outcomes. Assume that a random variable **X** has been defined and that it takes the value 0 with probability p and the value 1 with the probability $q = 1 - p$. Then the distribution of **X** is

x	$P(x)$
0	p
1	q

The cumulative distribution function for this random variable is

$$F(x) = \begin{cases} 0, & x < 0 \\ p, & 0 \le x < 1 \\ 1, & x \ge 1 \end{cases}$$

The expected value, variance, and standard deviation are

$$\mu = E(\mathbf{X}) = 0 \cdot p + 1 \cdot q = q$$
$$\sigma^2 = V(\mathbf{X}) = E(\mathbf{X}^2) - [E(\mathbf{X})]^2 = 0 \cdot p + 1 \cdot q - q^2 = q(1 - q)$$
$$\sigma = S(\mathbf{X}) = [q(1 - q)]^{1/2}$$

Figure 2.7 shows the Bernoulli distribution.

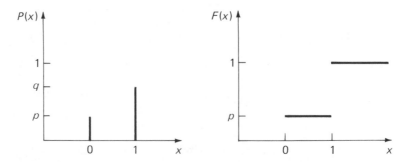

Figure 2.7
The Bernoulli distribution

Example 2.29   Consider the experiment of tossing a fair coin. Let **X** assume the value 0 if a head appears, 1 if a tail appears. Then $p = q = 1/2$, and

$$\mu = 1/2, \qquad \sigma^2 = 1/4, \qquad \sigma = 1/2$$

Binomial distribution

2.10.2   The binomial distribution is a discrete distribution that results from a sequence of independent Bernoulli trials. Assume that an experiment that has two outcomes is conducted n times, $n > 0$. Assume also that the probability of one outcome on any trial (call the outcome 0) is p and that the probability of the other outcome (call it 1) is $q = 1 - p$. Then the outcome 0 can occur any number of integral times from 0 to n, as can the outcome 1. The probability that the outcome 0 occurs precisely k times (1 occurs $n - k$ times) is

$$P(\mathbf{X} = k) = \frac{n!}{k!(n - k)!} p^k q^{n-k}, \qquad k = 0, 1, \ldots, n$$

The cumulative distribution function is given by

$$F(k) = \sum_{s=0}^{k} \frac{n!}{s!(n - s)!} p^s q^{n-s}, \qquad k = 0, 1, \ldots, n$$

The binomial distribution is illustrated in figure 2.8 for $n = 5, p = 0.5$.

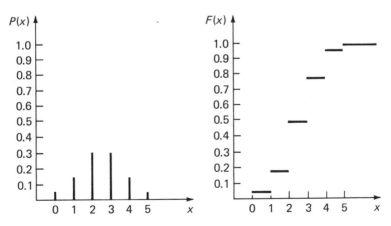

Figure 2.8
Binomial distribution (n = 5, p = 0.5)

The expected value and variance are easily calculated by treating the binomial as the sum of n Bernoulli random variables $\mathbf{X}_1, \mathbf{X}_2, \ldots, \mathbf{X}_n$. Then

$$\mu = E(\mathbf{X}) = E[\mathbf{X}_1 + \mathbf{X}_2 + \cdots + \mathbf{X}_n]$$

$$= q + q + \cdots + q = nq$$

$$\sigma^2 = V(\mathbf{X}) = V[\mathbf{X}_1 + \mathbf{X}_2 + \cdots + \mathbf{X}_n]$$

$$= pq + pq + \cdots + pq$$

$$= npq$$

Example 2.30 Suppose five fair dice are tossed, and one wants to compute the probability of 0, 1, 2, . . . , 5 sixes. If the outcomes 0 signifies "not a six" and 1 signifies "a six", then $p = 5/6$ and $q = 1/6$ and the mean and variance are given by

$$\mu = E(\mathbf{X}) = (5)(1/6) = 5/6$$
$$\sigma^2 = V(\mathbf{X}) = (5)(5/6)(1/6) = 25/36$$

Geometric distribution

2.10.3　The geometric distribution is also a discrete distribution that occurs as a result of n independent Bernoulli trials, just as the binomial distribution does. The geometric distribution measures the number of trials before the first success or failure. If p is taken as the probability of the 0 outcome (failure) on a given trial and q is the probability of the 1 outcome (success), then the probability function for the geometric distribution is

$$P(k) = P(\mathbf{Y} = k) = p^{k-1}q$$

where $\mathbf{Y}$ measures the number of trials until the first success, $k = 1$, 2, ... The cumulative distribution function is clearly

$$F(k) = \sum_{i=0}^{\infty} P(i) = \sum_{i=1}^{\infty} p^{i-1}q$$

Figure 2.9 shows the geometric distribution for $p = 0.7$.

The mean and variance for the geometric distribution are

$$\mu = 1/q$$
$$\sigma^2 = p/q^2$$

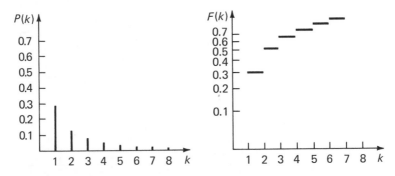

Figure 2.9
Geometric distribution (p = 0.7)

Example 2.31   Suppose a random experiment is conducted in which a biased coin is tossed until the first head appears. Further suppose the probability of a head on any toss is 1/5, while the probability of a tail if 4/5. Then

$$\mu = 1/(1/5) = 5$$
$$\sigma^2 = (4/5)/(1/25) = 20$$

Poisson distribution

2.10.4   The Poisson distribution, another discrete distribution, has been widely used to model arrival distributions and other seeming random events. It was originally developed to model telephone calls to a switchboard. The probability function is given by

$$P(x) = \frac{\lambda^x e^{-\lambda}}{x!} , x = 0, 1, 2, \dots$$

where λ is a constant called the *parameter* of the distribution. The cumulative distribution function is given by

$$F(x) = \sum_{i=0}^{x} \frac{\lambda^i e^{-\lambda}}{i!}$$

while its mean and variance are given by

$$\mu = \lambda, \qquad \sigma^2 = \lambda$$

Figure 2.10 illustrates the Poisson distribution for $\lambda = 4.5$.

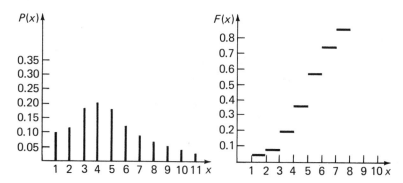

Figure 2.10
Poisson distribution $(\lambda = 4.5)$

Example 2.32 Calls to a switchboard are thought to be Poisson distributed with an average of five calls per minute. The probability of ten calls in the next minute is

$$P(\mathbf{X} = 10) = P(10) = \frac{\lambda^{10}e^{-10}}{10!}$$

$$= \frac{5^{10}e^{-10}}{10!} \doteq 0.0001$$

Uniform distribution

2.10.5 A continuous distribution, the uniform distribution, is one in which the density function is a constant.

$$f(x) = \begin{cases} 1/(b-a), & a \le x \le b \\ 0, & \text{otherwise} \end{cases}$$

This distribution is sometimes called the rectangular distribution. The interval [a, b] is called the range of the distribution. The cumulative distribution function is given by

$$F(x) = \int_{-\infty}^{x} f(t)dt = \begin{cases} 0, & x < a \\ \dfrac{x-a}{b-a}, & a \le x \le b \\ 1, & x > b \end{cases}$$

The mean and variance for this distribution are

$$\mu = \frac{a + b}{2}, \qquad \sigma^2 = \frac{(b - a)^2}{12}$$

Figure 2.11 shows the uniform distribution.

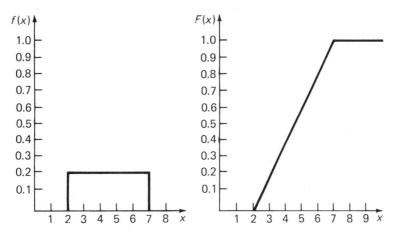

Figure 2.11
Uniform distribution (a = 2, b = 7)

This distribution is used to model truly random events. If a sequence of values is chosen at random on the interval $a \leq x \leq b$, it has the uniform distribution.

A particular uniform distribution in which $a = 0, b = 1$, called the standard uniform distribution, is of interest in generating random numbers. More will be said about it in chapter 4.

Normal distribution

2.10.6   Probably the most common continuous distribution is the normal distribution. It has been found useful in modeling most measurement phenomena, such as scores on a test, heights and weights, and errors made in manufacturing processes. The distribution is symmetrical, with the probability density function

$$f(x) = \frac{1}{\sigma\sqrt{2\pi}} \exp\left\{-\frac{(x - \mu)^2}{2\sigma^2}\right\}, \qquad -\infty < x < \infty$$

This distribution is unusual in that its cumulative distribution function cannot be computed exactly. Its cumulative distribution function is given by

$$F(x) = \int_{-\infty}^{x} \frac{1}{\sigma\sqrt{2\pi}} \, \exp\left\{-\frac{(t-\mu)^2}{2\sigma^2}\right\} dt$$

but this integral does not exist in closed form. To get around this problem, tables of values are available for the standard normal distribution, which has a mean of 0 and a variance of 1; that is,

$$f(z) = \frac{1}{\sqrt{2\pi}} \, e^{-z^2/2}$$

This function can be integrated numerically to obtain approximations for cumulative probabilities.

Cumulative probabilities for nonstandard normal distributions may be calculated from the standard tables of values. If **X** is normally distributed with mean μ and variance σ^2, then the random variable

$$\mathbf{Z} = (\mathbf{X} - \mu)/\sigma$$

is normally distributed with mean 0 and variance 1. Figure 2.12 shows the normal distribution with $\mu = 5.2, \sigma = 2.2$.

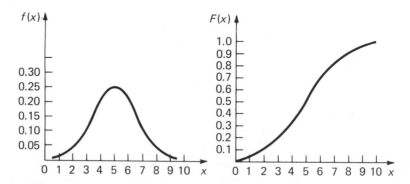

Figure 2.12
Normal distribution ($\mu = 5.2, \sigma = 2.2$)

Example 2.33   The grades on the final examination in a mathematics course were determined to be approximately normally distributed with mean 75 and variance 25. Then the standardized grades computed using $\mathbf{Z} = (\mathbf{X} - 75)/5$ are approximately normal with mean 0 and variance 1.

The normal distribution is probably the most useful distribution in modeling, not only because it accurately models many phenomena, but also because of the following reasons.

1. The sum of n independently and identically distributed random variables tends to be normally distributed as n tends to infinity. This result is known as the *central limit theorem*.

2. If $\mathbf{X}$ is distributed binomially, then as n tends toward infinity, $\mathbf{X}$ tends to be normally distributed with $\mu = nq$, $\sigma^2 = npq$.

3. If $\mathbf{X}$ is distributed according to the Poisson distribution, then as η gets large, $\mathbf{X}$ tends to be normally distributed with $\mu = \lambda$.

Thus the normal distribution is useful not only in its own right but also as an approximation to many other distribution.

Exponential distribution

2.10.7   Another continuous distribution that has wide utility is the (negative) exponential distribution. This distribution has been used to model "sudden and catastrophic" failures such as equipment failures due to manufacturing defects and light bulbs burning out. It has also been used to characterize service times and interarrival times in queueing systems. The probability density function for the exponential distribution is

$$f(x) = \alpha e^{-\alpha x}, \qquad 0 \le x < \infty$$

where α is a positive constant. The cumulative distribution function is

$$F(x) = \alpha \int_0^x e^{-\alpha t}\, dt = 1 - e^{-\alpha x}$$

The mean and variance are

$$\mu = E(\mathbf{X}) = \alpha \int_0^x x e^{-\alpha x}\, dx = 1/\alpha$$

$$\sigma^2 = V(\mathbf{X}) = \alpha \int_0^x (x - 1/\alpha)^2 e^{-\alpha x}\, dx = 1/\alpha^2$$

Thus the exponential distribution's mean and standard deviation are the same. The exponential distribution is illustrated in figure 2.13 for $\alpha = 1$.

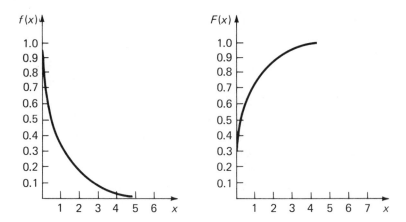

Figure 2.13
Exponential distribution ($\alpha = 1$)

Probably the most important aspect of the exponential distribution in modeling is that it has the "forgetfulness" property. This is summarized as follows.

PROPERTY 2.8   *Assume that the random variable **X** has an exponential distribution. Then for any x_1, $x_2 > 0$, $P(\mathbf{X} \leq x_2 \,|\, \mathbf{X} \geq x_1) = P(0 \leq \mathbf{X} \leq x_2 - x_1)$. The converse is also true.*

It is also interesting to note the relationship between the Poisson and exponential distributions.

PROPERTY 2.9   *Assume that the arrival process of customers to a queueing system follows the Poisson distribution, with arrival rate λ. Then the interarrival distribution (time between arrivals) will be exponential with parameter $1/\lambda$.*

This relationship will be explored more fully in chapter 5.

Example 2.34   The variable discussed in examples 2.20 and 2.21 has an exponential distribution with mean and variance equal to 1.

Chi-square distribution

2.10.8   A distribution that will be used extensively in goodness-of-fit testing is the chi-square distribution. The probability density function for this distribution is

$$f(\chi^2) = \frac{\chi^{2(\nu/2)-1} \, e^{-\nu/2}}{2^{\nu/2} \, \Gamma\left(\dfrac{\nu}{2}\right)}, \qquad \chi^2 > 0$$

In this formula, Γ is the standard Gamma function. The single parameter of this distribution is ν, known as the *degrees of freedom*. This distribution arises often when the squares of standard normal distributions are combined. If Z_i, $i = 1,2,\ldots,R$, are independent standard normal random variables, then $Z_1^2 + Z_2^2 + \cdots + Z_R^2$ is a chi-square distribution with R degrees of freedom.

Student's t-distribution

2.10.9   The t-distribution has been shown to be useful in hypothesis testing. Let Z and U be independent random variables, where Z follows a standard normal distribution and U a chi-square distribution with ν degrees of freedom. Then $t = Z/(U/\nu)$ follows a t-distribution. It, too, has only one parameter ν, which again denotes degrees of freedom. The t-distribution arises quite often when normal distributions are sampled. If X denotes the sample mean, S the sample standard deviation, and N the size of the sample, the random variable

$$t = N^{1/2} \, (X - \mu)/S$$

follows a t-distribution with $n - 1$ degrees of freedom.

F-Distribution

2.10.10   The F-distribution is also useful in hypothesis testing. Let U and V be two independent chi-square random variables with ν_1 and ν_2 degrees of freedom respectively. Then $(U/\nu_1)/(V/\nu_2)$ is distributed as an F-distribution with ν_1 and ν_2 degrees of freedom. This distribution arises when one is sampling from two normal populations. Let sample 1 consist of N_1 points from a normal population with mean μ_1 and variance σ_1^2, and let S_1^2 be the sample variance. Let sample 2 consist of N_2 points from a normal population with mean μ_2 and variance σ_2^2, and let S_2^2 be the sample variance. Then $(S_1^2/\sigma_1^2)/(S_2^2/\sigma_2^2)$ is distributed according to the F-distribution with $N_1 - 1$ and $N_2 - 1$ degrees of freedom.

Summary

In this chapter we have surveyed some of the fundamental aspects of probability and probability models. This material, along with statistical inference, random number generation, and queueing theory is fundamental to the simulation of systems. More detail on these concepts can be found in any of the many excellent references on probability.

Exercises

2.1   Three fair dice are tossed. Define the random variable **X** to denote the sum of the spots showing on all three dice. Determine the probability distribution, the expected value, and the variance of **X**.

2.2   A box contains six balls — three red, two black, and one white.
      a. Determine the probability that the white ball is drawn on a single draw.
      b. Determine the probability that the second ball drawn is black given that the first ball was white and that it was not replaced.
      c. Rework part b assuming that the white ball was replaced.

2.3   Let the random variable **X** count the number of boys in a family of six children. Assuming equal probabilities for boys and girls, determine the distribution, expected value, and variance of **X**.

2.4   Determine the probability that a student guesses seven of ten questions correctly on a true-false examination.

2.5   If the probability of a head on a single toss of a fair coin is 0.3, determine the expected number of tosses until the first tail appears.

2.6   The average number of calls to a switchboard is 30 per hour. Determine the probability that 10 calls will come in during the next 15 minutes.

2.7   A random variable **X** is distributed normally with mean 10 and variance 1. Determine the probability that an observation will lie within
      a. One standard deviation of the mean
      b. Two standard deviations of the mean
      c. Three standard deviations of the mean

2.8   A random variable **X** has mean 2 and variance 3. Find the mean and variance of
      a. $Y = 2X + 3$
      b. $Z = X - 3$

2.9   Assume that the height of men in the United States is distributed normally with a mean of 70 inches and a standard deviation of 2 inches. Determine the probability that a man selected at random is

   a. Exactly 72 inches tall
   b. Less than 68 inches tall
   c. Between 68 and 72 inches tall

2.10   A random variable **X** has probability density function $f(x) = 2e^{-2x}, x > 0$. Determine the expected value and standard deviation of **X**.

2.11   If the joint density function for two continuous random variables is given by

$$f_{XY}(x,y) = e^{-(x+y)}, \qquad x,y > 0$$

find
   a. $F_{XY}(x,y)$
   b. $F_X(x)$
   c. $F_Y(y)$

2.12   If **X** is a chi-square random variable, find
   a. $P(\mathbf{X} \geq 26.119)$ if $\nu = 14$
   b. $P(\mathbf{X} \leq 3.841)$ if $\nu = 1$
   c. $P(\mathbf{X} < 27.587)$ if $\nu = 17$

2.13   If **X** is a t random variable, find
   a. $P(\mathbf{X} > 1.372)$ if $\nu = 10$
   b. $P(1.333 < \mathbf{X} < 1.740)$ if $\nu = 17$

2.14   If **X** is an F random variable, find
   a. $P(\mathbf{X} \leq 19.5)$ if $\nu_1 = 40, \nu_2 = 2$
   b. $P(\mathbf{X} > 200)$ if $\nu_1 = 2, \nu_2 = 1$

2.15   Specifications for the diameter of a shaft are 1 ± 0.1 inches. If the manufacturing process produces shafts normally distributed with a mean of 1 inch and a variance of 0.0025, what is the probability that a shaft chosen at random will meet the specifications?

3

Estimation and statistical tests

At times a random variable **X** that is being used to represent some aspect of a simulation model is known to follow a particular distribution. If this is the case, the researcher's task is greatly simplified. More often than not, however, all that is known about the distribution of a random variable is what can be gleaned from the study of a set of sample values that has been collected through observations. Some technique is then needed to characterize the behavior of the random variable. Two general approaches have been taken in attempting to solve this problem. The first is to construct an empirical distribution using least squares or some other suitable curve-fitting technique. This approach should be used when the random variable does not appear to follow any of the common distributions. The second approach is to hypothesize that the random variable follows a particular distribution and to use statistical methodology to test the validity of this hypothesis. This approach is the more common of the two and, if successful, yields a distribution function that may be expressed analytically and whose behavior in most cases is well known. The normal distribution has been widely used and studied, and its characteristics are quite well known. The fortunate analyst who finds that the random variable of interest follows a normal distribution can draw on a wealth of knowledge available on that distribution.

Once a random variable has been found to follow a given distribution, the analyst's next task is to describe the distribution in easily understood terms. This task normally involves the estimation of the parameters (summary measures) of the distribution. When working with the normal distribution, for example, one is interested in estimating its mean and variance. The *t*-distribution, on the other hand, is categorized by the single parameter *degrees of freedom*.

The purpose of this chapter is to review the procedures used in constructing empirical distributions and the basic concepts of statistical inference and estimation. Four of the more common statistical tests are included. These tests will be used extensively in the subsequent chapters.

Empirical distributions

3.1
In some simulation studies it may not be possible or even necessary to establish that a random variable follows a particular known distribution. In this case the data samples gained from observations can be used to construct the cumulative distribution function directly.

To see how this is done, assume that N observations of a random variable **X** have been noted, and let the observations be ordered in a monotonic nondecreasing sequence as follows.

$$x_1 \leq x_2 \leq \cdots \leq x_N$$

Next form the sequence of numbers

$$y_n = n/N, \qquad n = 1, 2, \ldots, N$$

and plot the points $(x_1, y_1), \ldots, (x_N, y_N)$. By connecting these plotted points with some suitable function $y = F(x)$, where $F(x) = 0$ for $x < x_1$ and $F(x) = 1$ for $x > x_N$, one can obtain a curve satisfying all the properties of a cumulative distribution function. Such a function is known as an *empirical cumulative distribution function*.

Example 3.1   Suppose the following ten values were recorded for the random variable **X**: 1, −1, 2, 0, 4, 6, 7, 9, 10, 3. The points (x_n, y_n) are

n	1	2	3	4	5	6	7	8	9	10
x_n	−1	0	1	2	3	4	6	7	9	10
y_n	0.1	0.2	0.3	0.4	0.5	0.6	0.7	0.8	0.9	1.0

Plotting these points and joining the sequential observations with straight lines gives the empirical distribution function illustrated in figure 3.1.

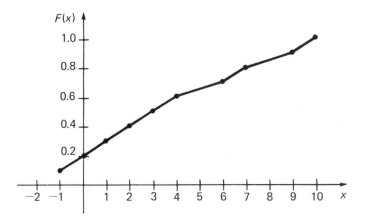

Figure 3.1
An empirical distribution function

A distribution function constructed in this fashion has the same problems that any quantity based on sample observations has. If it is based on too few observations, it may not be representative of the true process. Thus it is desirable to collect as many observations on the random variable of interest as is possible.

Construction of the cumulative distribution function by connecting sequential observations with straight-line segments as was done in example 3.1 is generally not desirable. If it is done in this fashion, each of the ordered pairs must be retained. If the number of observations is large, this can be inconvenient. A more satisfactory way is to fit a low-order polynomial

$$y = a_0 + a_1 x + \cdots + a_k x^k$$

to the points. Then only the coefficients of the polynomial need be stored. In many cases $k = 2$ or $k = 3$ is sufficient to describe the distribution.

A number of techniques are available for fitting a curve to the points. One of the most common techniques is the *method of least squares*. This technique is designed to fit a polynomial of kth degree

$$P(x) = a_0 + a_1 x + a_2 x^2 + \cdots + a_k x^k$$

to a set of $N \geq k$ points. This procedure yields a set of predicted values $\hat{y}_1, \hat{y}_2, \ldots, \hat{y}_N$ corresponding to each of the tabulated x_i, $i = 1, 2, \ldots, N$.

The difference between the ith predicted value $\hat{y}_i$ and the ith observed value y_i is referred to as the ith residual and is given by $\gamma_i = \hat{y}_i - y_i$. The basis of the least-squares method is to find the kth degree polynomial such that the sum of the squares of these residuals is a minimum.

Formally, let S be the sum of the squared residuals. Then

$$S = \sum_{i=1}^{N} \gamma_i^2 = \sum_{i=1}^{N} \left(y_i - \sum_{j=0}^{k} a_j x_i^j \right)^2$$

Since S is always positive, its minimum can be obtained by setting $\partial S / \partial a_j = 0$ for $j = 0, 1, 2, \ldots, k$ and then solving the resulting set of $k + 1$ linear equations for the coefficients $a_0, a_1, \ldots, a_k$. This technique will be illustrated by an example.

Example 3.2 Suppose we wish to fit the points of example 3.1 with a first-degree polynomial $P_1(x) = a_0 + a_1 x$. Then

$$S = \sum_{i=1}^{10} \gamma_i^2 = \sum_{i=1}^{N} (y_i - a_0 - a_1 x_i)^2$$

and

$$\frac{\partial S}{\partial a_0} = -2 \sum_{i=1}^{10} (y_i - a_0 - a_1 x_i)$$

while

$$\frac{\partial S}{\partial a_1} = -2 \sum_{i=1}^{10} x_i(y_i - a_0 - a_1 x_i)$$

Setting these derivatives equal to 0 and dividing by -2 yields the following equations

$$\sum_{i=1}^{10} (y_i - a_0 - a_1 x_i) = 0$$

$$\sum_{i=1}^{10} x_i(y_i - a_0 - a_i x_i) = 0$$

These equations may be rewritten as

$$10 a_0 + a_1 \sum_{i=1}^{10} x_i = \sum_{i=1}^{10} y_i$$

$$a_0 \sum_{i=1}^{10} x_i + a_1 \sum_{i=1}^{10} x_i^2 = \sum_{i=1}^{10} x_i y_i$$

Solving these two equations for a_0 and a_1 gives

$$a_1 = \sum_{i=1}^{10} x_i y_i \Big/ \sum_{i=1}^{10} x_i^2$$

$$a_0 = \bar{y} - a_1 \bar{x}$$

where $\bar{x}$ and $\bar{y}$ are the arithmetic means of the x's and y's respectively. Tabulation of the data necessary to compute these quantities for example 3.1 is given in table 3.1.

Table 3.1
Data for a regression example

i	x_i	y_i	x_i^2	$x_i y_i$	$\hat{y}_i$
1	-1	0.1	1	-0.1	-0.01
2	0	0.2	0	0	0.1
3	1	0.3	1	0.3	0.21
4	2	0.4	4	0.8	0.32
5	3	0.5	9	1.5	0.43
6	4	0.6	16	2.4	0.54
7	6	0.7	36	4.2	0.76
8	7	0.8	49	5.6	0.87
9	9	0.9	81	8.1	1.09
10	10	1.0	100	10.0	1.2
	41	5.5	297	32.8	

The respective means are $\bar{x} = 4.1$ and $\bar{y} = 0.55$, which yields

$$a_1 = \frac{32.8}{297} \doteq 0.11, \qquad a_0 \doteq 0.1$$

Thus the prediction equation is $\hat{y} = 0.1 + 0.11x$. The values of $\hat{y}_i$ for $i = 1, 2, \ldots, 10$ are given in the last column of table 3.1. Note that the curve does not appear to fit well. This is normally an indication that a higher-order polynomial is called for.

Estimation

3.2   Whether a random variable of interest in a simulation study is represented by an empirical distribution or is known to follow a particular distribution, the analyst encounters the problem of estimating the appropriate parameters of the distribution. For example, it is not generally sufficient to know that a random variable **X** follows a normal distribution without having some estimate of its expected value (mean) or standard deviation.

There are a number of desirable properties that any estimate of a population parameter should have. Some of these are as follows.

1. *Unbiasedness* An estimate $\hat{\theta}$ of some parameter θ is said to be unbiased if $\hat{E}(\hat{\theta}) = \theta$. For example, the sample mean $\mathbf{X} = n^{-1}\sum_{i=1}^{n} x_i$ is an unbiased estimate of the population mean μ. On the other hand, the sample standard deviation given by

$$S = \left(\sum_{i=1} (x_i - \bar{x})^2/(n - 1)\right)^{1/2}$$

is not an unbiased estimate of the population standard deviation σ.

2. *Minimum Variance* An estimate $\hat{\theta}$ of some population parameter θ is said to be a minimum variance estimate if $\sigma_{\hat{\theta}}^2 \leq \sigma_{\theta*}^2$ for any other estimate $\theta*$.

3. *Sufficiency* An estimate of $\hat{\theta}$ of some parameter θ is said to be sufficient if it utilizes all information in the sample.

4. *Consistency* An estimate $\hat{\theta}$ is said to be consistent if the estimate approaches the value of the parameter as the size of the sample increases.

It is not always possible to obtain an estimate that possesses all these (desirable) traits. For example, the sample standard deviation is normally used as an estimate of the population standard deviation even though it is not an unbiased estimate.

A point estimate of some population parameter provides some indication of the true value of that parameter. This indication may or may not be meaningful, since no indication of the possible degree of accuracy in the estimate is present. For this reason, estimates of population parameters are normally stated in the form of *confidence interval estimates*. This interval estimate is normally stated in the form $\hat{\theta} \pm \epsilon$, where ϵ is some positive quantity related to the size of the sample and to the standard deviation of the estimate. A confidence interval estimate normally carries some degree of assurance that the actual parameter falls within the specified interval. A number of techniques are available for constructing confidence interval estimates; the choice of a technique depends on the distribution being studied as well as the parameter being estimated. For this reason, no specific examples will be given here; instead, the techniques will be introduced as needed.

Tests of hypotheses

3.3 An alternative to constructing an empirical distribution is to hypothesize that the sample points of a random variable **X** come from some known distribution. Statistical methods can then be used to assess the validity of the hypothesis. In this section we review some of the fundamental concepts involved in making and testing statistical hypotheses. In later sections we examine particular tests and explore their application to simulation.

A *statistical hypothesis* is an assumption about the population being sampled. It could consist of theorizing that the population follows a given distribution or that a particular parameter of the population is a certain value. A *test* of a hypothesis is simply a rule by which a hypothesis is either accepted or rejected. This decision is normally based on statistics obtained from an examination of a sample or set of samples from the population. These sample statistics are referred to as *test statistics* when used to test hypotheses. The *critical region* of a test statistic consists of the values of the test statistic that result in rejection of the hypothesis.

Example 3.3   A simulation experiment is being designed to examine the operation of a service station. It is thought that customers arrive at the station at an average rate of 12 per hour. To test this assumption, the hypothesis could be stated as

$$H_0 : \mu = 12$$

The statement H_0 (called the null hypothesis) implies another hypothesis (called the alternate hypothesis) which is true if H_0 is determined to be false. For this experiment the alternate hypothesis can be stated as

$$A : \mu \neq 12$$

Suppose that the researcher decides to reject the null hypothesis if a sample collected yields an average arrival rate less than 10 per hour or greater than 14 per hour. The test statistic is then the sample mean **X**, while the critical region is $|\mathbf{X} - 12| > 2$.

Hypothesis testing is based on statistics gleaned from a sample. Anything based on sample statistics involves some likelihood of making an erroneous decision. The sample collected may not be representative of the true population; thus basing a decision on the sample could result in an incorrect decision. There are two types of errors that can be made.

If the sample statistics lead to rejection of a null hypothesis that is actually true, a type I error has been committed. The probability of making this type of error for a given test situation is normally denoted by α and is called the *level of significance*. If the sample statistics fail to reject a null hypothesis when it is actually false, a type II error has been made. The probability of making this type of error is normally designated β. The test situation and possible decisions are summarized in figure 3.2.

Test result	True situation	
	H_0 false	H_0 true
H_0 rejected	Correct decision	Type I error
H_0 accepted	Type II error	Correct decision

Figure 3.2
Decisions made in hypothesis testing

Obviously one of the objectives in hypothesis testing is to minimize α and β, the probabilities of making an incorrect decision. Unfortunately if one probability is reduced, the other is increased. In fact, the only way to simultaneously decrease both risks is to base the decision on a sample statistic obtained from a larger sample. In most testing situations α is set at some predetermined acceptable level and the decision rule is formulated to minimize β.

The steps taken in hypothesis testing can be summarized as follows.

1. State the hypothesis to be tested (establish H_0 and A).
2. Determine an acceptable risk of rejecting a true null hypothesis (set α at some level).
3. Choose some suitable test statistic by which to test H_0.
4. Assume H_0 is true and determine the sampling distribution of the test statistic.
5. Set up a critical region in which H_0 will be rejected $100\alpha\%$ of the time when α is true.
6. Collect a random sample of some predetermined size, compute the test statistic, and test the hypothesis.

Example 3.4   Consider the experiment described in example 3.3.

A test of the stated hypothesis following the procedure just described is as follows.

1. $H_0 : \mu = 12, A : \mu \neq 12$
2. Set $\alpha = 0.05$. That is, assume that a risk of rejecting a true null hypothesis 5% of the time is acceptable.
3. The test statistic to be used is $\overline{X}$, the average arrival rate determined from some sample. This statistic can be standardized as

$$\overline{X} : Z = \frac{\overline{X} - \mu}{\sigma/\sqrt{n}}$$

where σ is the true standard deviation of the population and n is the size of the sample.

4. $\overline{X}$ is normally distributed with mean μ and standard deviation $\sigma/\sqrt{n}$. This result follows from the central limit theorem if n is large enough.

5. The critical region on Z for a risk of $\alpha = 0.05$ is depicted in figure 3.3. Then H_0 will be rejected if

$$\left| \frac{\overline{X} - \mu}{\sigma/\sqrt{n}} \right| > 1.96$$

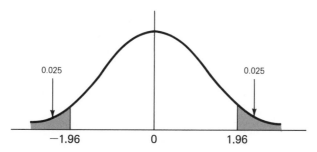

Figure 3.3
The critical region

6. Assume that a sample of size 16 was collected, that $\sigma = 2$, and that the sample yielded $\overline{X} = 14$. Then

$$Z = \frac{14 - 12}{1} = 2$$

So this sample would lead to rejection of H_0. The conclusion can then be drawn that $\mu \neq 12$.

The procedure outlined for testing a hypothesis did not consider β, the probability of a type II error. To compute β, one must assume H_0 false and some specific alternative true. For example, if H_0 in example 3.3 was assumed false and the alternate hypothesis $A : \mu = 14$ was assumed true, the situation would be as shown in figure 3.4. The shaded area is β and can be calculated from the normal distribution function as

$$\beta = P(\overline{X} \le 13.96)$$

$$= P\left(Z \le \frac{13.96 - 14}{1}\right)$$

$$= P(Z \le -0.04) = 0.4840$$

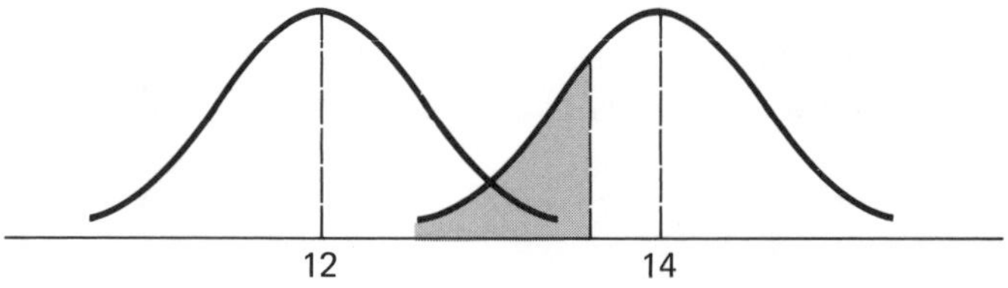

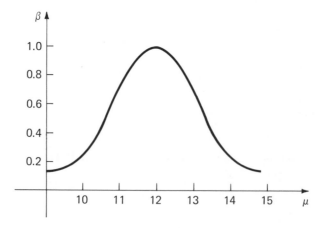

Figure 3.4
The value for β

By computing β for various alternate hypotheses and plotting β versus μ, one arrives at a curve known as the *operating characteristic* (OC) curve. The OC curve for the data of example 3.3 is shown in figure 3.5.

Figure 3.5
An operating characteristic curve

Frequently, rather than plot β versus μ, one plots the complement $1 - \beta$ versus μ. The quantity $1 - \beta$ is known as the *power* of the test, and a plot of $1 - \beta$ versus μ is known as the *power curve*. The power curve for the data of example 3.3 is shows in figure 3.6.

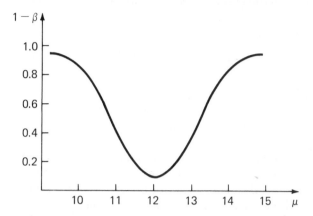

Figure 3.6
A power curve

Note that rejection of a null hypothesis is a positive action, whereas acceptance of the null hypothesis is no action. This is pointed out through examination of the OC or power curves. In the previous example, if the true mean was 12.5, the null hypothesis $H_0 : \mu = 12$ would be accepted with nearly as high a probability as if the mean was actually 12. Thus the test is not likely to detect small differences between the hypothesized and true parameter values. It will, however, detect large differences with a high probability. This is the reason for the statement that rejection of the null hypothesis is a positive action. Acceptance of the null hypothesis can be viewed as inconclusive. The hypothesis may be false, but we do not have sufficient evidence to prove it.

Many tests have been used in testing hypotheses. Which test to use depends on what one is trying to establish as well as how much is known about the underlying population. The next four sections will discuss four of the more useful tests, indicating the assumptions underlying their use as well as their utility.

The *t*-test

3.4   The *t*-test is used to test the hypothesis that two normal populations have the same mean. As the basis for the test, assume that we have two normally distributed populations, the first with mean μ_1 and variance σ_1^2 and the second with mean μ_2 and variance σ_2^2. In general, the variances are unknown, so they must be estimated from sample data. Assume further that a sample of size n_1, denoted $x_1, x_2, \ldots, x_{n_1}$, has been collected from the first population, while a sample of size n_2, denoted y_1, $y_2, \ldots, y_{n_2}$, has been collected from the second. The specific hypotheses we wish to test are

$$H_0 : \mu_1 = \mu_2, \qquad A : \mu_1 \neq \mu_2$$

or alternately

$$H_0 : \mu_1 - 0 \qquad A : \mu_1 - \mu_2 \neq 0$$

If the variables x_i, y_i are independent, a further assumption required to yield an exact test is that the variances σ_1^2 and σ_2^2, while unknown, are equal. If this assumption is not valid, no exact test exists. However, there are approximate tests that may be used. These approximate tests will not be discussed here but are available in most standard statistical texts. Under the assumption of equal variances, the test statistic for testing the equality of means is

$$t = \frac{(\bar{X} - \bar{Y})}{[S^2(1/n_1 + 1/n_2)]^{1/2}}$$

Where $\bar{X}$ is the sample mean from the first population, $\bar{Y}$ is the sample mean from the second population, and S^2 is an estimate of the variance given by

$$S^2 = \frac{[(n_1 - 1)S_1^2 + (n_2 - 1)S_2^2]}{(n_1 + n_2 - 2)}$$

S_1^2 is the sample variance from the first population, and S_2^2 is the sample variance from the second population. The sample variance S^2 is sometimes referred to as a pooled S^2. If the null hypothesis is true, t is distributed according to Student's t with $n_1 + n_2 - 2$ degrees of freedom. The critical region for the test is then $|t| \geq t_{(1-\alpha/2),(n_1+n_2-2)}$.

Example 3.5   Suppose that ten observations were taken on a random variable $\bar{X}$ and that the results were $\{1, 2, -1, 3, 7, 8, 9, 4, 3, 2\}$. Assume further that eight observations were taken on a random variable $\bar{Y}$ and that the results were $\{0, 3, 6, -2, 4, 0, 7, 8\}$. Assume that the observations come from normal populations and that the variances are equal. Then

$$\bar{X} = \sum_{i=1}^{10} \frac{x_i}{10} = 3.8 \qquad \bar{Y} = \sum_{i=1}^{8} \frac{y_i}{8} = 3.25$$

$$S_1^2 = \sum_{i=1}^{10} \frac{(x_i - \bar{x})^2}{9} = 10.4, \qquad S_2^2 = \sum_{i=1}^{8} \frac{(y_i - \bar{y})^2}{7} = 13.36$$

$$S^2 = \frac{(9(10.4) + 7(13.36))}{16} = 11.695$$

The hypotheses for testing for equality of means are

$$H_0 : \mu_1 - \mu_2 = 0, \qquad A : \mu_1 - \mu_2 \neq 0$$

The test statistic is

$$t = \frac{(\bar{X} - \bar{Y})}{[S^2(1 / n_1 + 1/n_2)]^{1/2}}$$

$$= \frac{(3.8 - 3.25)}{[(11.695)(1/10 + 1/8)]^{1/2}} = 0.34$$

If $\alpha = 0.05$, then $t_{0.05,16} = 2.120$. Since $t = 0.34 < 2.120$, we cannot reject the hypothesis that the means are equal.

Now suppose that the observations from the two populations cannot be considered independent but that corresponding observations can be paired. That is, they were both taken when conditions were similar (at the same time, and so on). This of course assumes that the size of each sample is the same, say n. Under these asssumptions, rather than consider each random variable separately, we consider the differences $D_i, i = 1, 2, \ldots, n$, as a random sample of size n from a normal distribution with mean $\mu = \mu_1 - \mu_2$ and variance σ^2. The test for equality of means is then

$$H_0 : \mu = 0, \qquad A : \mu \neq 0$$

The appropriate test statistic for testing this hypothesis is $t = n^{1/2}\bar{D}/S_D$ where $\bar{D}$ is the average difference and S_D is given by

$$S_D = \left[\frac{\sum_{i=1}^{n} (D_i - \bar{D})^2}{(n - 1)} \right]^{1/2}$$

If the null hypothesis is true, this statistic is distributed according to Student's t within $n - 1$ degrees of freedom. The critical region is then

$$|t| > t_{\alpha, n-1}$$

Example 3.6   Suppose the following paired observations were taken on the random variables $\overline{X}$ and $\overline{Y}$.

i	1	2	3	4	5	6	7	8
x_i	1	0	3	6	2	1	7	6
y_i	-2	4	-2	1	4	7	3	4
$d_i = x_i - y_i$	3	-4	5	5	-2	-6	4	2

Then

$$\overline{D} = \frac{\sum_{i=1}^{8} d_i}{8} = 0.875, \qquad S_D^2 = \frac{\sum_{i=1}^{8} (d_i - \overline{D})^2}{7} = 18.41$$

and the test statistic is $t = n^{1/2} \overline{D} / S_D = (8^{1/2})(0.875)/4.29 = 0.577$. If $\alpha = 0.05$, then $t_{0.05,7} = 2.365$. Again we are not able to reject the hypothesis of equal means.

The two tests examined in this section are two-tailed, meaning that we allowed rejection for extreme values above or below the hypothesized values. If one wished, for example, to test the hypothesis $H_0 : \mu_1 \leq \mu_2$ versus $A : \mu_1 > \mu_2$ where the samples are independent, a similar test is used, except that now rejection is possible only for large values of the test statistic. Rejection occurs only on one side of the hypothesized value. The only difference in the procedure is the calculation of the critical region. In this case the critical region is

$$t \geq t_{\alpha, \mu_1 + \mu_2 - 2}$$

A similar procedure exists for paired values.

To summarize, the t-test is designed to test for equality of means when samples have been drawn from two normal populations. If the samples are independent, an exact test exists only if it can be assumed that the variances of the two populations are equal. In the case of correlated samples the differences rather than the individual observations are considered.

The F-test

3.5   The t-test discussed in section 3.4 is used to test the hypothesis that two normal populations have the same mean. The F-test is used to test for equality of variances. Again an underlying assumption is that the two populations being sampled are normally distributed. Assume, just as in the previous section, that samples are taken from two normal populations with means μ_1 and μ_2 and variances σ_1^2 and σ_2^2 respectively. Let the sample taken from the first population be represented as $x_1, x_2, \ldots, x_{n_1}$ and the sample from the second population be represented as $y_1, y_2, \ldots, y_{n_2}$. The hypotheses that we wish to test in this case are

$$H_0 : \sigma_1^2 = \sigma_2^2, \qquad A : \sigma_1^2 \neq \sigma_2^2$$

The test statistic used to test these hypotheses is

$$F = S_1^2/S_2^2$$

where S_1 is the sample variance of the first sample and S_2 is the sample variance of the second sample. If the null hypothesis is true, this test statistic is distributed according to the F-distribution, with $\nu_1 = n_1 - 1$ and $\nu_2 = n_2 - 1$. The critical region for the test is then

$$F \geq F_{\alpha/2,(n_1-1,n_2-1)} \quad \text{or} \quad F \leq F_{(1-\alpha/2),(n_1-1,n_2-1)}$$

Example 3.7 Assume that samples are taken from two normal populations and that the following observations are recorded.

i	1	2	3	4	5	6	7	8	9	10
x_i	-5	4	-8	14	21	16	0	1	$-$	0
i	1	2	3	4	5	6	7	8		
y_i	0	1	-1	2	-2	0	1	2		

Then $S_1^2 = 73.73$ while $S_2^2 = 1.98$. The test statistic is

$$F = \frac{S_1^2}{S_2^2} = \frac{73.73}{1.98} = 37.2$$

If $\alpha = 0.05$, the critical region is

$$F \geq F_{0.025,(9,7)} = 0.238 \quad \text{or} \quad F \leq F_{0.975,(9,7)} = 4.82$$

Then the hypothesis of equal variances is rejected. Note that with these samples, the hypothesis would be rejected even if α were chosen as small as 0.00001. Thus one can say with a great deal of confidence that the population variances are not the same.

Recall from the previous section that to have an exact test for comparing the means of two normal populations when the samples are independent, we had to assume equal variances. The F-test is useful in testing this assumption.

Just as with the t-test, there are also one-sided F-tests. The test statistic used is the same as that for the two-sided test. Definition of the critical region does change, however. The appropriate hypotheses and critical regions for the one-sided tests are as follows.

Hypotheses	*Critical region*
$H_0 : \sigma_1^2 \leq \sigma_2^2$	$F \leq F_{(1-\alpha)(n_1-1, n_2-1)}$
$A \ : \sigma_1^2 > \sigma_2^2$	
$H_0 : \sigma_1^2 \geq \sigma_2^2$	$F \geq F_{\alpha,(n_1-1, n_2-1)}$
$A \ : \sigma_1^2 < \sigma_2^2$	

Example 3.8   The data in example 3.7 resulted in rejection of the hypothesis of equal variances. Using that data, let's test the hypotheses

$$H_0 : \sigma_1^2 \leq \sigma_2^2, \quad A : \sigma_1^2 > \sigma_2^2$$

If $\alpha = 0.05$, the critical region is $F \geq F_{0.05(9,7)} = 3.68$. Thus, with the computed F of 37.2, we would also reject this null hypothesis.

To summarize, the F-test is useful in comparing the variances of two normal populations. Both two-tailed and one-tailed tests exist. The test statistic is the same in each case, but the critical regions differ.

The chi-square goodness-of-fit test

3.6   One of the major difficulties facing a researcher designing a simulation experiment is the characterization of the random variables of interest. Before the operation of a service station can be modeled, for example, the distribution of customers arriving at the station must be characterized. In many cases the random variable cf interest is assumed to follow a particular distribution. Of course, the results obtained by the simulation study are usually very sensitive to this assumption. Thus there must be a method by which the assumption of a particular distribution can be checked. The chi-square goodness-of-fit test has proven useful in this regard.

This test makes a comparison between the actual and expected number of observations for various values of the random variable. The hypothesis that the observed and assumed distribution are the same is tested using the test statistic

$$\chi^2 = \sum_{i=1}^{r} \frac{(O_i - E_i)^2}{E_i}$$

where O_i is the observed frequency of observations in the ith interval and E_i is the frequency of observation if the assumed distribution is correct. A step-by-step procedure for conducting this test is as follows.

1. Construct a frequency table of the observed values of the random variable. The number of intervals is somewhat arbitrary; however, experience has shown that intervals with fewer than three to five observations tend to distort the test results.

2. Calculate the expected or theoretical frequencies for each interval under the assumption that the hypothesized distribution is correct. The parameters of the hypothesized distribution are usually estimated from the sample data.

3. Calculate the quantity $(O_i - E_i)^2/E_i$ for each interval, $i = 1, 2, \ldots, r$, where O_i is the actual frequency of observations in this interval and E_i is the frequency of observations expected under the hypothesized distribution.

4. Calculate the chi-square statistic using the formula

$$\chi^2 = \sum_{i=1}^{r} \frac{(O_i - E_i)^2}{E_i}$$

The degrees of freedom for this statistic are $r - p - 1$, where r is the number of intervals and p is the number of parameters estimated for the hypothesized distribution. As an example, suppose that there are ten intervals and that the distribution is assumed to be normal. Since both μ and σ^2 have to be estimated, the degrees of freedom for χ^2 are $10 - 3 = 7$. On the other hand, if the Poisson distribution is assumed, a single parameter needs to be estimated, so the degrees of freedom for χ^2 are $10 - 2 = 8$.

5. Choose a value for α and test the hypothesis, rejecting the hypothesis that the assumed and actual distributions are the same if

$$\chi^2 \geq \chi^2_{\alpha,r-p-1}$$

Example 3.9   A researcher is attempting to characterize the arrival pattern of customers to a service station. Through observation of the station over an extended period of time, the researcher constructed the following frequency table, where the quantity of interest is the number of customers arriving per hour.

Customers	Observed frequency
0–2	13
3–5	17
6–8	21
9–11	42
12–14	16
15–17	11
18–20	5

The researcher hypothesizes that the arrival pattern is Poisson. An estimate for λ, the average number of customers per hour, computed from this frequency table is $\overline{X} = 9.0$. From the cumulative Poisson table with $\lambda = 9.0$, the following table of observed versus expected frequencies can be tabulated.

Customers	Observed	Expected
0–2	13	0.75
3–5	17	13.75
6–8	21	42.5
9–11	42	43.375
12–14	16	19.5
15–17	11	4.0
18–20	5	1.125

Now combining the first two intervals and the last two intervals gives

$$\chi^2 = \sum_{i=1}^{5} \frac{(O_i - E_i)^2}{E_i}$$

$$= \frac{(30 - 14.5)^2}{14.5} + \frac{(21 - 42.5)^2}{42.5} + \frac{(42 - 43.375)^2}{43.375} + \frac{(16 - 19.5)^2}{19.5}$$

$$+ \frac{(16 - 5.125)^2}{5.125}$$

$$= 51.2$$

Then since $\chi^2 = 51.2 > \chi^2_{.01,3} = 11.3$, the hypothesis that the arrival pattern is Poisson can be rejected with $\alpha = 0.01$.

Example 3.10 The scores on an exam in a large mathematics course are thought to be normally distributed. The actual versus expected frequencies (calculated from the cumulative normal with estimated mean 73.3 and standard deviation 10.05) are as follows.

Score	Observed	Expected	$(O_i - E_i)^2/E_i$
50–59	16	11.98	1.35
60–69	31	39.39	1.79
70–79	72	58.84	2.94
80–89	26	34.65	2.16
90–99	9	8.33	0.05

Then $\chi^2 = 8.29$. If $\alpha = 0.01$, the critical region is $\chi^2 \leq \chi^2_{.01,2} = 9.21$. Thus we are unable to reject the hypothesis that the scores are normally distributed.

The Kolmogorov-Smirnov test

3.7   An alternative to the chi-square goodness-of-fit test is the Kolmogorov-Smirnov test. Like the chi-square test, it is used to test the hypothesis that a sample follows some hypothesized distribution. It is somewhat more powerful than the chi-square test. Thus it would be more likely to detect small differences in the actual and hypothesized distributions. The techniques used in this test are as follows.

1. Let $S(x)$ be the empirical cumulative distribution function constructed from a sample of N observations using the technique outlined in section 3.1.

2. Let $F(x)$ be the theoretical cumulative distribution function assuming that the null hypothesis is true.

3. For each of the N sample points, compute $F(x_i) - S(x_i)$. Let $D = \max_i |F(x_i) - S(x_i)|$.

4. Choose some value of α, and if the calculated value of D is greater than the tabulated critical value at that level of significance, reject the hypothesis.

Example 3.11   Consider the data of example 3.9. Using the right endpoint of each interval as the value of the sample, one can construct the following table.

x	$S(x)$	$F(x)$	$|F(x) - S(x)|$
2	0.104	0.006	0.098
5	0.240	0.116	0.124
8	0.408	0.456	0.048
11	0.744	0.803	0.059
14	0.872	0.959	0.087
17	0.960	0.995	0.035
20	1.000	1.000	0.000

In this table the hypothesized distribution was the Poisson distribution with $\lambda = 9.0$. The true sample mean for this sample was 9.02. It was rounded down to correspond to the table entries.

Now if $\alpha = 0.05$, the critical value from the table is $1.36/\sqrt{125} = 0.122$. Since $D = 0.124 > 0.122$, the hypothesis that the distribution is Poisson with mean 9.0 is rejected.

Example 3.12 Consider the data of example 3.10. Using the right endpoint of each interval as the value of the sample and the normal distribution (mean 73.3, standard deviation 10.05) as the hypothesized distribution, one can construct the following table.

x	S(x)	F(x)	|F(x) − S(x)|
59	0.10390	0.07780	0.0261
69	0.30519	0.33360	0.0284
79	0.77273	0.71566	0.0571
89	0.94156	0.94062	0.0009
99	1.000	0.99477	0.0052

If $\alpha = 0.01$, the critical value is $1.63/\sqrt{154} = 0.1313$. Since $D = 0.0571 < 0.1313$, we are unable to reject the hypothesis that the distribution is normal with mean 73.3, standard deviation 10.05.

Summary

In this chapter we have reviewed the fundamental concepts of estimation and hypothesis testing. We have also examined four of the more common statistical tests used in simulation studies. As in the previous chapter, the coverage was brief. The reader desiring more thorough coverage should consult any of many standard statistical texts.

Exercises

3.1 The following observations were recorded for a random variable **X**: $\{-2, 0, 6, 4, -1, -5, 12, 13, 3, 11\}$. Compute the sample mean and standard deviation.

3.2 Construct an empirical cumulative distribution function for the data of exercise 3.1 by connecting sequential observations with a straight line.

3.3 Construct an empirical cumulative distribution function for the data of exercise

3.1 by fitting the data with a second-degree polynomial $F(x) = a_0 + a_1 x + a_2 x^2$ using the method of least squares.

3.4 Assuming $\sigma = 6$ and $\alpha = 0.05$, test the following hypotheses for the data of exercise 3.1.
a. $H_0 : \mu = 4, A : \mu \neq 4$
b. $H_0 : \mu = 6, A : \mu \neq 6$
c. $H_0 : \mu \leq 5, A : \mu > 5$

3.5 Show that $S^2 = \sum_{i=1}^{n} (x_i - \bar{x})^2/(n-1)$ is an unbiased estimate of the population variance.

3.6 Independent samples were drawn from two normal populations and recorded as **X** and **Y**.

$$X : \{2,4,6,7,9,14,16,3\}$$

$$Y : \{-1, 4, 1, 6, 12, 12, 1, 0\}$$

Under the assumption of equal variances, test the hypothesis of equal means, with $\alpha = 0.05$.

3.7 Test the assumption of equal variances made in exercise 3.6.

3.8 If the observations in exercise 3.6 are paired rather than independent, test the hypothesis of equal means.

3.9 Messages arriving at a communications center are thought to follow a Poisson distribution. This of course implies that the interarrival distribution is exponential. Test this hypothesis using the chi-square test given the following frequency table of interarrival times.

Time	0–1	1–2	2–3	3–4	4–5	5–6	6–7
Frequency	2	6	12	16	21	11	6

3.10 Test the hypothesis of exercise 3.9 using the Kolmogorov-Smirnov test.

3.11 The following frequency table was recorded for some random variable **X**. Test the hypothesis that **X** comes from a normal distribution using the
a. Chi-square test
b. Kolmogorov-Smirnov test

Interval	0–5	5–10	10–15	15–20	20–25
Frequency	0	2	2	6	10
Interval	25–30	30–35	35–40	40–45	45–50
Frequency	20	28	32	32	28
Interval	50–55	55–60	60–65	65–70	70–75
Frequency	18	12	6	4	0

4

Generation of random numbers

In many simulations events appear to occur at random or to involve attributes whose values must be assigned somewhat by chance. This occurs because most simulations are based on knowledge expressed as general or historical relationships. For instance, in many cases the duration of an event is known to fall within a certain range. Simulation of the event requires that a particular value be assigned. Consider the simulation of a general-purpose computer system. One event that must be modeled is the retrieval of a record from a direct-access storage device. The duration of this event can be determined to fall within a certain interval; the actual value, however, is influenced by chance variables such as the position of the record relative to the read head when the request is made. Another instance in which chance appears to play a part is in the widespread use of decision logic in simulation. For example, suppose that in the operation of a system, a given path is known to be taken a certain percentage of the time. Simulation of the system requires a method for selecting this path over others so that the long-run behavior of the simulator is similar to that of the actual system. Since in most cases these decisions are nondeterministic, the choice is normally based on probabilistic relationships.

For these reasons and others, one of the requirements of almost any simulation model is some facility for generating random numbers. One must be able to assign a particular value to seeming random events on any given simulation run. In the previous example of the simulation of a computer system, one must assign a particular value to the time required to retrieve a record from a direct-access storage device each time a simulated request is received. In the case of a decision block one must be able to direct the simulator to take a given path on certain runs and other paths on other runs.

Modeling of random events, as described in chapter 2, is done using the uniform distribution. Thus random numbers can be generated by sampling from this distribution. Some sources of true random numbers that have been used are (1) a sack of unnumbered beads that can be sampled with replacement, (2) low-order digits on a microsecond clock, (3) a random electronic noise source whose output is quantized periodically. This last technique was used by the RAND Corporation to generate its widely published table of 1 million random digits (4.5). These techniques appear to generate random numbers, but they all have a common disadvantage when used in simulation studies: sequences generated by these techniques are generally not reproducible, and reproducibility is a requirement in most cases.

Pseudorandom numbers

4.1   A number of techniques have been applied to overcome the inherent nonreproducibility of random sequences. Before considering some of these, we might find it useful to discuss some of the requirements of a random number generator.

1. Numbers produced must follow the uniform distribution, because truly random events follow this distribution. Any simulation of random events must therefore follow it at least approximately.

2. Numbers produced must be statistically independent. The value of one number in a random sequence must not affect the value of the next number.

3. The sequence of random numbers produced must be reproducible. This allows replication of the simulation experiment.

4. The sequence must be nonrepeating for any desired length. This is not theoretically possible, but for practical purposes a long repeatability cycle is adequate. The repeatability cycle of a random number generator is known as its period.

5. Generation of the random numbers must be fast. In the course of a simulation run a large number of random numbers are usually required. If the generator is slow, it can greatly increase the time and thus the cost of the simulation run.

6. The method used in the generation of random numbers should use as little memory as possible. Simulation models generally have large memory requirements. Since memory is usually limited, as little as possible of this valuable resource should be devoted to the generation of random numbers.

With these requirements it is now possible to evaluate the approaches taken to compensate for the lack of reproducibility of random sequences. The first approach is to generate the sequence by some means and to store it, say on tape. This approach is generally unsatisfactory because of the time involved. Each time a random number is required, a read operation must be initiated, and this is a time-consuming operation. This technique also potentially suffers from a short repeatability cycle unless a large sequence is stored. The second approach is to generate a random sequence and hold it in memory. This approach would overcome the speed problem of the previous technique; however, to store a list large enough to satisfy the requirements of many simulation studies would require an inordinate amount of core. The third and most common approach is to use a specified input value to generate a random number using some algorithm. This technique overcomes the problems of speed and memory requirements but suffers from potential problems with independence and repeatability.

The use of an algorithm to generate random numbers seems to violate the basic principle of randomness. For this reason numbers generated by an algorithm are called synthetic or pseudorandom numbers. These numbers meet certain criteria for randomness but always begin with a certain initial value called the seed and proceed in a completely deterministic, repeatable fashion. Extreme care must be taken when using pseudorandom sequences to insure that a fair degree of randomness is present (that the uniform distribution is followed) and that the repeatability cycle is long enough. Random numbers are so important to simulation studies that much work has been done in devising and testing algorithms that produce pseudorandom sequences of numbers.

Algorithms for generating pseudorandom numbers

4.2   A lot of work has been done in designing and testing algorithms to produce pseudorandom number sequences. The algorithms differ not only in technique but in speed of generation, length of the repeatability cycle, and ease of programming. Some of the more common algorithms are surveyed in this section.

The midsquare method

4.2.1   The midsquare technique was developed in the mid 1940s by John von Neumann (4.3). The technique starts with some initial number, or seed. The number is then squared, and the middle digits of this square are used as the second number of the sequence. This second number is then squared, and the middle digits of this square are used as the third number of the sequence. The algorithm continues in this fashion.

Example 4.1   Suppose that one wishes to generate a sequence of four-digit random numbers using the midsquare method. Let the first number of the sequence be 3187. Then

$$x_0 = 3187$$

$$(3187)^2 = 10156969 \Rightarrow x_1 = 1569$$

$$(1569)^2 = 02461761 \Rightarrow x_2 = 4617$$

$$(4617)^2 = 21316689 \Rightarrow x_3 = 3166$$

$$(3166)^2 = 10023556 \Rightarrow x_4 = 0235$$

$$(0235)^2 = 00055225 \Rightarrow x_5 = 0552$$

$$(0552)^2 = 00304704 \Rightarrow x_6 = 3047$$

$$(3047)^2 = 09284209 \Rightarrow x_7 = 2842$$

This process could be continued to produce 0769, 5913, 9635, 8332, 4222, 8252, ...

This technique has a number of shortcomings. First, sequences generated by this technique generally have short repeatability periods. Second, whenever a zero is generated, all succeeding numbers will be zero. This phenomenon, if it occurred in the midst of a large simulation study could drive even the most conscientious analyst to distraction; it is illustrated by the following example.

Example 4.2   Suppose that one wishes to generate two-digit random numbers beginning with 44. Then

$$x_0 = 44$$

$$(44)^2 = 1936 \Rightarrow x_1 = 93$$

$$(93)^2 = 8649 \Rightarrow x_2 = 64$$

$$(64)^2 = 4096 \Rightarrow x_3 = 09$$

$$(09)^2 = 0081 \Rightarrow x_4 = 08$$

$$(08)^2 = 0064 \Rightarrow x_5 = 06$$

$$(06)^2 = 0036 \Rightarrow x_6 = 03$$

$$(03)^2 = 0009 \Rightarrow x_7 = 00$$

$$(00)^2 = 0000 \Rightarrow x_8 = 00$$

The problems with the midsquare method led to development of alternate algorithms to provide a more reliable source of random numbers.

The linear congruential method

4.2.2   Most of the random number generators used are modifications of the linear congruential scheme devised by Lehmer (4.4). In this algorithm successive numbers in the sequence are generated by the recursion relation

$$x_{n+1} = (ax_n + c) \bmod m, \qquad n \geq 0$$

The initial value x_0 is known as the *seed*, the constant a is the *multiplier*, the constant c the *increment*, and m the *modulus*. The selection of values for these constants has a dramatic effect on the length of the period of the generated sequence of random numbers.

Example 4.3   Let $a = 2, c = 3, m = 10$, and $x_0 = 0$. Then

$$x_0 = 0$$
$$x_1 = (2 \times 0 + 3) \bmod 10 = 3$$
$$x_2 = (2 \times 3 + 3) \bmod 10 = 9$$
$$x_3 = (2 \times 9 + 3) \bmod 10 = 1$$
$$x_4 = (2 \times 1 + 3) \bmod 10 = 5$$
$$x_5 = (2 \times 5 + 3) \bmod 10 = 3$$
$$x_6 = (2 \times 3 + 3) \bmod 10 = 9$$
$$x_7 = (2 \times 9 + 3) \bmod 10 = 1$$
$$x_8 = (2 \times 1 + 3) \bmod 10 = 5$$

Example 4.4   Let $a = 2, c = 0, m = 10$, and $x_0 = 1$. Then

$$x_0 = 1$$
$$x_1 = (2 \times 1) \bmod 10 = 2$$
$$x_2 = (2 \times 2) \bmod 10 = 4$$
$$x_3 = (2 \times 4) \bmod 10 = 8$$
$$x_4 = (2 \times 8) \bmod 10 = 6$$
$$x_5 = (2 \times 6) \bmod 10 = 2$$
$$x_6 = (2 \times 2) \bmod 10 = 4$$
$$x_7 = (2 \times 4) \bmod 10 = 8$$
$$x_8 = (2 \times 8) \bmod 10 = 6$$

Example 4.4 illustrates the case in which $c = 0$. This algorithm is called a *multiplicative congruential technique*. If $c \neq 0$, the technique is called a *mixed congruential scheme*. Both examples illustrate the repeatability of any sequence generated by this scheme. The sequence 3, 9, 1, 5 in example 4.3 repeats endlessly, while it is the sequence 2, 4, 8, 6 in example 4.4. Knuth (4.3) has shown that judicious choices of the constants a, c, x_0, and m can make the period sufficiently long for most studies. The arguments for each of the constants are summarized as follows.

1. *Choice of m.* Since the period will always be less than m, a large value of m is desirable. Furthermore, a value of m that facilitates the solution of the congruence relation should be used. For machines that utilize a binary number representation, a value of $2^k - 1$, where k is the word size of the machine, has proven excellent.

2. *Choice of a and c.* A sequence generated by a linear congruential scheme has period m if and only if

    a. c is relatively prime to m.

    b. $a - 1$ is a multiple of every prime dividing m.

    c. $a - 1$ is a multiple of 4 if m is a multiple of 4.

These constraints yield multiplier values of the form $a = z^p + 1$, where z is the radix used in the number representation of the computer, k is the word size of the computer (number of bits per word), $m = z^k$, and $z \leq p < k$. In particular, choices of $a = 2^{16} + 5 = 65541$ or $2^{16} + 3 = 65539$ have proved successful. As for the choice of c, it must only satisfy the requirement that it is relatively prime to m.

3. *Choice of x_0.* If the period of the sequence is m, the choice of x_0 is immaterial, since the entire sequence will be generated. Some care must be taken, since a choice of $x_0 = 0$, for example, will yield a degenerate sequence if the multiplicative congruential scheme is used.

Additive congruential generator

4.2.3 The additive congruential technique requires as its seed, a sequence of n numbers $x_1, x_2, \ldots, x_n$. This sequence of numbers can be generated using some other technique. Application of the algorithm will produce an extension to the sequence $x_{n+1}, x_{n+2}, x_{n+3}, \ldots$. Specifically the algorithm is

$$x_j = (x_{j-1} + x_{j-n}) \bmod m$$

The main advantage of this technique is speed; no multiplications are necessary. It can yield periods greater than m. As Knuth mentions (4.3), the theoretical behavior of this technique is not as well understood as the behavior of the mixed congruential technique. Thus careful validation of any number sequence generated by this technique is necessary.

Example 4.5   Let $m = 10$, and extend the sequence 1, 2, 4, 8, 6 generated in example 4.4.

$$
\begin{aligned}
x_1 &= 1 \\
x_2 &= 2 \\
x_3 &= 4 \\
x_4 &= 8 \\
x_5 &= 6 \\
x_6 &= (x_5 + x_1) \bmod 10 = (6 + 1) \bmod 10 = 7 \\
x_7 &= (x_6 + x_2) \bmod 10 = (7 + 2) \bmod 10 = 9 \\
x_8 &= (x_7 + x_3) \bmod 10 = (9 + 4) \bmod 10 = 3 \\
x_9 &= (x_8 + x_4) \bmod 10 = (3 + 8) \bmod 10 = 1 \\
x_{10} &= (x_9 + x_5) \bmod 10 = (1 + 6) \bmod 10 = 7 \\
x_{11} &= (x_{10} + x_6) \bmod 10 = (7 + 7) \bmod 10 = 4 \\
x_{12} &= (x_{11} + x_7) \bmod 10 = (4 + 9) \bmod 10 = 3 \\
x_{13} &= (x_{12} + x_8) \bmod 10 = (3 + 3) \bmod 10 = 6 \\
x_{14} &= (x_{13} + x_9) \bmod 10 = (6 + 1) \bmod 10 = 7 \\
x_{15} &= (x_{14} + x_{10}) \bmod 10 = (7 + 7) \bmod 10 = 4 \\
x_{16} &= (x_{15} + x_{11}) \bmod 10 = (4 + 4) \bmod 10 = 8 \\
x_{17} &= (x_{16} + x_{12}) \bmod 10 = (8 + 3) \bmod 10 = 1 \\
x_{18} &= (x_{17} + x_{13}) \bmod 10 = (1 + 6) \bmod 10 = 7 \\
x_{19} &= (x_{18} + x_{14}) \bmod 10 = (7 + 7) \bmod 10 = 4 \\
x_{20} &= (x_{19} + x_{15}) \bmod 10 = (4 + 4) \bmod 10 = 8
\end{aligned}
$$

Quadratic congruence generator

4.2.4   The quadratic congruence method, proposed by Coveyou (4.1), may be used when m is a power of 2. It is nearly equivalent to the double-precision midsquare method but has a longer period. The recursion relation for this method is given by

$$
x_{n+1} = (x_n(x_n + 1)) \bmod m, \qquad n \geq 0
$$

The seed x_0 must satisfy the relation $x_0 \bmod 4 = 2$.

Example 4.6   Let $x_0 = 2$, $m = 16$, and generate a random number sequence using the quadratic congruence generator.

$$x_0 = 2$$
$$x_1 = (2(3)) \bmod 16 = 6$$
$$x_2 = (6(7)) \bmod 16 = 10$$
$$x_3 = (10(11)) \bmod 16 = 14$$
$$x_4 = (14(15)) \bmod 16 = 2$$
$$x_5 = (2(3)) \bmod 16 = 6$$
$$x_6 = (6(7)) \bmod 16 = 10$$
$$x_7 = 14$$
$$x_8 = 2$$

Pseudorandom number generator

4.2.5 The pseudorandom number (PRN) technique is useful for generating pseudorandom numbers that fall in the interval $(0, 1)$. Let

$$x_{n+1} = \langle 10^p c x_n \rangle$$

where

$\langle a \rangle$ denotes the fractional part of a
p is the number of digits in the pseudorandom number
c is a constant multiplier, $0 < c < 1$

We shall not go into the details of how c is to be picked, but it has been established that a value of c equal to $10^{-p}(200\,A \pm B)$ will provide satisfactory results, where A is any nonnegative integer and B is any number from $\{3, 11, 13, 19, 21, 27, 29, 37, 53, 59, 61, 67, 69, 77, 83, 91\}$. The seed should be chosen to be $x_0 = 10^{-p}k$, where k is any integer not divisible by 2 or 5 such that $0 < k < 10^p$.

Example 4.7 Let $x_0 = 0.33$, $A = 0$, and $B = 11$. Suppose that two-digit numbers are desired. Then

$$c = 10^{-2}(11.0) = 0.11$$

and

$$x_0 = 0.33$$
$$x_1 = \langle 100(0.11)(0.33) \rangle = 0.63$$
$$x_2 = \langle 100(0.11)(0.63) \rangle = 0.93$$
$$x_3 = \langle 100(0.11)(0.93) \rangle = 0.23$$
$$x_4 = \langle 100(0.11)(0.23) \rangle = 0.53$$
$$x_5 = \langle 100(0.11)(0.53) \rangle = 0.83$$

The main disadvantage of this scheme is that it is slow because so many multiplications are required to generate the sequence of random numbers.

GPSS random number generator

4.2.6   GPSS/360 incorporates eight pseudorandom number generators specified as RN1–RN8. Each will produce the same sequence of numbers, or
it may be altered to provide up to eight unique sequences. The description of these generators that appeared in Felder (4.2) is summarized here.

Three eight-by-one arrays are maintained: a base number array containing the seed, a multiplier array containing the multiplier for each
generator (all are initially 1), and an index array containing the index
for each generator (all are initially 0). A random number is generated by
the following procedure.

1. The appropriate word from the index array points to the base
number array. Since each index is initially zero, the first base number is
used as the seed for all generators.

2. The appropriate multiplier is multiplied by the base number selected in step 1.

3. If the higher-order bit of the low-order 32 bits of this product is
a 1, the low-order 32 bits are replaced by their twos complement.

4. The low-order 31 bits of this possibly transformed product is
stored in the multiplier array for future use.

5. Three bits of the high-order 16 bits of the product are stored in
the index array, also for future use.

6a. If a fractional number is required, the middle 32 bits of the
product are divided by 10^6, and the remainder produced is the desired
six-digit number.

6b. If an integer is required, the middle 32 bits are divided by 10^3
and the remainder produced is the desired three-digit number.

This generator starts as if it were a multiplicative congruential generator but then diverges from that procedure because no recursion relation is used to produce successive numbers. The scrambling operation
is designed to reduce nonrandomness, but it precludes analysis of the
generator. For a further description of the generator see Felder (4.2).

Testing and validating
pseudorandom sequences

4.3   The generation of pseudorandom numbers is used to simulate the sampling from a continuous uniform distribution. Testing and validation of
a sequence of pseudorandom numbers normally entails the comparison
of the sequence with what would be expected from the uniform distribution. A multitude of tests are in use. Knuth (4.3) describes ten such

tests. In this section we will review some of the more common tests. For more detail see Knuth (4.3).

Frequency test

4.3.1   The frequency test is designed to test the uniformity of successive sets of numbers in the sequence. A procedure for this test is as follows.

1. Generate a sequence of M (say 10) consecutive sets of N (say 100) random numbers each.
2. Partition the number range into intervals (say 10).
3. Tabulate the frequency within each interval for each of the M groups.
4. Compare the results of the M groups with each other and with the expected values (continuous uniform distribution) using the chi-square goodness-of-fit test described in chapter 3.

Serial test

4.3.2   The serial test measures the degree of randomness between successive numbers in a sequence. A procedure for this test is as follows.

1 Generate a sequence of M (say 10) consecutive sets of N (say 100) random numbers each.
2. Partition the number range into k intervals (say 10).
3. For each group construct an array of size $k \times k$. The values of the array are initially 0. Examine the sequence of numbers from left to right, pairwise. Do not examine any number twice. If the left member of the pair is in interval i while the right member is in interval j, increment the (i, j) element of the array by 1.
4. When an array has been constructed for each group, compare the results of the M groups with each other and with the expected value (each pair should be equiprobable) using the chi-square test.

This test can be extended to examine triples, quadruples, and so on. The number of random numbers required for a valid test tends to become very large in these cases.

Kolmogorov-Smirnov test

4.3.3   The Kolmogorov-Smirnov test, described in chapter 3, is used to test the degree of randomness. Its utility in testing the hypothesis that a sequence of numbers are from a uniform distribution should be obvious.

Runs test

4.3.4   The runs test is used to test the randomness of oscillation of numbers in the sequence. A procedure for this test is as follows.

1. Generate N random numbers (say 10,000).
2. Build a binary sequence such that for any two consecutive numbers (x_j, x_{j+1}) of the sequence, the jth bit is 0 if $x_j < x_{j+1}$ and 1 otherwise.
3. Tabulate the frequency of occurrence of runs (consecutive 0's or 1's) of each length $(2, 3, 4, 5, \ldots)$.
4. Compare the tabulated frequencies with expected values. As Knuth points out (4.3), it is not possible to apply the chi-square statistics directly because consecutive runs are not independent. Knuth has devised a special statistic for use in this test, and any interested reader is referred to his work for the details.

Poker test

4.3.5   The poker test examines successive groups of five random numbers. The number of distinct values in the set of the five numbers is counted, giving five categories:

1. Five different
2. Four different (one pair)
3. Three different (two pairs or three of a kind)
4. Two different (full house or four of a kind)
5. One different (five of a kind)

The theoretical frequency of each category is calculated under the assumption that each number is equally likely, and the chi-square statistic is used to determine whether the random sequence conforms to the expected distribution.

Permutation test

4.3.6   The permutation test is a generalization of the poker test. The random sequence is broken into n subsequences, each with k elements. Each of the possible $k!$ permutations of the elements of each group is considered equiprobable, and the theoretical frequency of each obtained ordering is calculated. The chi-square statistic is then used to compare the actual frequency with the expected frequency.

Distance test

4.3.7 The distance test considers successive pairs of random numbers to be the coordinates of points in the unit square. For example, if the random sequence is $r_1, r_2, r_3, \ldots, r_n$, the points $(r_1, r_2), (r_3, r_4), \ldots, (r_{n-1}, r_n)$ would be plotted in an x-y plane. The square of the Euclidean distance D^2 is then calculated between each of the points. If the points are distributed randomly in the unit square (which they should be in the case of a truly random sequence), the probability that the observed value of D^2 is less than or equal to some value k is given by

$$
F(k) = \begin{cases}
\pi k - \dfrac{8}{3} k^{3/2} + \dfrac{k^2}{2}, & \text{for } k \le 1.0 \\[2ex]
\dfrac{1}{3} + (\pi - 2)k + 4(k - 1)^{1/2} + \dfrac{8}{3}(k - 1)^{3/2} \\[1ex]
\quad - \dfrac{k^2}{2} - 4k \text{ arc sec } \sqrt{k}, & \text{for } 1.0 \le k \le 2.0
\end{cases}
$$

That is

$$F(0.0) = 0$$
$$F(0.25) = 0.483$$
$$F(0.50) = 0.753$$
$$F(0.75) = 0.905$$
$$F(1.0) = 0.975$$
$$F(1.5) = 0.999$$
$$F(2.0) = 1.0$$

Using this distribution function, one can calculate the theoretical frequencies for the values of D^2 in any prescribed interval. Comparisons of the actual frequencies with the theoretical frequencies can be made with the use of the chi-square statistic.

Generation of nonuniform variates

4.4 All the generators used thus far are designed to generate sequences of numbers following a uniform distribution. However, other theoretical distributions such as the normal, exponential, Poisson, and gamma distributions are encountered more often in simulation studies than the uniform distribution. In many cases no appropriate theoretical distribution can be found, and an empirical distribution is used. Thus it is necessary to have a technique for generating random numbers that simulate the sampling of any arbitrary distribution. Note that all the techniques discussed start by generating one or more pseudorandom numbers from the uniform distribution. A transformation is then applied to this uniform variable to generate the nonuniform pseudorandom number.

The inverse transformation method

4.4.1   The inverse transformation technique is useful for transforming a standard uniform deviate into any other distribution. It is particularly useful when the distribution is an empirical one.

Suppose that we wish to generate a pseudorandom number from a distribution given by $F(x)$, where F satisfies all the properties of a cumulative distribution function outlined in chapter 2. This generation is done in two steps.

1. Generate a standard uniform random number using one of the techniques outlined in section 4.2.

2. If r is the standard uniform number generated in step 1, then $x_0 = F^{-1}(r)$ is the desired nonuniform variate.

This process is depicted graphically in figure 4.1.

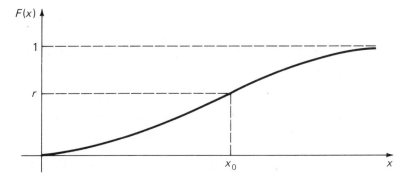

Figure 4.1
The inverse transformation method

Example 4.8   Suppose that the standard uniform random numbers 0.1021, 0.2162, and 0.7621 have been generated and that we wish to transform them into a distribution given by

$$F(x) = \begin{cases} 0, x < 0 \\ x, 0 \leq x < 1/4 \\ (3x + 1)/7, \quad 1/4 \leq x < 2 \\ 1, x > 2 \end{cases}$$

This distribution function is illustrated in figure 4.2. Then

$$F^{-1}(a) = \begin{cases} a, & 0 \leq a < 1/4 \\ (7a - 1)/3, & 1/4 \leq a \leq 1 \end{cases}$$

So

$$F^{-1}(0.1021) = 0.1021$$

$$F^{-1}(0.2162) = 0.2162$$

$$F^{-1}(0.7621) = 1.4449$$

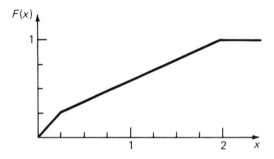

Figure 4.2
The distribution function for transforming variates

These numbers then are random numbers from the distribution given by $F(x)$.

The inverse transformation method is particularly useful when the cumulative distribution function is tabulated. The inverse function in this case is obtained simply by reversing the roles of the abscissa and the ordinate values of each tabulated point.

Example 4.9 Suppose a distribution has been tabulated as follows.

x	0.0	0.5	1.0	1.5	2.0	2.5	3.0
F(x)	0.0	0.1	0.2	0.5	0.7	0.9	1.0

Suppose further than the standard uniform random number is 0.25 has been generated. The corresponding transformed random number, obtained by using linear interpolation between 1.0 and 1.5, is 1.0833.

Generation of nonstandard uniform random numbers

4.4.2   Most standard routines to generate pseudorandom numbers are designed to simulate sampling from the standard uniform distribution. They produce random numbers in the range from 0 to 1. The nonstandard uniform distribution is given by

$$F(x) = \begin{cases} 0, x < a \\ (x - a)/(b - a), & a \le x \le b \\ 1, x > b \end{cases}$$

To produce nonstandard uniformly distributed random numbers from standard uniformly distribution random numbers, it is only necessary to scale the numbers. If r is a random number from a standard uniform distribution, then $x = a + (b - a)r$ is a random number from a nonstandard uniform distribution with the range from a to b.

Generation of normal random numbers

4.4.3   Random variables following a normal distribution are commonly encountered in simulation studies. A number of techniques are used in transforming standard uniform random numbers into normal random numbers. Two of the more common techniques are given here.

The first technique is to use the inverse transformation technique. In chapter 2 we showed that there is no closed-form functional representation of the cumulative distribution function for the normal distribution; thus a tabular representation must be used. A sufficient number of points must be included to give the desired degree of detail.

Example 4.10   Suppose that we want to obtain random numbers from a normal distribution with mean 3 and variance 4. Suppose further that standard uniform random numbers 0.2163, 0.3241, 0.1021, and 0.7621 have been generated. A 13-point tabular representation of the standard normal (mean 0, variance 1) is given in table 4.1.

The standard normal random numbers corresponding to the standard uniform random numbers in table 4.1, obtained by using linear interpolation, are -0.8077, -0.4594, -1.3070, and 0.7357.

To transform a standard normal variable z into a normal random variable x with mean μ and standard deviation σ, the relationship

Table 4.1
Tabular representation of the standard normal distribution

z	F(z)	z	F(z)
−3	0.00135	0.5	0.69146
−2.5	0.00621	1.0	0.84134
−2.0	0.02275	1.5	0.93319
−1.5	0.06681	2.0	0.97725
−1.0	0.15866	2.5	0.99379
−0.5	0.30854	3.0	0.99865
0.0	0.50000		

$x = \mu + \sigma z$ is used. The final transformed numbers are 1.3846, 2.0812, 0.3842, and 4.4714.

A second, more common technique for generating normally distributed random numbers is to use the central limit theorem. This theorem states that the sum of identically distributed independent random variables $X_1, X_2, \ldots, X_n$ has approximately a normal distribution with a mean $n\mu$ and variance $n\sigma^2$, where μ and σ^2 are respectively the mean and the variance of X_i. If the variables X_i, $i = 1, 2, \ldots, n$, follow the standard uniform distribution, then $\mu = 0.5$ and $\sigma^2 = 1/12$. Thus summing n standard uniform variates gives an approximate normal distribution with mean $0.5n$ and variance $n/12$.

The choice of n is largely up to the analyst. Of course, the larger the value of n chosen, the better the approximation to the normal distribution. Studies have shown that with $n = 12$ the technique provides fairly good results while at the same time maintaining calculation efficiency. This is because it yields $\sigma = 1$; so in the transformation from a nonstandard normal to the standard normal, a division operation is saved.

Example 4.11   Suppose the standard uniform random numbers 0.1062, 0.1124, 0.7642, 0.4314, 0.6241, 0.9443, 0.8121, 0.2419, 0.3124, 0.5412, 0.6212, 0.0021 have been generated. Generate a normal random number from a distribution with mean 25 and variance 9.

Summing the 12 standard uniform numbers gives $Y = 5.5135$. This number is from an approximate normal distribution with a mean of 6 and a variance of 1. The corresponding standard normal number is $Z = Y - 6 = -0.4865$. Now transforming this number to a normal distribution with mean 25 and a variance 9 generates the desired result.

$$X = \mu + \sigma Z = 25 + 3(-0.4865) = 23.5405$$

Generation of binomially distributed random numbers

4.4.4   The binomial distribution is used to model n successive trials of some experiment having two possible outcomes on each trial. The binomial random variable **X** counts the number of successes in each of these n trials, where the probability of a success on any given trial is p. To generate binomially distributed random numbers, one simulates the outcome of a trial of the experiment by generating a standard uniform random number. After all n trials have been simulated (n standard uniform numbers have been generated), the value of the binomially distributed random variable is simply a count of those standard uniform numbers that are less than or equal to p. This procedure is useful for small to moderate values of n. For large values of n, the normal approximation to the binomial should be used. Rather than generate binomially distributed numbers, generate numbers from a normal distribution with mean np and variance $np(1-p)$.

    Example 4.12   Generate a random number from a binomial distribution with $n = 7$, $p = 0.3$. To simulate seven trials, generate seven standard uniform numbers. Assume that the numbers are 0.02011, 0.85393, 0.97265, 0.61680, 0.16656, 0.42751, and 0.69994. Now two of these numbers are less than $p = 0.3$, so the desired binomial random number is **X** = 2.

Generation of exponentially distributed random numbers

4.4.5   The generation of exponentially distributed random numbers is easily accomplished with the use of the inverse transformation technique described in section 4.4.1. Recall that the cumulative distribution function for an exponentially distributed random variable **X** is

$$F(x) = 1 - e^{-\alpha x}, \qquad x > 0$$

The inverse of F is then

$$F^{-1}(a) = -\frac{1}{\alpha}\ln(1 - a)$$

If a is uniformly distributed, however, then $1 - a$ is also uniformly distributed, and the desired random numbers can be generated by using

$$F^{-1}(a) = -\frac{1}{\alpha} \ln (a)$$

Thus generating a standard uniform number r permits the formation of an exponentially distributed random number by

$$\mathbf{X} = -\frac{1}{\alpha} \ln (r)$$

Note that this method is simple to program, yet it is very time-consuming because it involves the calculation of the natural logarithm function. If computation time is a problem, tabulated values of the exponential distribution function can be used in the manner illustrated in section 4.4.1.

Example 4.13 Suppose we wish to generate random numbers from an exponential distribution with $\alpha = 1$. Then

$$F(x) = 1 - e^{-x}, \qquad x > 0$$
$$F^{-1}(a) = -\ln(1 - a)$$

Now if a standard uniformly distributed random number, say 0.02104, has been generated, the desired random number from the exponential distribution would be

$$\mathbf{X} = -\ln(0.02104) = -(-3.8613) = 3.8613$$

Generation of Poisson-distributed random numbers

4.4.6   Generation of random numbers from a Poisson distribution with a mean of λ can be accomplished by multiplying successively generated standard uniform random numbers. Specifically, multiply N standard uniform random numbers U_i until

$$\prod_{i=1}^{N} U_i < e^{-\lambda}$$

Then the value of the Poisson random variable $\mathbf{X}$ is $N - 1$.

Example 4.14   Suppose that we wish to generate a random number from a Poisson distribution with $\lambda = 2.5$. Suppose further that we have generated the standard uniform random numbers 0.91646, 0.89198, 0.64809, 0.16376, 0.91782, 0.45624, 0.31641. Then $e^{-2.5} = 0.08208$, and

$(0.91646)(0.89198) = 0.81746 > 0.08208$

$(0.91646)(0.89198)(0.64809) = 0.52979 > 0.08208$

$(0.91646)(0.89198)(0.64809)(0.16376) = 0.08675 > 0.08208$

$(0.91646)(0.89198)(0.64809)(0.16376)(0.91782) = 0.07963 < 0.08208$

Then $N = 5$ and hence the value of the Poisson-distributed random number is $\mathbf{X} = N - 1 = 4$.

Summary

In this chapter some of the more common techniques for generating pseudorandom numbers and tests for validating the corresponding random number generators have been reviewed. The generation of pseudorandom numbers can be viewed as the simulated sampling of a given distribution. This simulated sampling technique is generally referred to as the *Monte Carlo* technique. It is of great value when sampling is desirable but either impossible or impractical. Monte Carlo simulation has been applied to the solution of waiting-line problems, inventory control problems, and purchasing problems, as well as to the approximate solution of differential equations and integral equations. It is a valuable tool when the analytic model of the system under consideration is complex or unwieldy.

Exercises

4.1   Generate a sequence of ten pseudorandom numbers using the midsquare method and beginning with $x_0 = 0.6677$.

4.2   Use the linear congruential scheme to generate ten pseudorandom numbers beginning with $x_0 = 21, a = 4, c = 1$, and $m = 100$.

4.3   Repeat exercise 4.2 with $c = 0$.

4.4   Assess the choices of a, c, and m according to the criteria established in section 4.2.2. Could the generator be expected to have a full period?

4.5   Use the additive congruential generator of section 4.2.3 to extend the sequence generated in exercise 4.3 to a length of 25.

4.6   Generate a sequence of ten pseudorandom numbers using the quadratic congruence generator of section 4.2.4 with $x_0 = 10$ and $m = 128$.

4.7   Generate a sequence of ten two-digit random numbers using the pseudorandom number generator scheme of section 4.2.5, with $A = 0$ and $B = 13$. Start with $x_0 = 0.49$.

4.8   Use the inverse transformation method to generate a random number from a distribution with the probability density function given by

$$f(x) = \begin{cases} 1/4, & 0 \leq x < 1 \\ 3/4, & 1 \leq x \leq 2 \end{cases}$$

4.9   Generate a random number from a normal distribution with mean 10 and variance 16.

4.10   Generate a random number from a binomial distribution with $n = 10, p = 0.35$.

4.11   Generate a random number from an exponential distribution with $\alpha = 1.5$.

4.12   Generate a random number from a Poisson distribution with $\lambda = 4.0$.

4.13   Write a general purpose FORTRAN subroutine to implement the linear congruential scheme of section 4.2.2. Scale the output so that standard uniform random numbers are produced.

4.14   Write a FORTRAN subroutine that generates normal random numbers and uses the output of the subroutine of exercise 4.13. Input parameters should include the desired mean and variance.

4.15   Write a FORTRAN subroutine to generate exponentially distributed random numbers.

4.16   Write a FORTRAN subroutine to generate Poisson-distributed random numbers.

4.17   Using one of the generators developed in exercises 4.13–4.16, generate a list of 100 pseudorandom numbers. Use the Kolmogorov-Smirnov test to verify that these numbers have the desired distribution.

References

4.1   COVEYOU, R. R. "Serial Correlation in the Generation of Pseudo-Random Numbers." *J. ACM* 7 (1960): 72–74.

4.2   FELDER, H. "The GPSS/360 Random Number Generator." *Digest of the Second Conference of Applications of Simulation*, New York, December 1968.

4.3   KNUTH D. E. *The Art of Computer Programming*, vol. 2: *Seminumerical Algorithms*. Reading, Mass.: Addison-Wesley, 1969.

4.4   LEHMER D. H. *Proceedings of the Second Symposium on Large-Scale Digital Computing Machinery*. Cambridge, Mass.: Harvard University Press, 1951.

4.5   RAND CORPORATION. *A Million Random Digits with 100,000 Normal Deviates*. New York: Free Press, 1955.

5

Introduction to queueing theory

Waiting lines, or queues, are encountered in nearly every facet of life. Queues range from waiting lines at the barber shop, supermarket, or filling station to a backlog of messages at a communication center or jobs at a computing center. The reason that waiting lines form is quite simple: there are simply not enough serving facilities (or servers) to satisfy all the customers simultaneously. The reason for an inadequate number of servers is simple economics. Customers seem to arrive at random; thus to guarantee that there will be no waiting lines, the service station manager would have to hire as many servers as there are customers. This is not economically feasible, and hence a fixed number of servers are normally hired with the hope that the waiting lines do not become intolerably long. Should the customers become discouraged and leave before being served, the manager would want to hire more servers to avoid losing business.

Waiting lines or queues are so common in real life that it should not be surprising that one of the most common problems encountered in modeling or simulating the operation of a system involves queues. In fact, the requirements of queue handling led to the development of simulation languages.

A queueing system is a system in which customers arrive, wait if that service is not immediately available, receive the necessary service, and then depart. A simple queueing system is illustrated in figure 5.1.

There are a number of characteristics of any queueing system that need to be discussed.

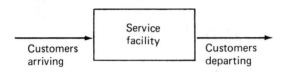

Figure 5.1
A queueing system

1. *The arrival pattern* concerns itself with the distribution of arriving customers, whether customers are allowed to balk (leave without receiving service), and whether customers arrive singly or in batches. A simple arrival pattern is one that is deterministic or devoid of all uncertainty. A more general, and more common, pattern includes some uncertainty.

2. *The service process* considers such details as the distribution of service time requested, whether customers are served singly or in batches, and whether the level of service changes or remains constant as the queue forms. The server could change its service depending on the length of the waiting line that is forming or as the demand requires.

3. *The queue discipline* considers the technique by which customers are selected from the queue for service. Probably the most common queue discipline is FIFO (first-in, first-out) in which the customer at the head of the line is selected for service. Other disciplines include LIFO (last-in, first-out) and priority schemes in which customers other than those at the head of the queue (line) may be selected for service.

4. *The system capacity* in most systems is finite. For instance, the length of the queue in a barber shop may be limited by the number of chairs available. The maximum backlog of a message-switching center, on the other hand, may be limited by the amount of buffer (reserve) space available to hold these messages. The maximum capacity of a system has a pronounced effect on the operation of the system; hence when the operation of the system is being simulated or otherwise modeled, these capacities must be considered.

5. *The number of parallel servers* varies. In some systems several servers simultaneously serve customers. These servers can all select customers from a single queue or each can service its own queue. Regardless of the queue mechanism, the servers are normally considered to be operating independently of one another.

To summarize these characteristics of queueing systems, Kendall (5.2) developed a widely accepted notational convention. With this convention, a queueing system is described by a series of symbols separated by slashes.

A/B/C/D/E

In this notation A represents the interarrival time distribution, B the service time distribution, C the number of parallel servers, D the system capacity, and E the queue discipline. Some of the more common interarrival distributions are M (exponential), D (deterministic), E_k (Erlang type k), and G (general). The same letters are also used to denote similar service time distributions. Queueing disciplines are indicated by FIFO (first-in, first-out), LIFO (last-in, first-out), SIRO (service in random order), PRI (priority), and GD (general discipline). For example, $M/M/1/\infty/$ FIFO indicates a single-server system with infinite system capacity, exponentially distributed interarrival times (Poisson-distributed arrivals), exponentially distributed service times, and a first-in, first-out queueing discipline.

Once a queueing model has been developed, the following are the items of interest concerning the model.

1. *Queue length.* Both the maximum and the average queue lengths are useful in characterizing the behavior of a system.

2. *Time in the system.* The expected length of time that a customer will spend in a system is of interest to the analyst as well as to the customer.

3. *Idle and busy time of the server.* Optimal utilization of the service facility is one of the aims of a system designer.

The rest of the chapter surveys techniques useful in the analysis of a queueing system. As the complexity of the queueing model grows, so does the complexity of the analysis; for this reason only relatively simple models are analyzed.

Review of the Poisson and exponential distributions

5.1   Many systems have been successfully modeled by a queueing model in which both the interarrival and the service distributions are exponentially distributed. In chapter 2 we showed that an exponential interarrival distribution implied that the arrival process is Poisson. Because the application of this model is widespread, the next two sections are devoted entirely to it. The properties of the Poisson and exponential distributions are reviewed in this section, and the equations necessary to analyze the model are developed in the next. The exponential and Poisson distributions are both single-parameter distributions with the following underlying assumptions (5.1).

1. The probability that a customer arrives within a small time interval Δt is $\lambda \Delta t + O(\Delta t)$, where λ is the arrival rate and $O(\Delta t)$ includes all higher-order terms in Δt such that $\lim_{\Delta t \to 0}[O(\Delta t)/\Delta t] = 0$.
2. The probability of two or more arrivals in Δt is $O(\Delta t)$ and hence can be neglected.
3. The number of arrivals in nonoverlapping time intervals is statistically independent.

It is easy to establish that if the arrival process is Poisson, then the interarrival distribution is exponential. Suppose that the arrival process to a queueing system is Poisson, with an arrival rate of λ. Let T be the random variable that measures the time between successive arrivals. Then

$$P(T > t) = P(\text{zero arrivals in time } t) = e^{-\lambda t}$$

from which

$$F(t) = P(T \le t) = 1 - P(T > t) = 1 - e^{-\lambda t}$$

This is precisely the exponential distribution function, proving the supposition. It is somewhat more difficult to prove the converse. The argument of this proof is given in Gross and Harris (5.1).

One of the main reasons the exponential distribution is so widely applicable is that it is memoryless. This property was mentioned in chapter 2 and is reviewed here. Assume that the random variable $\mathbf{X}$ has an exponential distribution. Then for any $X_1, X_2 > 0, X_2 > X_1, P(\mathbf{X} \le X_2 | \mathbf{X} \ge X_1) = P(0 \le \mathbf{X} \le X_2 - X_1)$. In terms of a queueing model this property states that the probability of an arrival in a given time interval is not affected by the fact that no arrival has taken place in the preceding interval or intervals. This fact greatly simplifies the analysis of queueing systems with Poisson arrivals and exponential services.

The Poisson distribution also possesses a property that is valuable in the analysis of many queueing systems: the aggregation and disaggregation property. Consider an arrival process that is the confluence of n independent Poisson arrival streams. Then the combined stream is Poisson, with rate $\lambda = \lambda_1 + \lambda_2 + \ldots + \lambda_n$. The converse also holds. That is, suppose a Poisson arrival stream with rate λ feeds n independent streams. Then the ith stream is also Poisson, and it has a rate equal to λP_i, where P_i is the probability that a given customer takes path i.

Recall from chapter 2 that the Poisson distribution is used to model random events. This idea is formalized as follows. Suppose that the input stream to a queueing system follows a Poisson distribution. Suppose also that an arrival has occurred during the interval $(0,t)$. Then the exact instant of the arrival follows the uniform distribution. That is, the arrival occurs at random in the interval.

Having mentioned some of the more useful properties of the exponential Poisson distribution, we are ready to analyze the first queueing model, the M/M/1/∞/FIFO system.

The M/M/1/∞/FIFO system

5.2   The M/M/1/∞/FIFO system is a single-server system whose interarrival and service times are exponentially distributed with parameters $1/\lambda$ and $1/\mu$ respectively. There is no restriction on the system's capacity, and the queue discipline is a first-in, first-out discipline.

Of crucial interest to the analysis of any queueing system is the number of customers in the system. Let S_j denote the state of the system when there are j customers present, $j \geq 0$. Let $P_j(t)$ denote the probability of state S_j at some time t. Now the system is in state S_j at time $t + \Delta t$ if and only if one of the following mutually exclusive events occurs.

1. The system was in state S_{j-1} at time t, and one arrival but no departures occur during the interval $(t, t + \Delta t)$.

2. The system was in state S_j at time t, and no arrivals or departures occur during the interval $(t, t + \Delta t)$.

3. The system was in state S_{j+1} at time t, and one departure but no arrivals occur during the interval $(t, t + \Delta t)$.

Now recall that the probability of a single arrival during the interval $(t, t + \Delta t)$ is $\lambda \Delta t + O(\Delta t)$, while the probability of a single departure during that same interval $(t, t + \Delta t)$ is $\mu \Delta t + O(\Delta t)$. The probability of multiple arrivals or departures during the interval is negligible. Then

$$P_j(t + \Delta t) = P_{j-1}(t)(\lambda \Delta t)(1 - \mu \Delta t)$$
$$+ P_j(t)(1 - \lambda \Delta t)(1 - \mu \Delta t)$$
$$+ P_{j+1}(t)(1 - \lambda \Delta t)(\mu \Delta t), \qquad j = 1, 2, \ldots$$

Simplifying gives

$$P_j(t + \Delta t) = \lambda \Delta t P_{j-1}(t) + (1 - (\lambda + \mu)\Delta t)P_j(t) + \mu \Delta t P_{j+1}(t), \qquad j = 1, 2, \ldots$$

Now rearranging terms gives

$$\frac{P_j(t + \Delta t) + P_j(t)}{\Delta t} = \lambda P_{j-1}(t) - (\lambda + \mu)P_j(t) + \mu P_{j+1}(t), \qquad j = 1, 2, \ldots$$

Taking the limit of both sides as $\Delta t \to 0$ gives

$$P_j'(t) = \lambda P_{j-1}(t) - (\lambda + \mu)P_j(t) + \mu P_{j+1}(t), \qquad j = 1, 2, \ldots$$

This equation holds for $j = 1, 2, \ldots$. The case $j = 0$ must be handled separately, since in this case S_{j-1} is not possible. Utilizing the same procedure gives

$$P'_0(t) = -\lambda P_0(t) + \mu P_1(t)$$

These equations can be summarized as a set of differential difference equations whose solution gives the distribution of the number of customers in the system.

$$P'_0(t) = -\lambda P_0(t) + \mu P_1(t)$$

$$P'_j(t) = \lambda P_{j-1}(t) - (\lambda + \mu)P_j(t) + \mu P_{j+1}(t), \qquad j \geq 1$$

This system of equations can be more readily solved once the system is in steady state. Steady state has been reached if the probability P_j of finding j customers in the system approaches a limiting value. Then time is no longer of essence in computing the probabilities. Another way of expressing this is that the system has reached statistical equilibrium. Under the assumption of steady state, $dP_j(t)/dt = 0$ for $j = 0, 1, 2, \ldots$. Then the system of equations becomes a set of simple difference equations of the form

$$P_1 = \frac{\lambda}{\mu} P_0$$

$$P_{j+1} = \frac{\lambda + \mu}{\mu} P_j - \frac{\lambda}{\mu} P_{j-1}, \qquad j \geq 1.$$

A number of approaches are useful in solving this set of difference equations. Two techniques are surveyed here. Both techniques work equally well for this simple system, but as the queueing system becomes more complex, one of the techniques may prove more advantageous over the other. An alternate derivation of these equations is also presented.

Solution by an iterative technique

5.2.1   Using the developed difference equations in an iterative manner gives

$$P_1 = \frac{\lambda}{\mu} P_0$$

$$P_2 = \frac{\lambda + \mu}{\mu} P_1 - \frac{\lambda}{\mu} P_0$$

$$= \left(\frac{\lambda + \mu}{\mu}\right)\left(\frac{\lambda}{\mu} P_0\right) - \frac{\lambda}{\mu} P_0 = \left(\frac{\lambda}{\mu}\right)^2 P_0$$

$$P_3 = \frac{\lambda + \mu}{\mu} P_2 - \frac{\lambda}{\mu} P_1$$

$$= \left(\frac{\lambda + \mu}{\mu}\right)\left(\left(\frac{\lambda}{\mu}\right)^2 P_0\right) - \left(\frac{\lambda}{\mu}\right)\left(\frac{\lambda}{\mu} P_0\right)$$

$$= \left(\frac{\lambda}{\mu}\right)^3 P_0$$

The general form of this iterative equation can be deduced using a straightforward induction argument.

$$P_j = \left(\frac{\lambda}{\mu}\right)^j P_0$$

To complete the solution of the steady-state equations, we need only to find P_0. Using this definition, we have

$$P_j = \rho^j P_0, \qquad j = 1, 2, \ldots$$

Now, as previously defined, the P_j, where $j = 0, 1, \ldots$, represent the probability that there are j customers in the system. By definition of probabilities,

$$\sum_{j=0}^{\infty} P_j = \sum_{j=0}^{\infty} \rho^j P_0 = 1$$

This equation can be rewritten to give a value of P_0, as required.

$$P_0 = \frac{1}{\displaystyle\sum_{j=0}^{\infty} \rho^j}$$

where $\displaystyle\sum_{j=0}^{\infty} \rho^j$ is a geometric series. This series converges if and only if $\lambda/\mu = \rho < 1$. When it converges, it converges to

$$\sum_{j=0}^{\infty} \rho^j = \frac{1}{1 - \rho}$$

If we assume that $\rho < 1$, the necessary condition for a system to reach steady state will be $P_0 = 1 - \rho$, and the solution to the steady-state equations is given by

$$P_j = \rho^j(1 - \rho), \qquad j = 0, 1, 2, \ldots$$

Solution using generating functions

5.2.2 The probability generating function

$$P(z) = \sum_{j=0}^{\infty} P_j z^j$$

introduced in chapter 2 can also be used to solve the steady-state equation. Using the previously defined utilization factor $\rho = \lambda/\mu$, we can write the steady-state equations as

$$P_1 = \rho P_0$$
$$P_{j+1} = (\rho + 1)P_j - \rho P_{j-1}, \qquad j \geq 1$$

Multiplying both sides of the second equation by z^j and rewriting gives

$$z^{-1}P_{j+1}z^{j+1} = (\rho + 1)P_j z^j - \rho z P_{j-1}z^{j-1}$$

Summing this equation from $j = 1$ to ∞ yields

$$z^{-1}\sum_{j=1}^{\infty} P_{j+1}z^{j+1} = (\rho + 1)\sum_{j=1}^{\infty} P_j z^i - \rho z \sum_{j=1}^{\infty} P_{j-1}z^{j-1}$$

This equation can be rewritten

$$z^{-1}\left[\sum_{j=-1}^{\infty} P_{j+1}z^{j+1} - P_1z - P_0\right] = (\rho + 1)\left[\sum_{j=0}^{\infty} P_jz^j - P_0\right] - \rho z\sum_{j=1}^{\infty} P_{j-1}z^{j-1}$$

Now

$$\sum_{j=-1}^{\infty} P_{j+1}z^{j+1} = \sum_{j=0}^{\infty} P_jz^j = \sum_{j=1}^{\infty} P_{j-1}z^{j-1} = P(z)$$

so

$$z^{-1}[P(z) - P_1z - P_0] = (\rho + 1)[P(z) - P_0] - \rho zP(z)$$

Since $P_1 = \rho P_0$, the equation can again be rewritten

$$z^{-1}[P(z) - (\rho z + 1)P_0] = (\rho + 1)[P(z) - P_0] - \rho zP(z)$$

Solving this equation for $P(z)$ yields

$$P(z) = \frac{P_0}{1 - z\rho} \tag{5.1}$$

Now $P(z) = \sum_{j=0}^{\infty} P_jz^j$, so

$$P(1) = \sum_{j=0}^{\infty} P_j1^j = \sum_{j=0}^{\infty} P_j = 1$$

From equation 5.1, $P(1) = P_0/(1 - \rho)$, so $P_0 = 1 - \rho, \rho < 1$. Substituting this value into equation 5.1 yields the generating function

$$P(z) = \frac{1 - \rho}{1 - z\rho} \tag{5.2}$$

To obtain probabilities from a generating function, one simply expands the generating function in a power series (sometimes more easily said than done) and utilizes the coefficients of the power of z. The probability $P(z)$ given in equation 5.2 can be easily expanded through long division. That is,

$$\frac{1 - \rho}{1 - z\rho} = (1 - \rho)\frac{1}{1 - z\rho}$$
$$= (1 - \rho)(1 + z\rho + (z\rho)^2 + \cdots)$$

Then the infinite series expansion of the generating function is

$$P(z) = \sum_{j=0}^{\infty} (1 - \rho)\rho^j z^j$$

The coefficient of the jth term gives the following relation:

$$P_j = (1 - \rho)\rho^j, \qquad j = 0, 1, 2, \ldots$$

This is the result previously obtained using the iterative technique.

Derivation using stochastic balance

5.2.3   The steady-state equations can also be easily derived using a method known as stochastic balance. This technique is based on the fact that in steady state, the expected rate of transitions out of state S_j is equal to the rate of transitions into state S_j. This can be seen from the state diagram in figure 5.2.

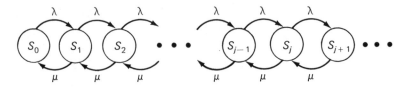

Figure 5.2
State transition diagram

The system moves from state S_j to S_{j+1} only if an arrival but no departure occurs; from state S_{j+1} to state S_j only if a departure but no arrival occurs; from state S_{j-1} to state S_j only if an arrival but no departure occurs; and from S_j to S_{j-1} only if a departure but no arrival occurs. The rate of transitions into state S_j is

$$\lambda P_{j-1} + \mu P_{j+1}$$

while the rate out of state S_j is $\mu P_j + \lambda P_j$. Equating the two gives

$$P_{j+1} = \frac{\lambda + \mu}{\mu} P_j - \frac{\lambda}{\mu} P_{j-1}$$

Using a similar approach, one can see that

$$P_1 = \frac{\lambda}{\mu} P_0$$

These are precisely the same equations obtained through the development of the differential difference equations. The foundations behind the two schemes are identical. This method is simply a shorthand version of the first technique. The equations must still be solved using either the iterative or the generating-function approach.

Summary measures for the $M/M/1/\infty/$ FIFO system

5.3   Once the steady-state equations for the $M/M/1/\infty/$FIFO queueing system have been solved, the distribution of the number of customers in the system is known, at least in steady state. This distribution can then be used to calculate various summary measures such as the expected number in the system and expected waiting time, and these measures can then be used to characterize the behavior of the system.

Expected number in the system

5.3.1   Let $\mathbf{X}$ denote the random variable that counts the number in the system. Then when the system is in a steady state,

$$P(\mathbf{X} = x) = P_x = (1 - \rho)\rho^x, \qquad x = 0, 1, 2, \ldots$$

The expected value of $\mathbf{X}$ can be calculated from

$$E(\mathbf{X}) = \sum_{x=0}^{\infty} xP_x = (1 - \rho) \sum_{x=0}^{\infty} x\rho^x$$

Now

$$\sum_{x=0}^{\infty} x\rho^x = \rho \sum_{x=1}^{\infty} x\rho^{x-1} = \rho \frac{d}{d\rho} \left[\sum_{x=0}^{\infty} \rho^x \right]$$

But since $\rho < 1$, $\sum_{x=0}^{\infty} \rho^x = 1/(1 - \rho)$. Then

$$\sum_{x=0}^{\infty} x\rho^x = \rho \frac{d}{d\rho} \left[\frac{1}{1 - \rho} \right] = \frac{\rho}{(1 - \rho)^2}$$

Then

$$E(\mathbf{X}) = (1 - \rho) \left(\frac{\rho}{(1 - \rho)^2} \right) = \frac{\rho}{1 - \rho}$$

This average number in the system is sometimes denoted L.

$$L = \frac{\rho}{1 - \rho} = \frac{\lambda}{\mu - \lambda}$$

Expected number in the queue

5.3.2 We sometimes want to calculate the average length of the queue rather than the average number in the system. Let $\mathbf{Q}$ denote the random variable that counts the customers waiting in the queue for service. Then

$$E(\mathbf{Q}) = 0P_0 + \sum_{j=1}^{\infty} (j - 1)P_j$$

$$= \sum_{j=1}^{\infty} jP_j - \sum_{j=1}^{\infty} P_j$$

$$= L - \sum_{j=1}^{\infty} P_j$$

But $\sum_{j=0}^{\infty} P_j = 1$, so $\sum_{j=1}^{\infty} P_j = 1 - P_0$, and $E(\mathbf{Q}) = L - (1 - P_0)$. Since $P_0 = 1 - \rho$,

$$E(\mathbf{Q}) = L - \rho = \frac{\rho}{1 - \rho} - \rho = \frac{\rho^2}{1 - \rho}$$

This quantity is sometimes denoted L_q. So the average queue length is given by

$$L_q = \frac{\rho^2}{1 - \rho} = \frac{\lambda^2}{\mu(\mu - \lambda)}$$

Expected time in the system

5.3.3 Another measure important in summarizing the behavior of a queueing system is the average time that a customer spends in the system, both waiting for and receiving service. The distribution of waiting times can be readily obtained from an expectation argument. However, if all that is desired is the average time in the system, it is easier to compute it using a relationship known as Little's formula (5.3).

Let W be the expected time in the system, L the expected number in the system, and λ the arrival rate of customers to the service facility. Then

$$L = \lambda W$$

The conditions under which this relationship holds are rather broad. For more details see Gross and Harris (5.1).

In section 5.3.1, we established that $L = \rho/(1 - \rho) = \lambda/(\mu - \lambda)$. Using this relationship along with Little's formula gives the expected time in the system.

$$W = \frac{L}{\lambda} = \frac{1}{\mu - \lambda}$$

Expected time in the queue

5.3.4   The average time that a customer must wait for service is also important, since it is while waiting that a customer becomes discouraged and leaves the system. Once service begins, the customer is usually committed. The average waiting time in the system queue W_q is related to the average time in the system by

$$W = W_q + \frac{1}{\mu}$$

Although this relationship will not be proved here, it should be intuitive. Then since $W = 1/(\mu - \lambda)$,

$$W_q = \frac{1}{\mu - \lambda} - \frac{1}{\mu}$$

or

$$W_q = \frac{\lambda}{\mu(\mu - \lambda)}$$

Another version of Little's formula relates the average waiting time in the queue to the average length of the queue.

$$L_q = \lambda W_q$$

Example 5.1 Consider a queueing system composed of a message-switching center that serves five remote send-only terminals, as illustrated in figure 5.3. Messages are received from each of the terminals

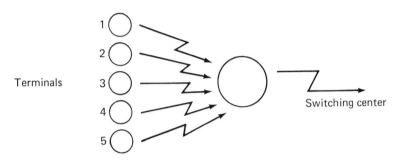

Figure 5.3
A message-switching diagram

according to the Poisson process with rates $\lambda_1 = 2$ per min, $\lambda_2 = 0.5$ per min, $\lambda_3 = \lambda_4 = 1$ per min, and $\lambda_5 = 3.5$ per min. The messages are then buffered before being processed and transmitted over a single line to another switching center. Assume that the time to process and transmit the messages can be considered exponentially distributed with an average service time of four seconds. Assume also that the switching center has infinite available storage so that the system's capacity is not a factor. Assuming steady state, determine (1) the probability that there are fewer than five messages in the system, (2) the average number of messages in the system, (3) the average number of messages buffered, (4) the average time spent by each message in system, and (5) the average time spent in the buffer by each message.

Since the arrival stream from each terminal is Poisson, the aggregate arrival stream will also be Poisson with a rate of $\lambda = \lambda_1 + \lambda_2 + \lambda_3 + \lambda_4 + \lambda_5 = 8$ per min. The service rate is $\mu = 60/4 = 15$ per min. Then the system can be considered an $M/M/1 /\infty/$FIFO system with utilization factor $\rho = \lambda/\mu = 6/15 = 0.4000$. The probability that there are fewer than five messages in the system is

$$P(\mathbf{X} < 5) = P(\mathbf{X} = 0) + P(\mathbf{X} = 1) + P(\mathbf{X} = 2) + P(\mathbf{X} = 3) + P(\mathbf{X} = 4)$$

$$= P_0 + P_1 + P_2 + P_3 + P_4$$

$$= (1 - \rho) + (1 - \rho)\rho + (1 - \rho)\rho^2 + (1 - \rho)\rho^3 + (1 - \rho)\rho^4$$

$$= (1 - \rho)(1 + \rho + \rho^2 + \rho^3 + \rho^4)$$

$$= 0.4666(2.053)$$

$$= 0.9567.$$

The expected number of customers in the system is

$$L = \frac{\rho}{1 - \rho} = \frac{0.5333}{0.4666} = 1.1429$$

The average number of messages buffered in the system is

$$L_q = \frac{\rho^2}{1 - \rho} = \frac{(0.5333)^2}{0.4666} = 0.6095$$

The average time spent by each message in the system is

$$W = \frac{1}{\mu - \lambda} = \frac{1}{15 - 8} = \frac{1}{7} \doteq 0.1429 \text{ min} \doteq 8.57 \text{ sec}$$

The average time spent by each message in the buffer is

$$W_q = \frac{\lambda}{\mu(\mu - \lambda)} = \frac{8}{15(7)} = 0.0762 \text{ min} \doteq 4.57 \text{ sec}$$

The *M/M/1/K/FIFO* system

5.4   Suppose that instead of allowing for an infinite system capacity as with the M/M/1/∞/FIFO system, the system is restricted so that a maximum of K customers can be present at any given time. In most instances this is a more realistic model. Difference equations may be derived for this model just as for the M/M/1/∞/FIFO system. In fact, as long as the number in the system is less than K, the equations are exactly the same as those previously developed. For j = K the following difference equation must be added.

$$P_K(t + \Delta t) = P_K(t)(1 - \mu \Delta t) + P_{K-1}(t)(\lambda \Delta t)(1 - \mu \Delta t)$$

This equation must be included since transitions to state S_{K+1} are not possible. An arriving customer is turned away from the system when the system is full. If the system is assumed to be in equilibrium, the steady-state equations are then

$$P_1 = \frac{\lambda}{\mu} P_0$$

$$P_{j+1} = \frac{\lambda + \mu}{\mu} P_j - \frac{\lambda}{\mu} P_{j-1}, \quad 1 \leq j \leq K - 1$$

$$P_K = \frac{\lambda}{\mu} P_{K-1}$$

The first two equations are identical to those of the $M/M/1/\infty/$FIFO system the third equation results from the additional difference equation.

Using the utilization factor ρ as well as the iterative procedure detailed in section 5.2.1, one can show that

$$P_j = \rho^j P_0, \qquad 1 \le j \le K$$

In this case, $\displaystyle\sum_{j=0}^{K} P_j = 1$, so $\displaystyle\sum_{j=0}^{K} \rho^j P_0 = 1$ and $P_0 = 1 \bigg/ \displaystyle\sum_{j=0}^{K} \rho^j$.

Now $\displaystyle\sum_{j=0}^{K} \rho^j$ is a finite geometric series whose sum is given by

$$\sum_{j=0}^{K} \rho^j = \begin{cases} \dfrac{1 - \rho^{K+1}}{1 - \rho}, & \rho \ne 1 \\ K + 1, & \rho = 1 \end{cases}$$

Thus

$$P_0 = \begin{cases} \dfrac{1 - \rho}{1 - \rho^{K+1}}, & \rho \ne 1 \\ \dfrac{1}{K + 1}, & \rho = 1 \end{cases}$$

from which the solution to the steady-state equations can be derived.

$$P_n = \begin{cases} \dfrac{(1 - \rho)\rho^n}{1 - \rho^{K+1}}, & \rho \ne 1 \\ \dfrac{1}{K + 1}, & \rho = 1 \quad n = 0, 1, 2, \ldots, K \end{cases}$$

Thus in this case steady state will be reached regardless of the utilization factor. This should not be surprising, since constraining the maximum number of customers in the system prevents the queue from growing without bound, as happens in the $M/M/1/\infty/$FIFO system when $\rho \ge 1$.

The summary measures for the $M/M/1/K/$FIFO system can be developed in a manner analogous to those measures used for the $M/M/1/\infty/$FIFO system. Little's formula holds for the system, if the effective arrival rate $\lambda' = \lambda(1 - P_K)$ is used in place of λ. The following relationships can be easily derived by using the procedure used for the $M/M/1/\infty/$FIFO system.

Expected number in the system

$$L = \begin{cases} \dfrac{K}{2}, & \rho = 1 \\[2ex] \dfrac{\rho[1 - (K + 1)\rho^K + K\rho^{K+1}]}{(1 - \rho^{K+1})(K - \rho)}, & \rho \neq 1 \end{cases}$$

Expected number in the queue

$$L_q = L - (1 - P_0)$$

Expected time in the system

$$W = \frac{L}{\lambda'} = \frac{L}{\lambda(1 - P_K)}$$

Expected time in the queue

$$W_q = W - \frac{1}{\mu} = \frac{L_q}{\lambda'} = \frac{L_q}{\lambda(1 - P_K)}$$

Example 5.2　Consider the system described in example 5.1. Instead of assuming an infinite storage capacity at the switching center, assume that there is sufficient storage to keep a maximum of ten messages. With these assumptions the system is an M/M/1/10/FIFO system.

The probability that there are fewer than five messages in the system is

$$P(\mathbf{X} < 5) = P_0 + P_1 + P_2 + P_3 + P_4$$

$$= \frac{(1 - \rho)}{1 - \rho^{11}} [1 + \rho + \rho^2 + \rho^3 + \rho^4]$$

$$= \frac{0.4666}{0.9990} (2.0503)$$

$$= 0.9577$$

The expected number of customers in the system is

$$L = \frac{\rho[1 - (K + 1)\rho^K + K\rho^{K+1}]}{(1 - \rho^{K+1})(1 - \rho)}$$

$$= \frac{0.5333[1 - 11(0.5333^{10}) + 10(0.5333)^{11}]}{(1 - (0.5333)^{11})(0.4666)}$$

$$= 1.1320$$

The average number of messages buffered in the system is

$$L_q = L - (1 - P_0)$$

$$= 1.1320 - \left(1 - \frac{(1 - \rho)}{(1 - \rho^{11})}\right)$$

$$= 1.1320 - \left(1 - \frac{0.4666}{0.9990}\right)$$

$$= 1.1320 - 0.5329$$

$$= 0.5991$$

The average time spent by each message in the system is

$$W = \frac{L}{\lambda'} = \frac{L}{\lambda(1 - P_K)}$$

$$= \frac{1.1320}{8(1 - 0.0009)} = 0.1416 \text{ min.}$$

$$= 8.50 \text{ secs.}$$

The average time spent by each message in the buffer is

$$W_q = W - \frac{1}{\mu} = 0.1416 - \frac{1}{15} = 0.0749 \text{ min}$$

$$= 4.496 \text{ sec}$$

As this example shows, when the system capacity is constrained, the summary measures are smaller than their respective counterparts of the $M/M/1/\infty/$FIFO system. This result should be expected, since in the $M/M/1/K/$FIFO system some customers are being turned away.

The $M/M/C/\infty/$FIFO system

5.5   Suppose that instead of having a single server as with the $M/M/1/\infty/$FIFO system, there are C servers, each with an independently and identically distributed exponential service time distribution with rate μ. The arrival process is still assumed to be Poisson. The system is illustrated in figure 5.4.

First consider the mean service rate of the system. If there are more than C customers in the system, all the servers are busy; hence, the mean service rate is $C\mu$. If there are fewer than C customers in the system, say k, some of the servers are idle, so that the mean service rate is $k\mu$. Using an approach similar to that used for the analysis of the $M/M/1/\infty/$FIFO system, we can obtain the following relationship for P_j, the probability that j customers are in the system.

$$P_j = \begin{cases} \dfrac{\lambda^j}{j!\mu^j} P_0, & 1 \le j \le C \\[3mm] \dfrac{\lambda^j}{C^{j-C}C!\mu^j} P_0, & j > C \end{cases}$$

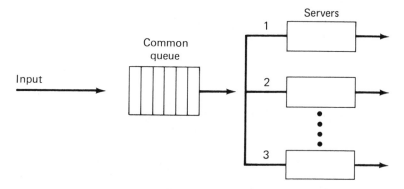

Figure 5.4
Multiserver queueing system

The calculation of P_0 for this system is considerably more complicated than for the previous systems because of the more complex relation for P_j. Again using the condition $\displaystyle\sum_{j=0}^{\infty} P_j = 1$ yields

$$P_0 \left[\sum_{j=0}^{C-1} \frac{\lambda^j}{j!\mu^j} + \sum_{j=C}^{\infty} \frac{\lambda^j}{C^{j-C}C!\mu^j} \right] = 1$$

Define $r = \lambda/\mu$ and $\rho = \lambda/C\mu$; this relationship can then be rewritten

$$P_0 \left[\sum_{j=0}^{C-1} \frac{r^j}{j!} + \sum_{j=C}^{\infty} \frac{r^j}{C^{j-C}C!} \right] = 1$$

Thus

$$\sum_{j=C}^{\infty} \frac{r^j}{C^{n-j}C!} = \frac{r^C}{C!} \sum_{j=C}^{\infty} \left(\frac{r}{C}\right)^{j-C}$$

$$= \frac{r^C}{C!} \sum_{j=0}^{\infty} \left(\frac{r}{C}\right)^{j}$$

$$= \frac{r^C}{C!} \sum_{j=0}^{\infty} \rho^{j}$$

$$= \frac{r^C}{C!} \left(\frac{1}{1-\rho}\right) \quad \text{if } \rho < 1$$

Finally

$$P_0 = \left[\sum_{j=0}^{C-1} \frac{r^j}{j!} + \frac{Cr^C}{C!(C-r)} \right]^{-1}$$

or

$$P_0 = \left[\sum_{j=0}^{C-1} \frac{1}{j!} \left(\frac{\lambda}{\mu}\right)^{j} + \frac{1}{C!} \left(\frac{\lambda}{\mu}\right)^{C} \left(\frac{C\mu}{C\mu - \lambda}\right) \right]^{-1}$$

This equation appears quite formidable, and as more restrictions on the $M/M/1/\infty/\text{FIFO}$ system are relaxed, the equations become worse to solve. Note that the requirement for the $M/M/C/\infty/\text{FIFO}$ system to reach steady state is $\lambda/C\mu < 1$, rather than $\lambda/\mu < 1$ as with the $M/M/1/\infty/\text{FIFO}$ system.

Obviously the development of the summary measures becomes somewhat cumbersome for the $M/M/C/\infty/\text{FIFO}$ system. The derivation of these measures can be found in Gross and Harris (5.1).

Expected number in the system

$$L = \frac{\lambda}{\mu} + \left[\frac{(\lambda/\mu)^C \lambda\mu}{(C-1)!(C\mu - \lambda)^2} \right] P_0$$

Expected number in the queue

$$L_q = \left[\frac{(\lambda/\mu)^C \lambda\mu}{(C-1)!(C\mu - \lambda)^2} \right] P_0$$

Expected time in the system

$$W = \frac{1}{\mu} + \left[\frac{(\lambda/\mu)^C \mu}{(C-1)!(C\mu - \lambda)^2} \right] P_0$$

Expected time in the queue

$$W_q = \left[\frac{(\lambda/\mu)^C \mu}{(C-1)!(C\mu - \lambda)^2} \right] P_0$$

It should be apparent from these relationships that Little's formula holds for the *M/M/C/∞/FIFO* system.

Example 5.3   Consider the system described in example 5.1. Suppose that there are four identical switch-line combinations at the switching center, each of which can service a message in an average of four seconds. The system can be analyzed as an *M/M/4/∞/FIFO* system. The quantities calculated in examples 5.1 and 5.2 can be recalculated for this system as follows:

1. $P_0 = \left[\sum_{j=0}^{3} \frac{1}{j!} \left(\frac{\lambda}{\mu} \right)^j + \frac{1}{4!} \left(\frac{\lambda}{\mu} \right)^C \left(\frac{C\mu}{C\mu - \lambda} \right) \right]^{-1}$

$= \left[1 + \frac{\lambda}{\mu} + \frac{1}{2} \left(\frac{\lambda}{\mu} \right)^2 + \frac{1}{6} \left(\frac{\lambda}{\mu} \right)^3 + \frac{1}{24} \left(\frac{\lambda}{\mu} \right)^4 \left(\frac{4\mu}{4\mu - 1} \right) \right]^{-1}$

But $\lambda = 8, \mu = 15$, so $\lambda/\mu = 8/15 = 0.5333$. Thus

$$P_0 = \left[1 + 0.5333 + \frac{1}{2}(0.5333)^2 + \frac{1}{6}(0.5333)^3 + \frac{1}{24}(0.5333)^4 \left(\frac{60}{52} \right) \right]^{-1}$$

$$= 1/1.7047 = 0.5866$$

Finally

$P(\mathbf{X} < 5) = P_0 + P_1 + P_2 + P_3 + P_4$

$= P_0 \left(1 + \frac{\lambda}{\mu} + \frac{1}{2} \left(\frac{\lambda}{\mu} \right)^2 + \frac{1}{6} \left(\frac{\lambda}{\mu} \right)^3 + \frac{1}{24} \left(\frac{\lambda}{\mu} \right)^4 \right)$

$= 0.5866 \left(1 + 0.5333 + \frac{1}{2}(0.5333)^2 + \frac{1}{6}(0.5333)^3 + \frac{1}{24}(0.5333)^4 \right)$

$= 0.5866 \, (1.70415)$

$= 0.9997$

2. $L = \frac{\lambda}{\mu} + \left[\frac{(\lambda/\mu)^4 \lambda\mu}{(3!)(4\mu - \lambda)} \right] P_0$

$= 0.5333 + \left[\frac{(0.5333)^4(8)(15)}{(6)(52)} \right] (0.5866)$

$= 0.5333 + 0.0182 = 0.5515$

3. $L_q = \left[\dfrac{(\lambda/\mu)^4 \lambda\mu}{(C-1)!(C\mu - \lambda)^2} \right] P_0$

$= 0.0182$

4. $W = L/\lambda = 0.5515/8 = 0.0689 \text{ min} = 4.1363 \text{ sec}$

5. $W_q = L_q/\lambda = 0.0182/8 = 0.0023 \text{ min} = 0.1365 \text{ sec}$

Note that with this system the calculated summary measures have decreased dramatically from those calculated for the $M/M/1/\infty/\text{FIFO}$ system.

Priority queueing systems

5.6   In all the previously surveyed queueing systems, the next customer selected for service in the system was the one at the head of the line. It is not uncommon for this selection to be based instead on a priority system, in which certain customers are given precedence over others. There are a number of reasons for applying priority disciplines. One is to reduce the average cost of the system. It may be more expensive to have certain customers wait in line rather than others. It would seem reasonable then to serve the high-cost customers first and thereby reduce the average total cost to the system. Another motivation might be to reduce the average number of customers in the system. The required service time for certain customers may be considerably shorter than for other customers in the system. By giving priority to customers who require the least service, it is possible to reduce the average number of customers in this system, an objective of particular interest for systems with a finite capacity.

Two general classes of priority queueing disciplines must be examined.

Nonpreemptive. Once the service of a given customer has started, it cannot be interrupted. If there are customers in the queue with different priorities, the next customer selected for service is the one with the highest priority. If there are customers in the queue with the same priority, some alternate discipline, normally first-in, first-out, is used to determine which customer is served next.

Preemptive. In this scheme, if an arriving customer has a higher priority than the customer currently being served, service is interrupted for the current customer, and the higher-priority customer gains control of the service facility. The interrupted customer rejoins the queue for service. The question then is, What happens when the interrupted customer is again selected for service? If the portion of service that the customer received is lost and service begins again, the discipline is known as a *preemptive repeat* discipline. If the service is resumed from the point of interruption, the discipline is known as a *preemptive resume* discipline.

Whether a given discipline is preemptive or nonpreemptive does not determine the priority of customers in the queue. Some techniques for assigning priorities to customers in the queue are the following.

Shortest service first. This scheme requires that the required service of each customer be known. Customers are then assigned priorities based on the required service, and the customer requiring the least amount of service is given the highest priority. This technique is generally used in nonpreemptive disciplines.

Willingness to pay. In some systems customers are allowed to buy a higher priority. Rates are set for various levels of priority, and a customer is charged according to the level of priority desired. This technique is normally used in nonpreemptive systems.

Round robin. Each customer in the queue is given some interval (quanta) of service before any customer receives a second interval. If the quanta is not sufficient to complete service on a given customer, service is interrupted and the customer rejoins the queue in a cyclic fashion. A number of techniques have been used to handle the customer who has received only part of the service. The customer can rejoin the original queue, for example, or join a second queue.

The development of the steady-state equations for priority queueing systems is a cumbersome job. For this reason, we refer the reader to Gross and Harris (5.1) for the details.

Nonpreemptive priority system

5.6.1   Suppose that a total of r priority classes of customers are serviced by a single-channel service facility. Assume that the priority class numbers are assigned such that a lower number implies a higher priority. Suppose also that the arrival process of the kth class is Poisson with rate λ_k, while the service time required for the kth class customer is exponential with rate μ_k. Then define

$$\rho_k = \frac{\lambda_k}{\mu_k}, \qquad 1 \le k \le r$$

and the system will reach steady state if $\sum_{k=1}^{r} \rho_k < 1$. It is convenient to define $\sigma_k = \sum_{i=1}^{k} \rho_i$. Then the requirement for the system to reach steady state is $\sigma_r < 1$.

If the system has reached steady state, the expected waiting time (time in the queue) for a customer in the ith priority class is given by

$$W_q^{(i)} = \frac{\sum_{k=1}^{r} (\rho_k/\mu_k)}{(1 - \sigma_{i-1})(1 - \sigma_i)}$$

The expected number of customers of the ith class who are in the queue is

$$L_q^{(i)} = \lambda_i W_q^{(i)} = \frac{\lambda_i \sum_{k=1}^{r} (\rho_k/\mu_k)}{(1 - \sigma_{i-1})(1 - \sigma_i)}$$

Then the total expected number in the queue is given by

$$L_q = \sum_{i=1}^{r} L_q^{(i)} = \sum_{i=1}^{r} \frac{\lambda_i \sum_{k=1}^{r} (\rho_k/\mu_k)}{(1 - \sigma_{i-1})(1 - \sigma_i)}$$

Preemptive priority system

5.6.2   The major difference between the preemptive and the nonpreemptive systems is that the preemptive priority system allows higher-priority customers to preempt lower-priority customers. The next consideration is whether the preemptive-repeat or the preemptive-resume technique is being used. If the service distribution is assumed to be exponential, the techniques used are immaterial because the distribution is memory-less.

With the same definitions as in previous sections, the expected number of customers in the ith priority class waiting in the queue is given by

$$L_q^{(i)} = \frac{\rho_i}{\left(1 - \sum_{n=1}^{i-1} \rho_n\right)\left(1 - \sum_{n=1}^{i} \rho_n\right)}$$

With this discipline a customer in the ith priority class is unaffected by customers in the $i + 1, i + 2, \ldots, r$ priority classes, so these priority classes have no effect on the expected waiting time. The expected waiting time for a customer in the ith priority class is identical to that of a customer in a nonpreemptive model with i priority classes. Thus

$$W_q^{(i)} = \frac{\sum_{k=1}^{i} (\rho_k/\mu_k)}{(1 - \sigma_{i-1})(1 - \sigma_i)}$$

Example 5.4   Consider the system described in example 5.1. Assume that messages arriving to the switching center are assigned priorities on the basis of their originating terminal, with messages received from terminal 1 assigned the highest priority, those from terminal 2 the second highest, and so on. Also assume that $\mu_1 = \mu_2 = \mu_3 = \mu_4 = \mu_5 = \mu$. Using the nonpreemptive model, calculate the average number of terminal-3 messages in the buffer awaiting retransmission and the average time that each of these messages remains in the buffer.

$\rho_1 = 2/15 = 0.1333$

$\rho_2 = 0.5/15 = 0.0333$

$\rho_3 = 1/15 = 0.0667$

$\rho_4 = 1/15 = 0.0667$

$\rho_5 = 1.5/15 = 0.1000$

From these we get

$$\sigma_2 = \rho_1 + \rho_2 = 0.1666, \qquad \sigma_3 = \rho_1 + \rho_2 + \rho_3 = 0.2333$$

Then

$$W_q^{(3)} = \frac{\sum_{k=1}^{5} (\rho_k/\mu_k)}{(1 - \sigma_2)(1 - \sigma_3)}$$

$$= \frac{1/15(0.1333 + 0.0333 + 0.0667 + 0.0667 + 0.1000)}{(1 - 0.1666)(1 - 0.2333)}$$

$$= \frac{0.0267}{(0.8334)(0.7667)}$$

$$= 0.0418 \text{ min} = 2.5 \text{ secs}$$

and

$$L_q^{(3)} = \lambda_3 W_q^{(3)} = (0.0418)(1) = 0.0418$$

Summary

This chapter has surveyed some of the more common queueing systems, deriving summary measures for some and merely listing those for others. We have of course ignored many systems. For example, we did not consider models in which arrivals or services occur in batches. We also ignored series and parallel queueing systems. As queueing systems become more complex, the mathematics involved becomes nearly intractable, and this complexity calls for simulation. If a system cannot be analyzed analytically using queueing models, it is normally simulated. Even if it can be analyzed analytically, it is sometimes more convenient to simulate it and use the analytic model to validate the simulation.

Exercises

5.1   The manager of a single-channel service facility wishes to study the operation of the facility. To this end the manager collects data for one hour. The data collected are as follows.

Customer	Arrival time	Service required
1	8:01	6
2	8:06	4
3	8:07	3

4	8:11	5
5	8:12	3
6	8:14	2
7	8:15	1
8	8:16	7
9	8:17	4
10	8:21	2
11	8:24	6
12	8:27	3
13	8:28	3
14	8:29	2
15	8:30	1
16	8:32	1
17	8:36	11
18	8:41	1
19	8:42	4
20	8:44	3
21	8:45	2
22	8:50	3
23	8:52	2
24	8:54	2
25	8:58	1

Construct an empirical distribution for the interarrival times and service times by connecting the points with straight-line segments, as described in section 3.1.

5.2 The manager of the system described in exercise 5.1 suspects that the arrival distribution is Poisson with an average arrival rate of 0.5 customers per minute, and that the service time distribution is exponential with an average of three minutes per customer. Do the data collected support these conjectures?

5.3 Suppose that the service facility described in exercise 5.1 closes at 9:00 but continues to service customers until all customers in line at the time of closing are served. Assuming a FIFO queueing discipline, determine the system state (number of customers in the system) at each point in time that this state changes. Determine the average queue length and the system idle time. How many customers were waiting at 9:00?

5.4 Repeat exercise 5.3 under the assumption that the shortest-job-first (SJF) queueing discipline is used. In this discipline the customer in the queue requiring the least service is selected when the server finishes serving the present customer.

5.5 Suppose that the service facility described in exercise 5.1 is composed of two identical servers working from a common queue. Repeat exercise 5.3 under this assumption.

5.6 Automobiles arrive at a single-bay service station according to a Poisson process at a rate of ten per hour. The time required to service the cars is exponentially distributed with an average of five minutes per car. Assuming infinite system capacity and steady state, determine the following.

a. The probability that the service station is idle
b. The average number of cars waiting for service
c. The average time each spends waiting for service

5.7 If the service station has only enough ramp space for ten cars, how will the answers to exercise 5.6 change?

5.8 If there are four bays with identically distributed service times, how will the answers to exercise 5.6 change?

5.9 Use the method of stochastic balance to derive the steady-state difference equations for the $M/M/1/K/FIFO$ system.

5.10 Failures of a given machine occur according to a Poisson process at a rate of five machines per hour. It costs $10 for each hour of downtime per machine. The manager of the facility must decide between two repair services. One service charge $5 per hour and can repair an average of six machines per hour. The other charges $6 per hour but can repair an average of eight machines per hour. Assuming that the service times are exponentially distributed, which service should be used?

5.11 A given service facility uses a nonpreemptive priority queueing discipline. There are three priority classes, with arrivals in each class followng a Poisson process at rates $\lambda_1 = 2$ per hour, $\lambda_2 = 3$ per hour and $\lambda_3 = 1$ per hour. The service requirements for each class are exponentially distributed, with rates of four per hour, eight per hour, and ten per hour. Determine the expected waiting time and average queue length for each priority class.

5.12 To simulate the operation of an $M/M/1/\infty/FIFO$ system, one would need a source of Poisson random numbers with which to simulate the arrival process and a source of exponential random numbers with which to simulate service completions. In addition, a clock would be necessary to control the simulator. Write a FORTRAN program to simulate this system using the random number generators developed in chapter 4. Collect statistics on the average number in the system and compare with the theoretical results.

References

5.1 GROSS, DONALD, and HARRIS, CARL. *Fundamentals of Queueing Theory.* New York: John Wiley and Sons, 1974.

5.2 KENDALL, D. G. "Stochastic Processes Occurring in the Theory of Queues and Their Analysis by the Method of Imbedded Markov Chains." *Ann. Math. Statistics 24* (1953): 338–354.

5.3 LITTLE, J. D. C. "A Proof for the Queueing Formula $L = \lambda W$." *Oper. Res. 16,* (1961): 651–665.

6

Discrete system simulation

An understanding of the basic concepts in probability, statistical methods, and queueing theory that were introduced in previous chapters is necessary for the full understanding of simulation methods. This chapter and the next discuss some of the factors that influence the development of a system simulation model. Let us review some of the simulation terminology introduced earlier.

An object is called an *entity*. The characteristics of an entity are referred to as *attributes*. The collection of entities and attributes for a given system is referred to as the *system state*, and it is generally expressed in a time frame of reference. Any process that changes the system state is referred to as an *activity*. The occurrence of such a change at a point in time is referred to as an *event*. An event may be a change in the value of some attribute, the creation or destruction of an entity, or the initiation or termination of an activity. A *discrete* system is characterized by changes in the system state that occur in discrete or quantum jumps; a *continuous* system is characterized by smooth, continuous changes in system state. This chapter is devoted to aspects of discrete system simulation, and a later chapter considers continuous system simulation. Some of the considerations are the same for both and will generally not be repeated.

The state of a system — continuous or discrete — is usually expressed as a function of time. Two time references are involved in the simulation of a system: simulation time and run time. The term *simulation time* is used to refer to the period of time simulated by the model — 30 minutes, 5 years, 100 years, whatever interval the researcher is interested in. This simulation time is usually set to 0 at the beginning of the simulation run and acts as a counter to the number of simulation time units. The *duration* of a simulation run is the difference between the initial clock setting and the setting at the termination of the run. The *run time* is simply the time that it takes the computer to simulate the period of interest. There is generally very little if any correlation between the two measures of time. The run time is influenced by factors such as the complexity of the simulation model and the number of events simulated, as well as by the duration of the run. Run time in most cases is considerably shorter than simulation time. For example, one can generally simulate the operation of this country's economic system over a period of years in minutes on a computer. In some cases, however, the run time is considerably longer than the simulation time. Consider, for example, the simulation of a computer system. Simulation time in this case is measured in microseconds and nanoseconds. But because of the complexity of any realistic computer system model and the number of events that generally occur in any period of interest, the run time would probably be several thousand times greater than the simulation time for this example. Unless otherwise indicated, references to time in this chapter and succeeding chapters are to simulation time. Run time, although crucial from an economic standpoint, is generally not as easily controlled by the analyst as simulation time. References to run time are made only to compare different simulation approaches.

Time management methods

6.1 Simulation models have been used to model both static (time-independent) and dynamic (time-dependent) situations. A static model shows the relationships between entities and attributes when the system is in a state of equilibrium. In this case, when the value of an attribute is changed to allow observation of its effect on the rest of the system, new attribute values can be derived for the rest of the system. No information can be obtained, however, on the manner in which this change occurred. The dynamic model allows the changes in attribute values to be derived as a function of time. The manner in which a change occurs can then be studied.

Most simulation models are dynamic models. Many static models can be solved analytically and provide better results than simulation. Analytic solutions of dynamic models often require many simplifying assumptions to make the model tractable and thus rarely yield useful results. Thus a simulation is generally a numerically solved dynamic mathematical model.

Dynamic models are time dependent. For that reason a simulator must generally include a means for depicting a time change in the system. This has resulted in the use of the phrase *time management*. There are a number of different ways of managing time in a simulator. Two of the more common ways are periodic scan and event scan.

The *periodic scan,* or fixed-time increment, technique adjusts the simulation clock by one predetermined uniform unit and then examines the system to determine whether any events occurred during that interval. If any occurred, the event or events are simulated; otherwise no action is taken. The simulation clock is then advanced another unit, and the process is repeated. An example of this time management procedure is illustrated in figure 6.1.

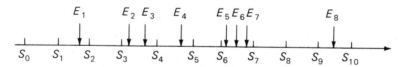

Figure 6.1
The periodic scan approach

In figure 6.1 no event occurs in the first unit of simulated time, so the clock is immediately advanced and the system scanned. Then event E_1 occurs in the second time increment. This event would be simulated and the clock advanced again. Since there is no event to simulate during the third interval, the clock is again advanced. During the fourth interval two events are to be simulated, E_2 and E_3. Following their simulation the clock is again advanced. This process of advancing the clock, scanning the system, and simulating events if necessary is repeated until the duration of the simulation run is reached. With this method the exact time of the occurrence of particular events is largely ignored. All events that occur during a given interval are treated as if these events occurred at the end of that interval.

Example 6.1   Consider the simulation of a single-bay service station for a period of ten minutes. Assume that the system is empty at the beginning and at the end of the period. Assume also that four customers are serviced, that arrivals occur at simulation times 1.8, 3.2, 6.1, and 7.4, and that service completions occur at simulation times 2.6, 4.8, 7.3, and 8.1. If a time interval of one minute is used, arrival events are denoted by A_1, A_2, A_3, and A_4 and completion events by C_1, C_2, C_3, and C_4. This system is shown in figure 6.2.

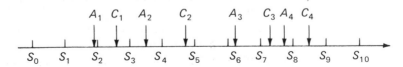

Figure 6.2
Arrival and completion of service events

In this example events C_3 and A_4 are both considered to have occurred at clock time 8.0, although C_3 actually occurred before A_4. Thus a problem with the periodic scan approach is that events separated in time appear to occur simultaneously. To an observer the system state would not appear to have changed with the simultaneous arrival and departure events, although the actual system was idle for a short period of time.

The initial consideration in using the periodic scan approach is the determination of the length of the interval to be used. As example 6.1 shows, if the time unit selected is too large, events separated in time appear to occur simultaneously, and information on the operation of the system is lost. Thus the time advance increment should generally be small relative to the likelihood of occurring events. More precisely, the time increment should be small enough that the probability of multiple events occurring during a single time interval is small. If the time unit selected in example 6.1 had been 0.1 minute rather than 1 minute, the time separation between events C_3 and A_4 would be detected.

From this discussion it appears that the time increment used in the periodic scan approach should be as small as possible to minimize the possibility of lost information, but a moment's reflection should reveal that this is not always the case. The smaller the time unit, the larger the number of calculations necessary to complete the simulation. Thus the actual run time of the simulation and hence the cost of the simulation is increased. There is obviously a trade-off between the need for the precise, detailed model that can be obtained by decreasing the time advance interval and the increasing cost of the computer simulation run. Conversely, the cost of the computer simulation run can be decreased by increasing the size of the time advance unit.

Even if the time advance unit is small enough that the likelihood of multiple event occurrences within a single interval is small, the precise point at which an event occurs within that interval is still uncertain. In some models the exact time of occurrence may be unimportant. However, if a great deal of precision is desired, the time of the exact occurrence might be crucial. There seems to be no solution to this problem, short of making the time advance interval even smaller and thus increasing the cost of the computer simulation.

In many simulation models there are periods of high activity separated by periods of inactivity. The periodic scan approach is not well suited to this type of behavior because it is designed to give equal attention to each interval when more emphasis should be given to the periods of high activity. This fact, along with the problems of determining the time advance interval length, suggests an alternative approach to time management — the event scan approach.

In the *event scan* approach the clock is advanced by the amount necessary to trigger the occurrence of the next, most imminent event, not by some fixed, predetermined interval. Thus the time advance intervals are of variable lengths. This approach requires some scheme for determining when events are to occur. When events are discovered or generated, they are generally stacked in a list, or queue, in time order. The length of the required time advance interval can then be determined merely by scanning the event lists to determine the next earliest event. The simulation clock is then advanced to that time, and occurrence of the event is simulated.

Example 6.2   Consider the simulation model described in example 6.1. If the event scan approach was used in lieu of the periodic scan approach, the simulation clock would initially be advanced to time 1.8 minute and event A_1 simulated. The clock would then be advanced to time 2.6 minutes and event C_1 simulated. The process would continue until all events have been executed or until the simulation duration had been met, whichever occurs first.

The event scan approach avoids some of the problems inherent in the periodic scan approach. The periodic scan approach requires that the analyst supply a fixed unit to be used to advance the simulation clock. The optimal size of this time unit is not known in advance and must be determined from a trade-off between precision and maximum run time. The event scan approach, on the other hand, does not require this artificial time increment; instead, the simulation clock is merely advanced to the next scheduled event occurrence time.

As pointed out in example 6.1, some information can be lost in the periodic scan approach because events that are actually separated in time may be treated as if they occur simultaneously. The event scan approach avoids this problem because the clock is advanced only to the next occurrence time. Thus in an event-scheduling approach two events will be treated as occurring simultaneously only if they actually occur simultaneously.

The third problem with the periodic scan approach is that the exact occurrence time of events is not known, because each event is treated as if it occurred at the end of the interval in which it occurred. The resulting loss of precision in the model can be overcome only by decreasing the size of the time advance interval and thus increasing the cost of the simulation run. This problem is not encountered in the event scan approach, since the simulation clock is advanced to precisely the instant at which the next event occurs.

Another problem with the periodic scan is that during periods of inactivity the simulator is cycling, doing nothing useful, merely advancing the clock. This problem may seem minor, but if the system is characterized by relatively long periods of inactivity separated by short periods of high activity, a significant percentage of the run time associated with a given simulation run might be devoted to merely updating the clock. This problem is again avoided by the use of the event scan approach.

This comparison of the two techniques shows that the event scan approach appears to be more efficient in terms of run time, while the periodic scan approach is more advantageous in ease of implementation and simplicity in bookkeeping.

Object generation

6.2   A system as defined in chapter 1 is a collection of objects with a well-defined set of interactions among them. Therefore when a system is being simulated, there must be some way of representing and introducing objects to the system.

An object or an entity of a simulation model must be uniquely identified in the program; in most cases this is done by the assignment of a serial number to the entity. For example, in a service station model customers might be numbered in the order of their arrival to the system. Along with the serial number, entities are characterized by a set of attributes. The state of an entity at any point in time is the current set of values of its attributes. The state of the system can be thought of as the collection of all present entities represented by their state vectors. Entities that will be present throughout the course of a simulation run are called *permanent*. Entities that will be introduced to the system, remain for a period of time, and then exit the system are called *transitory*.

Permanent entities are generally input to the simulation model during the initialization of that model. Transitory entities, on the other hand, are introduced at particular points in the course of the simulation run and then removed from the model. Thus the generation of a transitory entity involves the generation of an arrival time as well as the assignment of values to various attributes.

The arrival of a transitory entity to the system is an event. It alters the state description of the system by adding one more entity. Arrivals can be made to occur at regular fixed intervals or in some random fashion by sampling the interarrival distribution. A bootstrapping scheme is commonly used in generating the arrival times for successive transitory entities. The arrival time for the first entity is generated by sampling the appropriate distribution and placing the arrival event on the event list. When the simulation clock has advanced to that point at which the event is completed, the system state is updated and the arrival time for the second entity is generated. An alternative to this bootstrapping scheme is to generate all the arrival times at once. This scheme, however, requires the storage of arrival times, thus increasing the storage requirements of the model.

Example 6.3   Again consider the problem of simulating the operation of a message center. The transitory entities for this system are the messages themselves. Suppose that the messages arrive according to a Poisson distribution with a mean rate of λ. The interarrival times for the messages can then be obtained by generating exponentially distributed random numbers using the techniques outlined in chapter 4.

Once the arrival time for the transitory entity is determined, values must be assigned to the various attributes. Attribute values can be generated either at the time the arrival time is generated or at the instant at which the arrival event actually occurs (6.2). The factor that determines which of these two times is to be used is whether the assignment of attribute values is state dependent. State-dependent attribute values should be assigned at the time the arrival actually occurs. And, as with the arrival times, attribute values are normally assigned by the simulated sampling of a given distribution, using the random number generation techniques outlined in chapter 4.

Example 6.4   Consider the message center example outlined in example 6.3. Once the arrival time has been determined through simulated sampling from the exponential distribution, attribute values are assigned. Two attributes of interest are the message precedence and the message length. Suppose that messages are equally likely to be one of three precedences — routine, priority, and emergency. Suppose also that the message length is approximately normally distributed with mean μ and variance σ^2. The assignment of message precedence can be accomplished by the generation of a standard uniform random variate. If the random number is between 0 and 0.33, routine precedence is assigned; between 0.33 and 0.66, priority precedence; and between 0.66 and 1.00, emergency precedence. Assignment of message length can be accomplished by the generation of an appropriate random normal deviate.

Events and event synchronization

6.3   An event is the occurrence of a change in the system state at some point in time. In this sense an event has no duration but exists as an instant in time. An important aspect of a discrete system simulation is the scheduling and synchronization of events.

Events can be categorized by type. Events that involve similar changes to the system state are said to be of the same type. There are two broad event types: system events and program events. A *system event* is an event that represents a simulation of a comparable event in the real system. A *program event* has nothing to do with the system being simulated but deals only with the simulation program itself. Program details such as when the collected statistics are to be printed out are program events. Although these program events may seem artificial, they must be scheduled just as system events must be scheduled.

System events can be further broken down. The scheduled occurrence time for certain types of system event as well as the effect of their occurrence on the system state may be altered by some event that occurs after the event is scheduled but before it actually occurs. Such events are referred to as *contingent events*. System events that cannot be modified by any intervening event once they are scheduled are referred to as *noncontingent events*.

Example 6.5   Consider the simulation of a single-bay service station. Suppose that an arrival event to the service station is scheduled for some time in the future. Suppose furthermore that after the arrival event was scheduled but before it actually occurred, the event "station capacity reached" occurs. The arrival event then would be cancelled. The arrival event in this case could be thought of as a contingent event.

System events can also be categorized as decision or nondecision events. A *decision event* is one in which some decision must be made about the event's effect on the system state. A *nondecision event* is one for which no decision is required to determine the effect of the event's occurrence. This breakdown of event types is mentioned merely to point out that special bookkeeping routines may be necessary to handle the various types.

Event sequencing and synchronization are important aspects of a discrete system simulation. Events are represented as instances in time. Once an event is scheduled and the simulation clock is advanced to the scheduled time, an event execution routine for that particular type of event is invoked to update the system state, thus simulating the effect that event would have on the real system. As long as scheduled events are separated by some interval of time, there is no problem with event sequencing. If two or more events are by chance scheduled to occur simultaneously, the simulation model must decide which event is to be executed first. The decision logic of the simulation model should reflect as much as possible the decision rule in effect in the real system. In other cases, in which either the simultaneity does not occur in the real system or the events are actually handled simultaneously by the real system, some ordering of the simultaneous events must be made so that the execution routines can be invoked. Possible orderings of simultaneous events range from elaborate priority schemes to simple random selection schemes.

The proper sequencing of events is crucial because the effects of certain events can have consequences on other events. For example, some events generate the occurrence of other scheduled events, while yet others may cause a cancellation of some already scheduled event. Events not sequenced in their proper order can have drastic effects on the system's performance.

Events are scheduled in most discrete system simulation programs by an event calendar or event chain. The events generated by the model join a time-ordered list. As the simulation clock is advanced using the periodic scan approach, the event calendar is scanned for events that should have occurred in the last time unit. Execution routines for those events are then invoked, and after they are completed, the simulation clock is again advanced. On the other hand, if the event scan approach is used, the simulation clock is actually controlled by the event calendar. The event calendar is scanned for the earliest scheduled occurrence of an event. The simulation clock is then advanced to this time, and the appropriate execution routine invoked. After this routine is completed, the event calendar is again scanned and the process repeated.

The number of events and the complexity of the corresponding execution routines are the primary determinants of the run time and consequently the cost of the simulation. For example, if there are a large number of contingent events, just updating the event calendar can be time-consuming.

Queue management and list processing

6.4   Waiting lines, or queues, are encountered in almost every system that is modeled because nearly all systems use some limited resource, whether it is the number of servers in a service station or the number of available I/O channels on a general-purpose computing system. Queues arise because of the competition for these limited resources. Thus a major consideration in developing a simulation model of a system is the representation and manipulation of queues. In chapter 5 queues were distinguished by their corresponding queueing disciplines, that is, by the manner in which the next customer gained control of the resource and was selected from the waiting line. The most common queueing discipline is the first-in, first-out (FIFO) discipline, in which the customer who has been waiting the longest is given control. Other disciplines include last-in, first-out (LIFO), in which the customer who has been waiting in the queue the shortest time is given control; random (RAND), in which a customer is selected at random from the queue; and a myriad of priority (PRI) disciplines, in which some customer is selected based on a particular value associated with one attribute.

Whenever an arriving entity is generated and scheduled, the values of its attributes are also assigned, either through the simulated sampling from given distributions or through some other preestablished procedure. In many cases the entity is also assigned a distinguishing serial number to allow unique identification. A convenient means of representing the entity arriving in the system is through an activation record such as that illustrated in figure 6.3. As the entity makes its way through the system model, the values of its attributes are adjusted to reflect event occurrences. Eventually the entity should traverse the entire system, at which time it ceases to be an active entity and becomes part of the summary statistics.

Serial number	Arrival time	Attribute 1	• • •	Attribute n

Figure 6.3
An activation record

Just as the activation record is a convenient way of representing an arriving entity to the system, a convenient way of representing a queue (nothing more than a collection of arriving entities waiting for a common resource) is a list. The organization of queues in a list supports such operations as inserting a new record (adding another entity to the queue), deleting a record (selecting an entity to gain control of the resource and thus eliminating it from those waiting), and accessing a particular record from a list to examine the value of one of its attributes.

With list processing, objects are represented in a computer in a manner that shows the relationship among these objects in an ordered set of entries. It is this ordering that makes the list so convenient for the representation of queues. The manner in which list processing is performed depends largely on the structure of the list.

There are a number of considerations in the construction of lists. First, the *dimension of the list* must be defined. A list comprising single entries is a one-dimensional list; a list of sublists is a two-dimensional list, and so on. Second, the *density of the list* must be considered. Objects in the list may be stored in contiguous or widely separated memory locations. Third, the *sequence of the list* should be determined. For example, a one-dimensional list can be sequenced from top to bottom or from bottom to top.

A number of factors influence the construction of a list. One is the type of application. The list must be constructed in the manner that best fits the application. Inappropriately constructed lists can lead to high processing overhead. A second factor important for the construction of a list is the search technique to be used. The search technique should be matched to the application and the construction scheme. A third factor is the alteration of the list. Consideration must be given to changes likely to result from adding, deleting, or altering elements.

A list is a collection of records in which the extent of the list must be delineated. Objects may be located in a variety of ways depending on the construction of the list. First, the item may be serially locatable. In this scheme the list is sequentially searched until the desired record is found. Second, the item may be directly locatable. A key is assigned to each record, and this key is used to extract the desired record directly from the list. A third scheme is indirect locatability. In this scheme items of the list are linked or chained by pointers. There may be single or multiple pointers to enhance locatability.

The linked, or threaded, list is commonly used to implement a queue structure. The linking or chaining in this queue structure is accomplished by appending a pointer to each record in the list. The pointer indicates the next item in the chain. If multiple chaining is desired, multiple pointers can be appended. Linked lists are therefore composed of records and pointers to the next item on a chain. The main advantage of the linked list is that the list can be altered easily. Items may be added or deleted from the list simply by manipulating pointers rather than entire records. An example of a *singly linked list* is given in figure 6.4. A *doubly linked list* can be obtained from the singly linked list by appending a pointer that links in the opposite direction. That is, record 109 would point to 108, 108 to 107, and so on. A *circular linked list* could be obtained by linking the tail of the chain (record 109) back to the head. In a singly linked list there is normally a separate pointer that points to the first record in the chain, while there may or may not be a separate pointer to the last record in the chain.

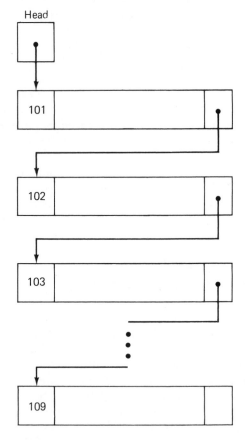

Figure 6.4
A singly linked list

At this point it might be useful to indicate how the singly linked list of figure 6.4 could be changed. Suppose that record 102 is to be deleted from the list. This could be accomplished merely by changing the pointer appended to record 101 to point to record 103, thus severing all ties to record 102. Note that information in record 102 is no longer retrievable. The storage used by record 102 should then be reclaimed by some "garbage collection" routine and reused. Suppose that instead of deleting record 102 we wish to add a new record, call it 102a, between records 102 and 103. This could be accomplished by appending a pointer to record 102a which points to the address of record 103, and then changing the pointer appended to record 102 to point to record 102a. Note that this scheme does not require record 102a to be located contiguous to record 102; record 102a can be located anywhere since it is locatable through the pointer appended to record 102. This avoids the need to shift entire records as would be necessary if a simple sequential arrangement were used.

Most of the common queueing disciplines can be readily implemented by using linked lists. To simulate the operation of a FIFO queue, a singly linked list would be sufficient. Arriving entities would join the tail of the queue. This of course would necessitate a separate pointer to the tail of the list. The processing of the queue (list) begins at its head, thus simulating first-in, first-out processing. A LIFO queue is also easily simulated using a singly linked list. Arriving entities are placed at the head of the list, and the queue is processed from its head. Priority queues are readily simulated using linked lists if the linking is based on the value of the attribute that determines the priority rather than on the time of arrival to the queue. An example may clarify this point.

Example 6.6 Consider a queueing system composed of a single server. Arriving entities are characterized by an assigned serial number by the time that they arrive in the queue, and by the estimated length of service that they require. Suppose that there are five objects in the queue awaiting service having the following attributes.

Serial number	101	102	103	104	105
Arrival time	1013	1009	1011	1015	1014
Service required (min)	2	4	6	1	5

These arriving entities could be represented to the system by an activation record consisting of the fields illustrated in figure 6.5. If the

Serial number	Arrival time	Service required	Pointer to next record

Figure 6.5
Activation record for arriving customers

queueing discipline to be simulated is a FIFO discipline, the following list arrangement is used.

Head

| 102 |

101	1013	2	105
102	1009	4	103
103	1011	6	101
104	1015	1	
105	1014	5	104

Tail

| 104 |

Processing then begins with record 102 and, following the chain, proceeds with 103, 101, 105, and 104; each record is deleted as it is processed. When a new arrival occurs (say record 106), it is added to the list by entering record 106 into the pointer field of record 104 and changing the tail pointer to point to record 106.

If a LIFO discipline is to be simulated, the following list arrangement must be used.

Head

| 104 |

101	1013	2	103
102	1009	4	
103	1011	6	102
104	1015	1	105
105	1014	5	101

In this arrangement processing begins with record 104 and, following the chain, proceeds with records 105, 101, 103, and 102. If a new arrival (again say record 106) occurs, it is added to the queue by changing the head pointer to 106 and by placing 104 in the pointer field of record 106.

A common priority scheme used in service demand systems is the shortest-job-first discipline, in which the priority is based on the amount of resources requested. The highest priority is given to the arrival that requires the least service. Only a moment's reflection is necessary to be convinced that this discipline minimizes the average waiting time. This simple priority scheme can be simulated for our example by using the following list arrangement.

Head

| 104 |

101	1013	2	102
102	1009	4	105
103	1011	6	
104	1015	1	101
105	1014	5	103

Processing begins with record 104 and proceeds to records 101, 102, 105, and 103 in that order. If a new arrival occurs, it is placed in the proper place in the list based on its requested service time. For example, if record 106 arrives requesting three minutes of service time, it is placed in the chain between records 101 and 102 by placing the address of record 102 in the pointer field of record 106 and by changing the pointer field of record 101 to point to record 106.

This example illustrates how linked lists can be used to simulate three of the more common queueing disciplines. More complex queueing disciplines can be simulated by including more pointers. For example, the RAND (random) discipline requires that every record be locatable from every other record. When the linked list is used care should be taken so that the overhead (storage requirements for the pointers) does not become excessive. As items are deleted from the list, some mechanism must be included to reclaim the storage occupied by that record (garbage collection).

Collecting and recording simulation data

6.5
A simulation model that produces no output is not very useful to the researcher. Thus an important aspect in the design, development, and use of the simulation model is the means by which data are collected and summarized. One of the major advantages of using a special-purpose simulation language rather than a general-purpose language such as FORTRAN is that a special-purpose language facilitates data collection. Depending on the system being simulated, different data of the system's performance must be recorded so that the system can be analyzed under varying conditions. This section describes some of the more general types of data that are usually collected and used to characterize a simulation run.

The most common type of data collected from a simulation run is count data — for example, the number of occurrences of a given type of event, the number of entities in each queue of the model at each interval of time, and the total clock time that an entity remains in the system. These count data are then manipulated at the completion of the simulation run to provide summary measures of the system's performance. Count data are easily collected through the use of counter variables initialized at the beginning of the simulation run and updated whenever an event occurs that affects the item of interest.

Example 6.7   Suppose that a simulation model has been developed for a single-bay service station and that one item of interest is the number of arrivals that occurs over the duration of the run. This information can be recorded by initializing a count variable NRARR to zero at the beginning of the simulation run and incrementing it each time that the occurrence of an arrival event is processed. Another item of interest might be the total time that entities remain in the system. This information could be collected by initializing a count variable NTIME to zero at the beginning of the simulation run. Then each time the simulation clock is incremented, the amount of the increment is multiplied by the total number of entities in the system and added to NTIME. Of course, the total number of entities in the system would be collected by initializing a count variable NRENT to zero at the beginning of the run, incrementing it whenever an arrival occurs and decrementing it whenever a departure occurs.

Particular attention must be given to the place in the simulation model where the data are collected. The most obvious place to collect the data is during the processing of an event occurrence that affects the variable of interest. For instance, in example 6.7, the count variable NRARR should be incremented either when the routine is invoked to process the arrival event occurrence or in the arrival event occurrence routine itself. Care should be taken to ensure that the data are collected at each point in the simulation model where an event occurrence affects the variable of interest. If arrival events are processed at two points in the model, data on the number of arrivals must be collected at both points.

The type of summary statistics to be calculated influences the type of data collected. For example, the mean and standard deviation of some variable may be desired. To calculate these two items of interest, one would need to accumulate the sum of the observations of the variable, the sum of the squares of the observations, and the number of observations on which these accumulated sums are based.

Example 6.8   Suppose that we want to calculate the mean and standard deviation of the length of the queue in the queueing system described in example 6.7. This could be accomplished by collecting the following data. Three count variables SUM, SUMSQ, and NTIM are initialized to zero. Then when the simulation clock is incremented, the number in the queue, call it NRQUE, is added to SUM, the square of NRQUE is added to SUMSQ, and NTIM is incremented by 1. At the end of the simulation run the mean and standard deviation of the queue length are calculated using the standard formulas

$$MEAN = SUM/NTIM$$

$$STDDEV = \frac{[(SUMSQ)^2 - (NTIM)(MEAN)^2]^{1/2}}{(NTIM - 1)}$$

In addition to count data, frequency data are often recorded during a simulation run. The recording of these data makes it possible to summarize certain aspects of the system's performance through the use of a frequency histogram. Frequency data are usually recorded for events such as interarrival times and queue lengths.

Example 6.9   Suppose that the analyst wishes to summarize the interarrival distribution to the single-bay service station discussed in example 6.7. This could be done as follows. A number of classes are established for the interarrival times. In this example suppose that the times between successive arrivals to the system have been recorded using the count variable INTARR. Suppose also that the classes have been established as

Class 1	$0 \le INTARR < 1$
Class 2	$1 \le INTARR < 2$
Class 3	$2 \le INTARR < 3$
Class 4	$3 \le INTARR < 4$
.	.
.	.
.	.
Class 10	$9 \le INTARR < 10$

An array composed of ten elements, ARRDIST, is then initialized to 0. Each time an arrival event is processed, INTARR is checked to determine the event's class, and the appropriate array element is incremented. Note that INTARR must be reinitialized after each arrival. After the simulation run has been completed, the interarrival distribution is summarized in array ARRDIST in the form of a frequency table. This can then be subjected to goodness-of-fit testing or presented as a summary of that aspect of the system's performance. If a relative frequency table is desired, each element of the array ARRDIST is divided by the total number of arrivals, which could be accumulated with another count variable NRARR.

The data collected and the analysis methods used on the data are nearly as numerous as the types of simulation models. In this section we have surveyed some of the more common types of data and collection techniques. The analyst has to tailor the data collection methods to the requirements of the system being modeled.

Analysis of simulation results

6.6   Once the simulator has been designed, tested, and debugged, the actual simulation study can be carried out, the results can be interpreted, and inferences about the operation of the true system can be drawn. Numerous pitfalls await the unsuspecting analyst in the interpretation of simulation run data. In this section we survey some of these problems and review some of the techniques that can be used to overcome them.

A simulation study is normally conducted to investigate various aspects of a system's operation for certain operating conditions. The aspects of the system that are under study are normally referred to as the *performance measures* or *response variables*. The aspects of the system's operation that are controllable and are normally varied by the analyst to observe the effect on the response variables are referred to as the *control variables* or *input parameters*.

Example 6.10   Consider a single-channel queueing system like the one illustrated in figure 6.6. In this model customers arrive for service according to some interarrival distribution, possessing some required interval of service that is assigned from some service-time distribution. If the service facility is idle, the customer moves immediately into service and departs after receiving the required service. Otherwise the customer joins a queue and waits to be selected for service. Note that the $M/M/1/\infty/$FIFO queueing system discussed in chapter 5 is an example of this type of model. A performance measure for this system could be the average number of customers in the queue. Control variables could include the interarrival distribution, service-time distribution, queueing discipline, and system capacity.

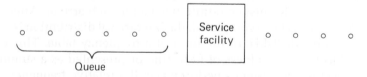

Figure 6.6
A single-channel queueing system

A problem commonly encountered in simulating systems similar to the one described in example 6.10 is that the performance measures observed during the initial part of a simulation run are not typical of the system's true operation. This *transient* period normally occurs because the starting conditions chosen for the simulation model are not characteristics of the system. It normally takes some time for the effect of the unrealistic starting conditions to become insignificant and for the simulation model to stabilize, or reach *steady state*. The analysis of the simulation results under steady-state conditions is desirable, since it is normally under these conditions that the true system's operation is simulated.

If the problem is to obtain performance measures for the model under steady-state conditions, then the analyst must eliminate the biasing effect of statistics generated during the start-up phase of the simulation. Consider, for example, the effect on the queue length of the different queueing disciplines in the system described in example 6.10. If the starting conditions are not characteristic of the true operating conditions of the system, the statistics that are generated (average queue length) will be biased because they include this transient phase. Ideally, then, statistics should be collected only after the system has reached steady state. Such a selective collection of statistics is virtually impossible to program. Thus statistics are normally collected for an entire simulation, and then an attempt is made to eliminate the bias of the transient phase.

Two problems with this approach are immediately apparent. First, how can one recognize that steady state has been achieved? Second, how can the biasing effect of the transient phase be eliminated? Several techniques have been used to determine when the system has reached steady state. One of the simplest is to compute a moving average of the performance measure. The steady state is assumed to have been reached when successive computations no longer vary significantly. A second approach, recommended by Emshoff and Sisson (6.1), is to examine a sequence of observations of the performance measure from the run. When the number of observations above the mean observation is approximately equal to the number of observations below it, it can be assumed that the steady-state condition has been reached.

Once the system has reached steady state, the analyst must decide how to reduce or eliminate the bias in the performance measures introduced during the transient phase. One obvious way is to lengthen the duration of the simulation run, making the steady-state phase much longer than the transient phase. A disadvantage of this approach is that long computer runs are expensive; moreover, the biasing effect of the transient phase is reduced but not eliminated. A second method is to impose steady-state conditions on the model as initial conditions. With this approach the analyst must be able to estimate the steady-state conditions from observations of the real system or from a preliminary run of the simulation model. A third technique is to introduce a start-up period to allow the simulator to achieve steady-state conditions. The accumulated statistics are then cleared and the collection of the statistics begun anew. Either of these latter two techniques is more desirable than an inordinately long computer run. They both minimize the required length of the simulation run, and if the estimate of steady-state conditions is relatively close, they eliminate the bias caused by the transient period.

In some simulation studies it is desirable to study transient periods rather than let the simulation model reach steady state. In fact, some systems never reach steady state; they are in a state of constant flux. In this case the collection of statistics such as the average queue length in the previous example would be of limited value, since the observations are likely to be widely scattered about their average value.

Another problem encountered in the analysis of simulation output is deciding which methodology produces a valid statistical sample. A valid statistical sample is, of course, required before one can make valid inferences about the true value of a performance measure. Determining the appropriate methodology is generally restricted to the case in which there is uncertainty in some phases of the model. (The model is stochastic. In stochastic models the events generated are only a subset of the total event set.) If the model is both finite and discrete, the total event set could eventually be generated if the duration of the simulation run is long enough. This is not the case if the model is continuous. Even in the discrete case, few analysts can afford to let the simulator run as long as would be required to generate the entire event set. Thus the objective in most cases is to limit the total computer time used (minimize the cost of the simulation runs) and at the same time achieve a reliable performance measure. Statistical sampling techniques are needed to obtain some estimate of the reliability of the derived performance measures.

As an illustration of the procedures involved, suppose that the desired performance measure is the mean of some parameter. From the central limit theorem we know that the sampling distribution of the mean is approximately normal if sufficient observations are taken. Thus there is a probability of approximately .997 that the sample mean lies within three standard errors of the true population (or process) mean. The standard error of a sample is $\sigma/n^{1/2}$, where σ is the standard deviation of the true process and n is the number of observations. Thus if we know the size of the error that is acceptable, as well as the standard deviation of the process, we can calculate the number of observations needed to provide a valid estimate of the mean. Once the required size of the sample is determined, the analyst is confronted with the task of obtaining the sample.

Emshoff and Sisson (6.1) discuss several approaches for generating a valid sample. The first method is applicable when the underlying process is thought or known to be normally distributed. In this case a single run is considered to be a sample, and individual observations of the performance measure are considered to be members of that sample. Next the standard deviation of the sample is taken as an estimate of the standard deviation of the true process and a confidence interval estimate of the true parameter is calculated. For example, if the performance measure is the mean of some quantity, a confidence interval estimate for the true process mean can be calculated from

$$I = \overline{X} \pm (t_{\alpha,n-1}) \, (s/n^{1/2})$$

where $\overline{X}$ is the sample mean, s is the sample standard deviation, and t is the appropriate value of the t-statistic.

If the underlying process is not known to be normal, a confidence interval estimate can still be obtained by resorting to the central limit theorem, which says essentially that the sampling distribution of the mean is normally distributed if sufficient samples are obtained. Then if a sample of sample means is generated, the performance measure may be estimated from this sample using the preceding statistical method.

One procedure by which the sample of sample means can be generated is *replication* of the simulation run. This provides independent samples. The procedure is somewhat expensive, however, and has the undesirable problem of having to repeat the transient phase; hence it is inefficient. A second technique involves subdividing one run of the simulator into subintervals, or *blocks*, and treating each block as a sample. This blocking technique is generally more efficient than replication, but it introduces the problem of autocorrelation. That is, the observations obtained from successive blocks may not be independent. The bias introduced by this autocorrelation between successive observations must be reduced or eliminated. Emshoff and Sisson (6.1) include a survey of techniques that have been used to deal with autocorrelated simulation output. One technique is to estimate the autocorrelation function by running the simulator and obtaining test data to calculate an estimate of the correlation between pairs of observations. This estimate is then used to refine the estimates of the variance. Another technique is to group the time series output into blocks of consecutive observations so that each block represents an independent sample and then use standard statistical techniques. For details on dealing with autocorrelated data see the work by Emshoff and Sisson (6.1).

Evaluation of the simulation model

6.7   Once a simulator has been designed and coded, the analyst must evaluate the validity of the model. Evaluating a model is determining how well the simulation model predicts the real system's performance. The ability of a simulation model to accurately predict the performance of the real system depends on both the validity of the model and the reliability of the performance measures produced. In this section we discuss problems in these areas and survey some techniques that have been used to enhance reliability and to demonstrate validity.

The validity of a simulation model depends on the accuracy of the model representing the real system. Also of concern to the analyst is the detail of the model. The model must be sufficiently detailed to provide the analyst with information on the aspects of the system's performance that are of primary interest. The only truly satisfactory method of validating a simulation model is to judge its performance. If the inferences drawn from the analysis of the simulator's output allow correct conclusions to be drawn about the system or the situation being modeled, then the simulation model can be assumed to be valid for that particular situation. However, using this test for the validation procedure has some drawbacks. Courses of action not taken or decisions not made by the simulator could provide some added insight into the true validity of the model. Thus it may not be sufficient to assess the validity of the simulation model only from observations of the model's performance.

A number of methods for assessing the validity of a model use techniques other than direct observation of its performance. These methods, just like the observation technique, do not guarantee that the model is valid, but they do provide a basis for assuming that the model is valid. The first of these methods deals with validating the design of the model. This form of validation is simply a checking procedure in which the design of the model is verified at different stages of its development. The process of modeling a system is broken into two phases, the conceptual phase and the implementation phase (6.3).

In the conceptual phase the logical flow of the system being modeled is determined, and the relationships between the various subsystems are formulated. During this phase the factors likely to influence the performance of the model are isolated and tentatively selected for inclusion. There are two procedures by which the model is validated at this stage. The first is to have the model reviewed by a disinterested qualified observer. If this observer confirms the decisions made by the model designer, the judgment of the model's validity is reinforced. Another method is to trace through the model in reverse order. This technique is somewhat analogous to verifying the accuracy of an arithmetic result by applying the inverse operation to the result.

The implementation phase of the model includes selecting and quantifying procedures for the model, coding the model, and actually using the model. Martin (6.3) suggests that the only practical method of ascertaining the validity of the model during this phase is to check the model at preestablished milestones by comparing it with the previous stages of the model development. The following milestones are suggested.

    1. Following the development of the logical flow chart of the model

    2. Following the program coding of each model subsystem

    3. Following the integration of the subsystem modules into a complete coded model

At the second milestone each subsystem should be tested with sample input before it is incorporated into the model. When all subsystems have been separately tested, the model as a whole should be tested.

    Emshoff and Sisson (6.1) have suggested other validity tests, including internal validity tests and variable-parameter validity tests. The *internal validity test* consists of performing several simulations using the same model and the same input parameters and then comparing the outputs to detect variability. If the variability of results is high, the model will probably prove of little value as a predictor, since it will be difficult to assess whether changes in output are due to changes in input parameter settings, the model's inherent variability, or a combination of the two. The limiting effect of this internal variability on the usefulness of the model can also be viewed in light of the real system's possible behavior under similar circumstances. It is unlikely that any real system of interest, when presented with identical operating conditions, will produce radically different results.

    The *variable-parameter validity test* consists of varying parameters and variables to determine their effect on the simulator and the subsequent output. If the impact of certain variables or parameters is large compared with the initial estimate of their impact, the validity of the model must be questioned.

    Probably no analyst is ever completely sure of the validity of the simulation model. In many cases validity is assumed until the contrary is shown. This could happen long after the original analyst has completed the work. The analyst must, however, make a serious attempt to validate the model before using it.

Summary

In the course of this chapter we have surveyed some of the factors and techniques that have been considered and employed in the development of computer simulation models. By this time you should have some idea how to develop a simulator. In the next chapter we will survey some of the more common discrete-event simulation languages. These languages were developed largely to ease the analyst's burden of developing the simulation model. Some additional considerations in the development of a simulation model will be introduced as features of the various languages are discussed.

Exercises

6.1 Develop a FORTRAN subroutine ARR that simulates the arrival of a customer to a queueing system. The arrival process to be simulated is Poisson. Parameters to be passed to ARR are the time of the last arrival and the mean arrival rate. The returned value should be the time of the next arrival.

6.2 Develop a FORTRAN subroutine SERVE that assigns required service times to the arrivals to a queueing system. The service-time distribution to be simulated is the exponential distribution. The mean service rate should be passed to the subroutine as a parameter. The returned value should be the service time required by the next arriving customer.

6.3 Develop a FORTRAN subroutine POSTQ that enters arriving customers into the queue. The maximum queue length should be passed as a parameter. Customers attempting to enter a full queue should be turned away. The attributes to be entered for each customer are customer number, arrival time, and required service time. Assume that the queueing discipline is FIFO.

6.4 Develop a FORTRAN subroutine REMOVQ that removes the first customer from the queue and moves the remaining customers up accordingly (simulate a FIFO queue). An attempt to remove a customer from an empty queue should be signaled by setting a flag.

6.5 Develop a logical flowchart of a single-channel queueing system ($M/M/1/K/$FIFO) using the periodic scan approach to time management.

6.6 Develop a logical flowchart of a single-channel queueing system ($M/M/1/K/$FIFO) using the event scan approach to time management.

6.7 Code the model depicted in the flowchart developed in exercise 6.5. The routines developed in exercises 6.1–6.4 should be used.

6.8 Code the model depicted in the flowchart developed in exercise 6.6. The routines developed in exercises 6.1–6.4 should be used.

6.9 Run the simulation models developed in exercises 6.7 and 6.8 with an average service rate of $\mu = 18$ per minute and an average arrival rate of $\lambda = 6$ per minute. Collect statistics on the number in the queue. Assume a maximum queue capacity of 25.

6.10 Compare and contrast the models developed in exercises 6.7 and 6.8 in terms of complexity and results obtained.

6.11 Use the model developed in exercise 6.8 to investigate the detection of steady state.

6.12 Modify the model developed in exercise 6.8 to allow for multiple servers.

6.13 Run the simulation model developed in exercise 6.12 with $\lambda = 6$ per minute, $\mu = 18$ per minute, a maximum queue length of 25, and two servers. Collect statistics on the average queue length and waiting time.

6.14 Modify the model developed in exercise 6.8 to allow the SJF (shortest-job-first) queueing discipline. In this discipline the customer in the queue who requires the least service is selected.

6.15 Run the simulation model developed in exercise 6.14 with $\lambda = 6$ per minute, $\mu = 18$ per minute, and a maximum queue length of 25.

References

6.1 EMSHOFF, J. R., and SISSON, R. L. *Design and Use of Computer Simulation Models.* New York: Macmillan, 1970.

6.2 GORDON, GEOFFREY. *System Simulation.* Englewood Cliffs, N.J.: Prentice-Hall, 1978.

6.3 MARTIN, F. F. *Computer Modeling and Simulation.* New York: John Wiley and Sons, 1968.

7

Languages for discrete system simulation

Once the aspects of the system to be simulated have been decided and the model formulated in terms of a logical flowchart, the model must be translated into a form suitable for the computer. That is, the model must be coded using some language. The coding process is probably one of the best understood of the steps in model building, yet difficult decisions sometimes accompany the choice of a suitable programming language. The range of programming languages that have been used in discrete system simulation covers the entire spectrum, from the low-level, machine-oriented assembly languages to the specialized simulation-oriented languages such as GPSS. A number of factors can influence the choice of a language, including the programmer's familiarity with the language; the ease with which the language is learned and used if the programmer is not already familiar with it; the languages supported at the installation where the simulation is to be done; the complexity of the model; and the need for a comprehensive analysis and display of the results of the simulation run.

In this chapter we survey some of the characteristics that any simulation language should have. We also discuss briefly how a simulation model may be implemented in FORTRAN and in three of the more common specialized simulation languages: GPSS, SIMSCRIPT, and GASP.

The purpose of this chapter is not to provide the analyst with the required level of expertise to code a detailed simulation model. Rather it is to survey the characteristics of each language and to aid the analyst in choosing a suitable language. After choosing a language, the analyst should consult the programming manuals and texts devoted to that language to obtain all the details. The choice of a language should not be made lightly, however, since this choice can have a significant impact on the time required to develop the simulation model and on the expense of running the simulation.

Language characteristics

7.1   Many simulation models perform similar functions. Some of these functons are

1. Generating random variates
2. Managing simulation time
3. Handling routines to simulate event executions
4. Managing queues
5. Collecting data
6. Šummarizing and analyzing data
7. Formulating and printing output

Many systems are characterized by some stochastic behavior, whether it is the interarrival times and service requirements in a queueing system or the time between equipment failures in a production system. To simulate such probabilistic events usually requires the use of the simulated sampling techniques outlined in chapter 4. Then any language to be used in implementing a simulation model should either provide or allow easy development of a facility to generate and transform standard uniform random variates.

Whether the periodic scan (fixed-time increment) or the event scan (variable-time increment) method of time management is employed, some means of representing time is required. This is important not only for controlling or "driving" the simulator but also for collecting, summarizing, and analyzing the data. A simulation programming language must allow for easy representation and manipulation of simulation time.

When a scheduled event is to be executed, the simulation program normally effects the required changes in system state by invoking a program module designed specifically for that purpose. Depending on the complexity of the required changes, the execution could be simulated with one or two statement routines inserted at the appropriate points in the model or with more complex, lengthy routines implemented as sub-programs.

Queue management is common to many models because many systems involve competition for limited resources. The representation and manipulation of waiting lines can be accomplished in many ways. A convenient way of representing queues is by a list because the primary operations in queue management are the addition and deletion of members. These two operations are easily performed using the list representation and the manipulation of pointers. Thus a language with efficient list-processing capability offers a significant advantage in simulation.

Many simulation models are implemented to assess the effect on the system of varying certain conditions or parameters. This measurement and comparison requires some facility for the collection of data. This requirement is not a strong criterion, however, because the most common data collected are count data, and these are easily represented and collected by integer variables. Nearly all languages that have gained any degree of recognition have this capability.

In most cases the simple collection and representation of raw data are not enough. In addition, some summarization and analysis of the data are normally required. This analysis could be relatively simple, requiring only the calculation of summary measures such as means or standard deviations. This simple form of analysis can be easily done in nearly all languages, although some languages carry out these calculations as standard functions, while others require that the programmer provide these routines. Other simulation projects may require a more extensive analysis of the data, perhaps regression analysis, analysis of variance, time series analysis, or other sophisticated tools of statistical analysis. A language that provides this level of analysis as part of its normal operation offers an advantage in simulation. The programmer can spend much time designing and coding the statistical analysis modules if they are not automatically provided in the programming language.

Some simple simulation models may require only simple output. Others may require extensive report writing. In any case the model must be able to display the results of a simulation run. A language that allows flexibility in formatting and presenting the data offers a significant advantage, particularly if the model is complex and if the results are to be presented to management personnel.

In addition to assessing how well each candidate language supports these seven common functions, another major consideration in selecting the best language is the assistance provided during the debugging phase of program development. In some versions of assembly language, for example, one must analyze a system dump, which is a snapshot of all or portions of the computer's memory, to verify that the results obtained are the correct ones or to trace an error in the code's logic or syntax. This is a tedious, seemingly interminable operation. Some languages, particularly the special-purpose simulation languages, provide extensive debugging assistance. The impact that the selection of a language with debugging assistance can have on a simulation project has been pointed out by Emshoff and Sisson (7.3). They report that it is not uncommon to reduce the time spent on coding and debugging a simulation model by a factor of ten through the use of a language with facilities that enhance the debugging process.

Another criterion for choosing a suitable programming language is the programmer's knowledge of the language. A programmer will probably choose a familiar language to implement a simulation model even if some other language provides better support of the common functions or better debugging assistance. This tendency is natural, and in most cases the decision is wise. Becoming familiar enough with a language to write efficient programs is time-consuming. The time needed to learn the new language may well be greater than the time needed for coding additional routines to support the common functions or debugging in the old language. A related consideration is the ease of use and ease of learning. Given two languages equally suited for the task, one would normally select the language that is easiest to learn and easiest to use.

A final consideration in selecting a simulation language is the inherent flexibility of the language. Having selected and learned a simulation language, the analyst is likely to use it for more than one model. It must therefore have a capability for expansion and adaptation, which would allow it to be applied to a wide range of models.

In summary, then, the languages available on a given computer system should be rated according to their

1. Support of the basic functions
2. Debugging assistance provided
3. Familiarity to the programmer
4. Ease of learning and use
5. Flexibility

The relative weights given to these factors depend somewhat on the problem. The aim in all cases, however, is, to minimize the time spent in the coding and debugging phases.

Use of multipurpose languages

7.2   Many programmers tend to select multipurpose languages such as FORTRAN, ALGOL, and PL/I for use in simulation. One of the chief reasons is the widespread availability of the languages. Even a very small computer installation probably has a FORTRAN, ALGOL, or PL/I compiler. Along with COBOL, FORTRAN is probably the most common programming language in use and is probably the first language to which a programmer is exposed. It is understandable then that this language would be selected for implementing a simulation model. In this section we survey some of the advantages and disadvantages of using multipurpose languages such as FORTRAN, ALGOL, and PL/I in simulation projects. Although there are significant differences in the capabilities of these languages, we consider them as a group in assessing their applicability to simulation projects. To assess these languages we ask, How well do these languages support the basic functions of simulation? What assistance is provided in debugging? How flexible are the languages?

There is no express capability in any of these languages to generate random variates. Many installations have among their library routines a function that generates standard uniform variates. Programmers are sometimes reluctant to use these standard functions; they may not understand the techniques used and thus may shy away from the generation of numbers using the black-box approach, preferring to write their own routines. Even if they use the standard functions to generate the uniform variates, they still must code the routines to transform the standard uniform variates to a normal, exponential, or Poisson distribution. Most of these routines are fairly trivial to code and do not significantly increase the time required to develop the simulation model.

Management of simulation time is generally easily done in the procedure-oriented multipurpose languages. A counter variable, say CLOCK, can be initialized at the beginning of the simulation run. If the periodic scan approach is used, some fixed increment is added to CLOCK each time the simulation clock is to be advanced. If the event scan approach is used, the pending events must be scanned to determine the size of the increment before it is added to CLOCK. In any case the programmer must define and initialize the clock and code routines to update the clock, but management of simulation time is not a big problem in these languages.

FORTRAN, ALGOL, and PL/I all have well-defined subprogram capabilities for simulating event executions. Generally they define a subroutine or procedure for each type of event to be executed. For example, in the simulation of a single-channel queueing system, such events are the arrival of a customer to the system, the completion of service to a customer (the customer's departure from the system), and the action taken when the system is full or closed. For each type of event a routine is coded that effects the changes in the system state in a way that reflects the event occurrence in the real system and takes care of housekeeping chores such as updating statistics. Since the definition and invocation of subprograms is straightforward in these languages, no major problems should be incurred in this function.

Languages such as PL/I offer some advantages over FORTRAN in queue management. List processing in FORTRAN is weak and is usually implemented by arrays. This approach can cause problems, since the maximum size and dimension of the arrays must be determined and declared beforehand. Hence it is not really possible to simulate the operation of say an $M/M/1/\infty$ FIFO queueing system. Manipulation of pointers in FORTRAN is also inefficient, since pointers are normally included as a part of a multidimensional array. Accessing a particular pointer can then become time-consuming. The actual penalty that results from FORTRAN's list-processing capability depends on the model. The amount of list processing required in the model has to be assessed and balanced against FORTRAN's advantages such as widespread availability and programmer familiarity. PL/I eases the problem of inefficient list processing at the cost of losing some advantage in availability and familiarity.

The collection of count data in FORTRAN, ALGOL, or PL/I is normally done with integer variables. The variables are initialized at the beginning of the simulation and incremented when an event occurs. Frequency data can be accumulated through the definition of classes and the use of arrays, as illustrated in the previous chapter.

The summarization and analysis routines required in most simulation programs can greatly lengthen the programming time. Each routine must be coded by the programmer. Some statistical analysis routines are complex, and care must be taken to interface them properly with the model. Models that do not require a great deal of analysis pose less difficulty.

When using multipurpose languages, the programmer must consider the formatting and printing of results. Unlike the specialized languages, multipurpose languages have no automatic output. Input and output routines that are part of the implementation of multipurpose languages provide for flexible formatting, under programmer control. Many installations provide plot routines that may be invoked to provide a visual presentation of the output. However, some effort is required on the part of the programmer to define, interface, and initialize the parameters needed by these routines.

Debugging aids in the multipurpose languages are somewhat limited. They all identify syntactic errors, such as the use of undefined variables and errors made in keypunching. Errors in logic, however, must be detected by the programmer. To do this, the programmer must have some idea of what results to expect from the model. The model is then run and its output compared with the expected results. Debugging in these languages is in many respects a trial-and-error process. The programmer finds one bug and eliminates it, only to expose another.

In summary, then, multipurpose languages can be used successfully in the programming of simulation models. In fact, there may be more simulation models in FORTRAN than in any other language. The main drawback to using these languages is that the entire model must be coded by the programmer. The languages provide few simulation-oriented functions and little debugging assistance other than pointing out syntactic errors. The advantages of these languages, however, are numerous. First, most programmers have at least been exposed to FORTRAN. Thus user familiarity is not likely to be a problem. Second, FORTRAN is one of the most common languages now available. Thus the installation is likely to support FORTRAN. Third, models developed in standard FORTRAN are likely to be highly portable because different implementations of the language are similar. A model developed at one location can probably be run at another location with only minor changes. Models developed in these general-purpose languages are likely to cost less to run. The programmer does not have to share the cost of a large software system, of which only a small part may be used. Another advantage, which may be hard to quantify for a particular project, is that programmers using one of the general-purpose languages to develop a simulation model are likely to be more conversant with the details of the model than if the model was coded in one of the especially designed simulation languages. Since a programmer is required to address each aspect of the model, the programmer obviously will be familiar with the design details. In selecting a language for a simulation model, then, one must weigh the advantages of the general-purpose languages against the almost guaranteed longer program development and debugging time.

Example 7.1   Consider the following system as an example of how a multipurpose programming language, such as FORTRAN, can be used.

Arrivals occur to a single-channel queueing system according to the Poisson distribution with arrival rate λ. The arrivals, each requiring an exponentially distributed service time, immediately try to enter the service facility. If the facility is busy, they join a queue. If the service time required is assigned when the arrival event occurs, there is no need to distinguish between the arrivals as far as the service facility's operation is concerned. If the periodic scan approach is used, the operation of this system can be simulated using the model depicted in the flowchart given in figure 7.1.

Suppose that the statistics of interest are the average time an arrival spends in the queue, the average queue length, the average number in the system, and the total time the system is idle. The model could be implemented using the following FORTRAN program. In most cases the actions are well documented; others should be apparent after careful scrutiny.

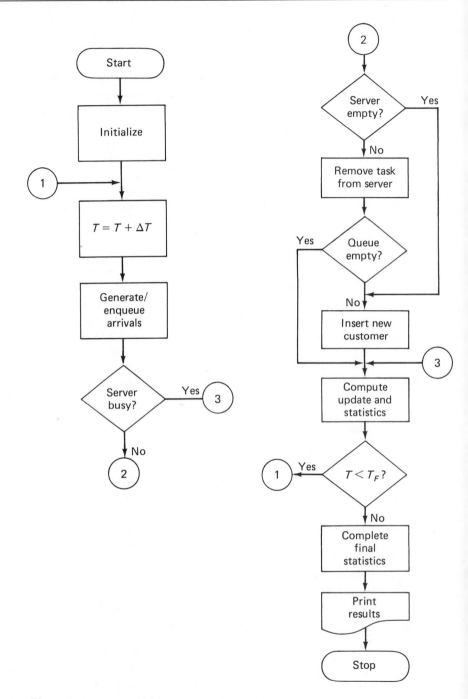

Figure 7.1
Flowchart for the simulation of a queueing system

```
C
C       SIMULATION OF A SINGLE-CHANNEL QUEUE
C
C       THIS PROGRAM SIMULATES THE OPERATION OF A SINGLE-CHANNEL
C       QUEUEING SYSTEM WITH POISSON ARRIVALS AND EXPONENTIAL SERVICE
C       TIMES.
C
C       THE INPUT DATA IS
C          DELT—THE TIME INCREMENT
C          SLEN—THE LENGTH OF THE SIMULATION
C          LAMBDA—THE ARRIVAL RATE
C          MU—THE SERVICE RATE
C          ISEED—AN INTEGER SEED TO PRIME THE RANDOM NUMBER GENERATOR
C
        INTEGER QUEUE
        LOGICAL SFULL
        REAL LAMBDA,MU
C
C       INITIALIZATION
C
        T=0.
        TIDLE=0.
        AVEQ=0.
        AVES=0.
        NSER=0.
        WTIME=0.
        ARRTIM=0.
        TSER=0.
        QUEUE=0.
           SFULL=.FALSE.
        READ(5,500)DELT,SLEN,LAMBDA,MU,ISEED
500     FORMAT(4F10.5,I5)
        LAMBDA=1./LAMBDA
        MU=1./MU
C
C       SIMULATION ROUTINE
C
C       GENERATE FIRST ARRIVAL
        CALL URANDX(ISEED,IRAND,URAND)
        ISEED=IRAND
        ARRTIM=-LAMBDA*ALOG(URAND)
C       CHECK IF ARRIVAL HAS OCCURRED
1       IF(ARRTIM.LE.0.)CALL  ARRVL(ARRTIM,QUEUE,ISEED,LAMBDA)
C       CHECK IF SERVICE TIME HAS EXPIRED
        IF(TSER.LE.0.)CALL SERCOM(TSER,QUEUE,ISEED,NSER,MU,SFULL)
```

Figure 7.2
Program listing for the simulation of a queueing system

Figure 7.2 — Continued

```
C       COMPUTE UPDATES
        IF(QUEUE.NE.0)GO TO 40
        IF(SFULL)GO TO 40
        TIDLE=TIDLE+DELT
40      AVEQ=AVEQ+QUEUE
        IF(SFULL)AVES=AVES+1
        AVES=AVES+QUEUE
        WTIME=WTIME+QUEUE*DELT
C       TEST TO SEE IF PERIOD HAS EXPIRED
        T=T+DELT
        ARRTIM=ARRTIM-DELT
        TSER=TSER-DELT
        IF(T.LT.SLEN)GO TO 1
C
C       COMPUTE AND PRINT FINAL STATISTICS
        AVEQ=AVEQ/(SLEN/DELT)
        AVES=AVES/(SLEN/DELT)
        IF(SFULL)I=1
        WTIME=WTIME/(NSER+I+QUEUE)
        WRITE(6,610)
610     FORMAT(1X)
        WRITE(6,603)DELT
603     FORMAT(1X,'FOR A DELTA—T OF',5X,F10.5,5X,'MIN THE RESULTS WERE')
        WRITE(6,600)NSER,QUEUE,I
600     FORMAT(1X,'THERE WERE',5X,I3,5X,'ITEMS SERVICED,',5X,I3,5X,'ITEMS
       +LEFT IN THE QUEUE AND',5X,I1,5X,'ITEM(S) LEFT IN SERVICE.')
        WRITE (6,601)AVEQ,AVES,WTIME
601     FORMAT(1X,'AVERAGE QUEUE LENGTH WAS',5X,F5.2,5X,'AVERAGE NUMBER
       +IN THE SYSTEM WAS',5X,F5.2,5X,'AVERAGE WAITING TIME WAS',5X,F5.2,5X,
       +'MIN.')
        WRITE(6,602)TIDLE
602     FORMAT(1X,'THE SYSTEM WAS IDLE FOR A TOTAL OF',5X,F5.2,5X,'MIN.')
        STOP
        END
C
        SUBROUTINE URANDX(JSEED,IRAND,URAND)
C
C       THIS ROUTINE GENERATES A PSEUDORANDOM STANDARD UNIFORM VARIATE.
C       THE PARAMETERS FOR THIS ROUTINE ARE
C       JSEED—AN INPUT PARAMETER EQUAL TO THE INTEGER SEED READ IN.
C       IRAND—AN OUTPUT PARAMETER REPRESENTING A PSEUDORANDOM VARIATE
C               USED AS THE SEED FOR THE NEXT ITERATION.
C       URAND—AN OUTPUT PARAMETER REPRESENTING A PSEUDORANDOM
C               STANDARD UNIFORM VARIATE.
C
        IRAND=JSEED*65539
        IF(IRAND)5,6,6
```

Figure 7.2 — Continued

```
5       IRAND=IRAND+2147483647+1
6       URAND=IRAND
        URAND=URAND*.4656613E-9
        RETURN
        END

        SUBROUTINE ARRVL(ARRTIM,QUEUE,ISEED,LAMBDA)
        INTEGER QUEUE
        REAL LAMBDA
C
C       ROUTINE TO SIMULATE AN ARRIVAL TO THE SYSTEM
C
        QUEUE=QUEUE+1
        CALL URANDX(ISEED,IRAND,URAND)
        ISEED=IRAND
        ARRTIM=-LAMBDA*ALOG(URAND)
        RETURN
        END

        SUBROUTINE SERCOM(TSER,QUEUE,ISEED,NSER,MU,SFULL)
        REAL MU
        INTEGER QUEUE
        LOGICAL SFULL
C
C       ROUTINE TO SIMULATE A SERVICE COMPLETION
C
        IF(SFULL)NSER=NSER+1
        IF(QUEUE.NE.0)GO TO 10
        SFULL=.FALSE.
        RETURN
10      QUEUE=QUEUE-1
        CALL URANDX(ISEED,IRAND,URAND)
        ISEED=IRAND
        TSER=MU*ALOG(URAND)
        SFULL=.TRUE.
        RETURN
        END
```

Special-purpose languages: GPSS

7.3   Special-purpose simulation languages were developed (beginning in the late 1950s) because many simulation projects needed similar functions across various applications. Although several such languages were created, few have gained any degree of acceptance. This section introduces three of the more commonly used languages, GPSS, SIMSCRIPT, and GASP.

The General Purpose Simulation System (GPSS) language was first published in 1961 by Gordon (7.4). The language has evolved over the years to the point where there are now two versions: GPSS/360 and GPSS V. The language was designed for the express purpose of simulating the operation of discrete systems. The system that is to be simulated is represented by a set of blocks connected by lines. Each block represents some activity, and each line represents a path to the next activity. The programmer is usually responsible for the contents of the blocks in programming languages that use block diagrams, but GPSS has 48 predefined blocks to which the programmer is restricted. Each block symbol is unique, thus providing a ready interpretation of the block diagrams. For a more complete description of GPSS, see Gordon (7.5) or Bobillier, Kahan, and Probst (7.1).

The entities that pass through the system are called *transactions*. Some examples of transactions are customers arriving at a service station, messages passing through a communications center, and jobs arriving for processing at a computer system. The *attributes* of these entities, such as the required service time, are represented as *parameters*.

Transactions enter the system with the GENERATE block, which is represented by the following symbol.

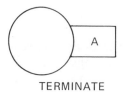

GENERATE

The operands for the GENERATE block are A, the mean interarrival time; B, the spread or mean modifier; C, the time of the generation of the first arrival; D, the total number of arrivals to be generated; E, the priority level of the transaction; F, the number of parameters to be attached to the transaction; G, the parameter type (F, fullword; H, halfword). If some of these parameter fields are omitted, default values are assumed. See the particular implementation for appropriate default values.

Transactions leave the system by way of the TERMINATE block, which is depicted by the following symbol.

TERMINATE

The operand A for this block indicates the number by which the termination counter is incremented. The number may be zero, but at least one TERMINATE block in the model must have a nonzero operand (value).

GPSS automatically keeps track of where each transaction is in the system and when it is to be moved. Transactions are classified according to priorities (0–127), and the transaction with the highest priority is moved first. If more than one transaction has the same priority, transactions are moved in a first-come, first-serve manner or in the order in which they were generated. A transaction's progress through the system may be held up for two reasons. First, it may enter an ADVANCE block, depicted by the following symbol.

ADVANCE

The ADVANCE block represents some activity that involves an expenditure of time, such as when a customer is receiving service at a service station. For the ADVANCE block operand A is the mean and operand B is the mean modifier such that the time that the transaction is delayed is equal to A ± B. This time is selected so that any time within the interval has equal probability. When a transaction encounters an ADVANCE block, its progress is blocked and the system will advance another transaction. A transaction's progress may also be halted if it attempts to enter a block already occupied by another transaction. In this case the system holds the transaction at the preceding block until the requested block is free.

A transaction always goes to the next sequential block unless a TRANSFER block is encountered. This block is depicted by the following symbol.

TRANSFER

The selection factor S specifies a decision rule used to determine which of two specified paths is to be taken. There are nine selection rules. The simplest rule is to set S to a three-digit fraction that specifies the percentage of time that the second of the two specified paths is to be taken. Of course, the first of the two paths is taken the remainder of the time. Normally the path selection is made at random, so that only the long-run frequency (or steady-state behavior) approaches this specified percentage.

With these concepts, it may be useful to assess GPSS in terms of the criteria of section 7.2. We will then give a simple example showing the application of GPSS to the modeling of a system.

GPSS provides eight random number generators, RN1–RN8; each provides a source of standard uniform pseudorandom numbers. To allow for the generation of nonuniform random numbers, the concept of a function is provided. The function accepts the output of one of the random numbers as its input and provides as output a random variate from the appropriate distribution. The method used is the inverse transformation method, which was discussed in section 4.4. The programmer must still define the appropriate function but does not have to program a random number generation routine. An example of a function used in this way is included as a part of example 7.2.

The management scheme used by GPSS more closely resembles the event scan approach than the time increment mechanism. The simulation clock is maintained by the GPSS control program. The progress of transactions through the system is monitored by using two lists: the current events chain and the future events chain. One attribute of every transaction is the block departure time (BDT), or the simulation time at which the transaction is scheduled to depart its current block. All transactions whose current BDT is less than or equal to the current clock time reside on the current events chain; all transactions whose current BDT is greater than the current simulation time reside on the future events chain. Transactions with a BDT earlier than the current clock time can still be on the current event chain because a transaction in the next block could have precluded the first transaction from departing the current block. The two event chains are ordered within each priority class by ascending BDT. The simulation control program scans the current events chain for a transaction to move. Once it has selected a transaction, it moves that transaction through the system a far as it can, that is, until the transaction encounters an ADVANCE block or becomes blocked. At this time the control program selects another transaction from the current events chain and repeats the process. Transactions are moved from the future events chain to the current events chain whenever their BDT is reached by the simulation clock. Transactions are moved from the current events chain to the future events chain whenever an ADVANCE block is encountered.

Since GPSS uses 48 different blocks, no more than 48 events can be simulated. The GPSS control program takes whatever actions are necessary whenever a transaction enters any of the blocks. Thus the programmer does not have to handle any event simulation routines; these are handled automatically. The programmer does have to ensure that the proper blocks are included in the proper sequence to effect the required actions of the model.

    Many systems have entities that compete for limited resources. It is this competition for limited resources that results in the formation of queues. In GPSS there are two types of resources for which transactions compete—facilities and storages. A *facility* can be used by only one transaction at a time, whereas a *storage* resource can be used by multiple transactions as long as its maximum capacity is not exceeded. Four controlling blocks are associated with facilities and storages. These four blocks are given in figure 7.3.

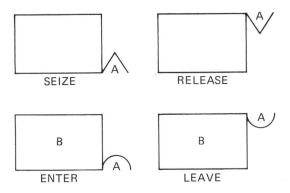

Figure 7.3
Block symbols for managing storages and facilities

    In each block the operand A specifies the number (programmer-assigned) of the facility or the storage involved. The SEIZE and RE-LEASE blocks allow a transaction to engage or disengage a facility if it is available, while the ENTER and LEAVE blocks serve the identical purpose for a storage. The B operand of the ENTER block specifies the amount of storage capacity that the transaction is requesting. If it is omitted, a default value of one unit is assumed. If transactions attempt to enter a SEIZE block for a facility already in use or an ENTER block for a storage with insufficient residual capacity to satisfy the request, it is prohibited from entering the block. Blocked transactions remain on the current events chain in ascending order of BDT within each priority class. These queues are then serviced on a FIFO basis.

    A queueing system could be coded and run in GPSS using only the blocks outlined so far. If this is done, however, no data would be collected or statistics prepared on the system's performance. Four additional control blocks are needed to gather data. These four block diagrams are illustrated in figure 7.4.

    Queues formed by transactions attempting to enter a block are as-

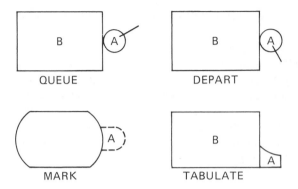

Figure 7.4
Block diagrams for data gathering

signed a number or name by the programmer. The QUEUE block increases the size of the queue named by operand A by the amount specified by operand B, with a default value of one. The DEPART block decreases the size of the queue in a similar manner. The MARK and TABULATE blocks are used to compute the transit time for a transaction between two points of the model. The time that a transaction passes through the MARK block is noted. When the same transaction traverses the TABULATE block, the transit time between the two blocks is computed and stored in a table named by operand A of the TABULATE block. The TABULATE block can be used without the MARK block. In this case the time computed is the total time elapsed since the transaction was generated.

The QUEUE, DEPART, MARK, and TABULATE blocks are used for gathering statistics. The statistics that are automatically generated by GPSS include the utilization of storages and facilities, lengths of queues (both maximum and average), and the frequency distribution of transit times. The GPSS data-gathering and summarization capabilities are extensive and in most cases provide all the information required.

Output routines in GPSS are precoded and formatted. Thus the results of a GPSS run are output in a report form at the conclusion of the run. The programmer therefore need not be concerned with the coding of output routines.

GPSS handles nearly all the details of the basic simulation functions. This is not surprising, since the language was designed for this purpose. These built-in features can drastically reduce the amount of time that must be devoted to coding and debugging a simulation model. This benefit is not gained without cost; most simulation models written in GPSS execute more slowly and hence are more expensive than models written in high-level general-purpose languages such as FORTRAN. Furthermore GPSS is not as widely available as FORTRAN.

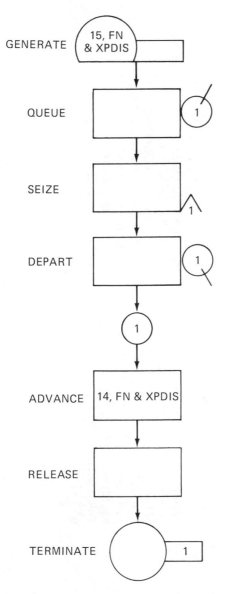

Figure 7.5
GPSS block diagram for the simulation of a queueing system

GPSS provides much assistance in debugging a simulation model. These aids are not restricted to the assembly phase but extend to execution errors as well. The diagnostic messages are usually descriptive and helpful in eliminating routine errors.

BLOCK NUMBER	*LOC	OPERATION	A,B,C,D,E,F,G	COMMENTS
		SIMULATE		
	*			
	*	FUNCTION AND VARIABLE DEFINITION		
	*			
	XPDIS FUNCTION	RN1,C24	EXPONENTIAL DISTRIBUTION FUNCTION	

0.0/.1,.104/.2,.222/.3,.355/.4,.506/.5,.69/.6,.915/.7,1.2/.75,1.38/.8,1.6/.84,1.83/.88,2.12/.9,2.3/.92,2.52/.94,2.81/
.95,2.99/.96,3.2/.97,3.5/.98,3.9/.99,4.6/.995,5.3/.998,6.2/.999,7/.9998,8

	*			
	*	SIMULATION ROUTINE		
	*			
1		GENERATE	15,FN$XPDIS	GENERATE ARRIVAL
2		QUEUE	1	QUEUE ARRIVAL
3		SEIZE	1	SEIZE CONTROL OF SERVER
4		DEPART	1	REMOVE CUSTOMER BEING SERVED
5		ADVANCE	20,FN$XPDIS	DELAY FOR SERVICE
6		RELEASE	1	RELEASE SERVER
7		TERMINATE	1	DEPART SYSTEM
		START	100	
	*END			
		END		

Figure 7.6
GPSS program listing for the simulation of a queueing system

FACILITY	AVERAGE UTILIZATION	NUMBER ENTRIES	AVERAGE TIME/TRAN	SEIZING TRANS. NO.	PREEMPTING TRANS. NO.
1	.999	100	19.289		

QUEUE	MAXIMUM CONTENTS	AVERAGE CONTENTS	TOTAL ENTRIES	ZERO ENTRIES	PERCENT ZEROS	AVERAGE TIME/TRANS
1	46	24.978	146	1	.6	330.191

$AVERAGE TIME/TRANS	TABLE NUMBER	CURRENT CONTENTS
332.468		46

$AVERAGE TIME/TRANS= AVERAGE TIME/TRANS EXCLUDING ZERO ENTRIES

Figure 7.7
Statistics gathered by the GPSS model

One of the best features of GPSS is its flexibility. Logical changes in a system's operation can normally be effected by changing or replacing one or two statements. This feature is in sharp contrast to a language such as FORTRAN, in which entire routines may have to be rewritten.

Example 7.2 Consider the simulation of a single-channel queueing system. Arrivals occur to the system according to a Poisson distribution. Service-time requirements are exponentially distributed. This model can be expressed in block-diagram form as illustrated in figure 7.5.

Coding from this block diagram is quite straightforward, as given in figure 7.6. Most of the actions should be clear from the previous discussion of the blocks. The function denoted XPDIS is a tabular representation of the inverse of the cumulative distribution function. It is used in conjunction with the system's random number generation routines to produce the interarrival and service times for transactions in the model. In line 1 the GENERATE block produces the arrival time for the next arrival by multiplying the mean interarrival rate, in this case 15, by the output of function XPDIS. When the scheduled arrival occurs, that transaction enters QUEUE 1 through the block in line 2. It then attempts to seize facility 1 (the server). Having seized the server, it departs the queue through the DEPART block on line 4. It then enters the ADVANCE block of line 5, where it is delayed an exponentially distributed service time. Control of the server is released in line 6 and departs the system (line 7). The START block controls the length of the simulation. In this case the simulation will proceed until 100 customers have been served. The statistics automatically produced by this run are given in figure 7.7.

Special-purpose languages:
SIMSCRIPT II.5

7.4   SIMSCRIPT is probably the second most commonly used special-purpose programming language developed for simulation modeling. The original version of SIMSCRIPT was developed at the RAND Corporation in the early 1960s by Markowitz, Karr, and Hausner (7.6). Although a number of versions of SIMSCRIPT have been produced, the features of the language described in this section are specifically those of SIM-SCRIPT II.5. Unlike GPSS, SIMSCRIPT approaches a general-purpose language and can therefore be taught to the beginning programmer as a first language. The language possesses powerful simulation verbs, however, by which it is possible to simulate highly complex systems. The language is free format and similar to English in structure, which enhances both the learning of the language and the readability of the finished model.

SIMSCRIPT II.5, as described by CACI (7.2), is organized into five separate levels, supposedly structured to aid the beginning programmer in learning the language. Level 1, when considered alone, is a simple language designed to introduce the beginner to programming. Level 5 is a self-contained simulation language. This discussion concerns the features of level 5.

The terminology involved in SIMSCRIPT is consistent with that introduced earlier. The objects of the simulation model are called *entities*, which are characterized by a fixed collection of parameters called *attributes*. *Sets* are collections of individual entities having common properties. The state of the system at any given time is completely described by the current list of individual entities, their attributes, and set memberships. *Temporary entities* are created and destroyed during the course of the simulation, while *permanent entities* remain throughout. Changes in the system state at discrete points in system time are called *events*. When an event is scheduled, an *event notice* is created that causes the transfer to the appropriate event routine. This language distinguishes between exogenous and endogenous events.

A SIMSCRIPT program is generally composed of three parts: the preamble, the main program, and the appropriate event routines. The preamble contains a description of all data structures used in the model. Each entity must be named and described by listing its attribute. The computational mode is also specified in the preamble. The default mode is single-precision real arithmetic. Example 7.3 shows the types of information contained in the preamble. The main program consists of initialization of all entities, plus the instructions used to control the simulation. The instructions are like English in structure and hence self-explanatory most of the time. No attempt will be made in this brief introduction to include the many instructions available in SIMSCRIPT. The purpose of this section is only to provide a flavor of the language. There must be an event routine for each event named in the preamble. The event routine effects the appropriate changes in the system state called for by the occurrence of that event.

In assessing how SIMSCRIPT supports the basic simulation functions, note that the programmer must write more of the routines than was necessary with GPSS. In GPSS the programmer was limited to the 48 predefined blocks. The action required by the use of each block was well defined and handled entirely by the system. This is not the case with SIMSCRIPT.

SIMSCRIPT supports the generation of random numbers by supplying ten independent streams. The technique used in generating each stream is the multiplicative congruential method outlined in section 4.2.2. Each of the ten generators uses the same multiplier, $a = 14^{29}$, and the same modulus, $m = 2^{31} - 1$. The difference in the generators is in the seed used. The seeds that are automatically supplied by the system are as follows.

SEED.V(1) =	524267	SEED.V(6)	=	1157240309
SEED.V(2) =	683743814	SEED.V(7)	=	15726055
SEED.V(3) =	964393174	SEED.V(8)	=	48108509
SEED.V(4) =	1217426631	SEED.V(9)	=	1797920909
SEED.V(5) =	618433579	SEED.V(10)	=	477424540

Users can supply their own seeds if they wish. This may be desirable if one is performing replications of the same basic experiment. Access to the random number generators is by a function call. For example, if a uniformly distributed number is desired, the call would appear as

RANDI.F(A,B,N)

The first two parameters specify the range desired (for a standard uniform variate, A = 0 and B = 1) while the third parameter specifies the random number stream (N can range from 1 to 10). Generation of non-uniform deviates is also supported for most of the common distributions. For example, an exponentially distributed random variable can be obtained from a call such as

EXPONENTIAL.F(A,N)

where A is the mean of the distribution, and N specifies the random number stream.

SIMSCRIPT uses the event scan method of time management. When an event is scheduled by using the SCHEDULE statement, an event notice is created. The existing event notices are scanned, and the earliest event is selected for execution. The simulation clock is then advanced to that scheduled time, and the appropriate execution routine invoked. To reflect the instantaneous nature of an event occurrence, the simulation clock is not advanced during the time an event routine is executing. The current value of the simulation clock can be accessed by way of the system variable TIME.V. This variable measures the simulation time in days; thus if another unit of time is to be used, the value of TIME.V has to be scaled.

An event routine has to be defined for each possible event. The types of event notice to be created are named in the preamble. The event routines are given the same names and are simply subprograms to effect the given changes to the system state. Example 7.3 provides a sample of an event routine.

If a queueing system is to be modeled, the preamble must list that the system has a queue, as well as the queueing discipline that is to be used. These tasks are accomplished through the two statements

```
THE SYSTEM OWNS THE QUEUE
DEFINE QUEUE AS A FIFO SET
```

Most of the standard queueing disciplines are supported. As with GPSS, the user does not have to be concerned with the management of the queue; it is handled by the system.

The data collection and analysis features of SIMSCRIPT are quite flexible. Data is collected by the use of statements such as TALLY and ACCUMULATE. Statistics are computed using the COMPUTE verb. SIMSCRIPT provides a number of standard functions that support statistical analysis, including

```
AVERAGE
MEAN
SUM
VARIANCE
STD.DEV
SUM.OF.SQUARES
MEAN.SQUARE
```

The uses of some of these functions appear in example 7.3.

The input-output features of SIMSCRIPT are also flexible. The language allows for free format of input, with data items separated by one or more blanks. Output is produced by the PRINT statement, which lists the variables to be printed along with the format. Thus the programmer controls the desired output.

Debugging aids in SIMSCRIPT are not as extensive as in GPSS, because more of the coding is left to the programmer. Syntactic errors are detected and reported by the compiler, just as in FORTRAN and the other general-purpose languages. The English-like structure of SIM-SCRIPT aids in debugging, since the language can be essentially self-documenting. The ease of debugging in SIMSCRIPT can probably be best described as somewhere between that of FORTRAN and that of GPSS.

SIMSCRIPT does provide some flexibility in model development. Major changes in a model can be made by replacing or modifying event routines. Minor changes can be effected by reading in different data or possibly modifying statements.

Example 7.3 Consider the single-channel queueing system outlined in example 7.1. This system can be simulated in SIMSCRIPT using the program given in figure 7.8.

```
PREAMBLE
NORMALLY, MODE IS INTEGER
EVENT NOTICES INCLUDE ARRIVAL AND CLOSING EVERY SERVICE. END
     HAS A CUSTOMER
TEMPORARY ENTITIES
EVERY PERSON HAS AN ARR TIME, AND MAY BELONG TO THE QUEUE
DEFINE ARR. TIME AS A REAL VARIABLE
THE SYSTEM OWNS THE QUEUE
DEFINE QUEUE AS A FIFO SET
DEFINE IDLE, NRCUST AS VARIABLES
DEFINE LAMBDA, MU AS REAL VARIABLES
DEFINE SYSTIME, QTIME AS DUMMY REAL VARIABLES
ACCUMULATE LQ AS THE AVG OF N.QUEUE
ACCUMULATE L AS THE AVG OF NRCUST
TALLY WQ AS THE AVG OF QTIME
TALLY W AS THE AVG OF SYSTIME
END


MAIN
PRINT 1 LINE THUS
SINGLE-CHANNEL QUEUEING SYSTEM—EXAMPLE 7.3
SKIP 3 OUTPUT LINES

PRINT 2 LINES THUS
ARRIVAL   SERVICE   LENGTH   LQ  L  WQ  W
RATE       RATE      OF SIM
READ LAMBDA, MU, LEN.SIM
LET IDLE=1
SCHEDULE AN ARRIVAL NOW
SCHEDULE A CLOSING IN LEN.SIM HOURS
START SIMULATION
```

Figure 7.8
SIMSCRIPT program listing for the simulation of a queueing system

Figure 7.8—*Cont.*
PRINT 1 LINE WITH LAMBDA, MU, LEN.SIM, LQ, L,
    WQ*HOURS.V*MINUTES.V, AND W*HOURS.V*MINUTES.V THUS
*.**/HR   *.**/HR   *   *.**   *.**   *.**MIN   *.**MIN
STOP
END

EVENT ARRIVAL SAVING THE EVENT NOTICE
CREATE PERSON
LET ARR.TIME(PERSON) = TIME.V
IF IDLE = 0 FILE PERSON IN QUEUE
    GO NEXT.ARRIVAL
ELSE
LET IDLE = 0
SCHEDULE A SERVICE.END(PERSON) IN EXPONENTIAL.F(1./MU,1) HOURS
'NEXT.ARRIVAL'
RESCHEDULE THIS ARRIVAL IN EXPONENTIAL.F(1./LAMBDA,2) HOURS
RETURN
END

EVENT SERVICE.END(PERSON)
LET SYSTIME = TIME.V-ARR TIME
DESTROY PERSON
LET NRCUST = NRCUST-1
IF QUEUE IS EMPTY, LET IDLE = 1
    RETURN
ELSE
REMOVE FIRST PERSON FROM QUEUE
LET QTIME = TIME.V-ARRTIME
SCHEDULE A SERVICE.END(PERSON) IN EXPONENTIAL (1./MU, 1) HOURS
RETURN
END

EVENT CLOSING
CANCEL THE ARRIVAL
DESTROY THE ARRIVAL
RETURN
END

This example should be self-explanatory if one keeps in mind the events that are necessary to simulate a queueing system.

Special-purpose languages: GASP IV

7.5   GASP IV is the latest in a series of simulation programming languages carrying the GASP name. This version was developed by A. A. B.

Pritsker in the early 1970s. Rather than being an independent programming language in the vein of GPSS and SIMSCRIPT, GASP IV is a package of FORTRAN subroutines used to perform the basic simulation functions. As described by Pritsker (7.7) the routines of GASP IV are designed to accomplish the following functions: event control, state variable updating, information storage and retrieval, initialization, data collection, program monitoring and event reporting, statistical computation, report generation, and random deviate generation. The GASP IV package to support these functions contains a total of 34 subprograms coded in ANSI standard FORTRAN. No attempt will be made here to describe all these subprograms, since the work of Pritsker (7.7) provides detailed descriptions and program listings. In addition to the GASP IV subprograms, there is an interface for a number of user-defined subprograms. These user-defined modules are used to simulate event occurrences, initialize state variables, provide additional error messages, and provide output in addition to the standard GASP IV output. These routines are represented in the GASP IV package as stubs, or dummy subprograms, eliminating the need for all the routines to be present when only a few are needed.

GASP IV generates standard uniform deviates by a function that employs the multiplicative congruential scheme described in chapter 4. As mentioned by Pritsker (7.7), the effectiveness of the multiplicative scheme is affected by the machine on which GASP IV is implemented. For this reason Pritsker provides a generalized version of the function DRAND, as well as two specialized versions for CDC and IBM equipment. The GASP IV package includes, in addition to the function DRAND, functions to produce deviates from the uniform, triangular, normal, lognormal, Erlang, gamma, beta, and Poisson distributions. An exponentially distributed deviate can be obtained from the function that produces Erlangian distributed variates.

GASP IV, when used to model discrete systems, uses the event scan method of time management. The scan of the future events list, as well as the advancing of the simulation clock, is accomplished by a system subprogram called GASP. The language can also be used to model continuous as well as hybrid systems. In these cases a modified method of time advance is used.

The user must supply routines to simulate the occurrence of a given event. A subroutine called EVNTS is defined to handle all events, with a computed GO TO statement used to invoke the appropriate routines.

Since GASP IV is composed of FORTRAN subprograms, the management of queues is just as handicapped in GASP IV as it is in FORTRAN. The lack of an efficient list-processing capability in FORTRAN makes queue handling somewhat inefficient. As with FORTRAN, the user must assess this disadvantage as it applies to the particular model.

GASP IV provides an extensive and flexible data collection, computation, and reporting capability. Eight subprograms support these functions. See Pritsker's work for the details of these routines (7.7). The user may define a subprogram, subroutine OTPUT, to provide output other than that automatically provided by GASP IV. The subroutine exists in stub form, so the user need only supply the particular logic.

GASP IV, composed of FORTRAN routines, enjoys many of the advantages of FORTRAN. GASP IV can be used at any installation equipped with a FORTRAN compiler. Programmers who are proficient in FORTRAN will need only to study the overall makeup of GASP IV and its naming conventions to be able to use the language.

In addition to the diagnostic capabilities provided by the FORTRAN compiler (compile-time errors), GASP IV possesses a subroutine ERROR to assist in debugging the simulation model. This subroutine is called whenever an illogical condition is detected. The routine identifies the type of error and provides a snapshot of the system state at the time that the error was detected. The user can define a subroutine UERR which can be written to provide any other information desired.

GASP IV, then, provides a great deal of assistance in the development of a simulation model. It retains many of the advantages of its parent language, FORTRAN, while at the same time relieving the programmer of the responsibility for coding many of the common routines. Because of the overall size of the GASP IV package, no example of its use is given here. See Pritsker (7.7) for more details of the language and numerous examples of its use.

Summary

In this chapter we have attempted to explain why new languages were designed for programming simulation models. We described functions common to many models: the generation of random variates, management of simulation time, simulation of event occurrences, queue management, data collection, summarization and analysis of data, and the formatting and printing of output data. In the later sections of this chapter we showed how three of the more popular simulation languages accomplished these functions. These three languages were selected because of their widespread use in this country. A fourth language, SIMULA, widely used in Europe and based on ALGOL, has failed to gain widespread acceptance in this country outside the academic community.

The choice of a suitable programming language is an important consideration in the development of a simulation model. The choice must be made based on the characteristics of the individual project. Considerations such as the languages supported at the installation, the programmer's level of proficiency, and the complexity of the model being developed all have an impact on this decision.

Exercises

7.1   Customers arrive at a barber shop according to a Poisson process at an average of five per hour. The shop is open from 8:00 a.m. to 5:00 p.m., and customers waiting at the time the shop closes are served. There is a single barber, who can give a haircut in an average of 15 minutes. This service time can be assumed to be exponentially distributed. The shop has chairs to seat ten customers in addition to the one being served. Customers who arrive and find the shop full leave. Develop a FORTRAN simulation model of this system and use it to simulate one day's activity. How many customers are lost during the course of the day? How many customers remain in the shop at closing time?

7.2   Develop a GPSS simulation model for the system described in exercise 7.1.

7.3   Develop a SIMSCRIPT simulation model for the system described in exercise 7.1.

7.4   Develop a GASP IV simulation model for the system described in exercise 7.1.

7.5   Compare and contrast the models developed in exercises 7.1–7.4

7.6   Suppose the barber operating the shop described in exercise 7.1 purchases seating for five additional customers. How does this affect the average number of customers waiting, the number of customers lost, and the number remaining at the time the shop closes?

7.7   Jobs arrive at a monoprogrammed computer facility according to a Poisson process of an average of 500 per hour. The CPU-time requirements are exponentially distributed with an average of 10 seconds. The shortest-job-first dispatching scheme is used. Develop a FORTRAN simulation model for this system, and collect statistics on the average number in the system and the average waiting time.

7.8   Develop a GPSS model for the system described in exercise 7.7.

7.9   Develop a SIMSCRIPT model for the system described in exercise 7.7.

7.10   Develop a GASP IV model for the system described in exercise 7.7.

7.11   Suppose that the jobs arriving to the system are assigned one of three priorities, priority 1 being the highest, and that the total job mix is distributed as follows: 20% in priority 1, 25% in priority 2, and 55% in priority 3. As the CPU finishes one job, it is assigned to the highest-priority job that is waiting. The tie-breaking discipline within each priority class is shortest-job-first (SJF). Develop a GPSS model for this system and simulate one hour of operation.

7.12   Develop a SIMSCRIPT model for the system described in exercise 7.11.

7.13   Change the program of example 7.1 to allow multiple servers. Investigate the impact of multiple servers on factors such as the average queue size, average time in the system, and average time in the queue.

7.14   Using one of the languages surveyed in this chapter, design and implement a model to simulate the operation of a banking facility. Why did you choose that particular language?

7.15   If you were to design a simulation programming language, what features would you include? What general-purpose language would you base it on and why?

References

7.1   BOBILLIER, P. A., KAHAN, B. C., and PROBST, A. R. *Simulation with GPSS and GPSS V.* Englewood Cliffs, N.J.: Prentice-Hall, 1976.

7.2   CONSOLIDATED ANALYSIS CENTERS, INC. *SIMSCRIPT II.5 Reference Handbook.* Santa Monica, Ca., 1971.

7.3   EMSHOFF, J. R., and SISSON, R. L. *Design and Use of Computer Simulation Models.* New York: Macmillan, 1971.

7.4   GORDON, GEOFFREY. "A General Purpose Systems Simulation Program." in *Proc. EJCC, Washington, D.C.* New York: Macmillan, 1961.

7.5   GORDON, GEOFFREY. *System Simulation.* 2d ed. Englewood Cliffs, N.J.: Prentice-Hall, 1978.

7.6   MARKOWITZ, N. M., KARR, H. N., and HAUSNER, B. *SIMSCRIPT: A Simulation Programming Language.* Englewood Cliffs, N.J.: Prentice-Hall, 1963.

7.7   PRITSKER, A. A. B. *The GASP IV Simulation Language.* New York: John Wiley and Sons, 1974.

8

Introduction to continuous system simulation

The text to this point has been oriented toward the simulation of discrete systems, systems whose changes in the system state can be thought of as occurring in quantum jumps at discrete points in time. The models for discrete systems, in which the primary interest is the detection of events, are usually stated in terms of logical equations. These logical equations delineate the conditions that must be present for an event to occur. Since the events occur at discrete points in time, it is possible to advance the simulation time in small increments and to check after each such advance whether an event occurred. Alternatively, the sequence of events could be planned in advance, and the time advance incremented to the occurrence of the next most imminent event. These approaches are referred to as the periodic scan and event scan techniques respectively.

In this chapter we survey the simulation of continuous systems. Recall that a continuous system is characterized by smooth, continuous changes to the system state. The models of continuous systems generally consist of sets of differential equations; the description of a continuous system generally involves the specification of the rate at which certain attributes change. Examples of continuous systems that have been modeled include fluid moving through a conduit or pipe, aircraft in flight, a spacecraft in orbit about the earth, and electrical circuits.

Many of the considerations in the design and modeling of discrete systems also need to be considered in the modeling of continuous systems. In fact, planning for the simulation project is nearly identical, and there is a similar need for verification and validation of the continuous model. The major differences between the two modes of simulation are the form in which the model is stated and the implementation technique used. In this chapter we point out additional considerations that are unique to the simulation of continuous systems. We do not, in general, repeat aspects already discussed for the simulation of discrete systems.

Models of continuous systems

8.1 The specification of a mathematical model for a continuous system generally involves a set of differential equations. In this section we examine a number of real-world systems that are amenable to simulation using the methods surveyed in this chapter.

Example 8.1 This example deals with the decay of a radioactive substance. One technique for modeling this system is to assume that the rate of decay of the substance is proportional to the amount of the substance present. Then a mathematical model for the system is

$$\frac{dx}{dt} = -kx$$

where x is the amount of undecayed substance at time t and k is some proportionality constant. Then if the initial amount is known, the process of decay could be simulated to determine the amount that would remain at some arbitrary time in the future.

Example 8.2 In many biological studies the rate of growth of a given species, say bacteria, is of interest. A simple model of this growth is obtained by assuming that the rate of change of the population is directly proportional to the number present.

$$\frac{dx}{dt} = kx$$

where x represents the population present at a given time t and k is again a positive constant of proportionality. Although quite simple, this model is not realistic, since it allows the population to grow without bound. Various limitations on food supply, space, and so forth, lead one to expect that the population will grow until it reaches a certain point and will then level off. A more realistic model might then be

$$\frac{dx}{dt} = kx(s - x)$$

where again x is the number present at time t and k and s are fixed constants. Once the number present exceeds s, the population will actually decrease.

Example 8.3   Consider the problem of a body falling under the influence of gravity. Newton's second law of motion is the basis for modeling this problem. This law states that the rate of change of the momentum of a body is proportional to the sum of the forces acting on it. Considering the mass of the object to be constant yields the more familiar expression $\mathbf{F} = m\mathbf{a}$, where $\mathbf{F}$ is the sum of the forces, m is the mass of the body, and $\mathbf{a}$ is its acceleration. Because $\mathbf{a}$ is the second time derivative of displacement, the model can be written

$$m\frac{d^2x}{dt^2} = F$$

Variations of this model can be obtained depending on the assumptions made. For example, if all forces other than gravity are ignored, and if it is assumed that the body is falling near the surface of the earth, the model is represented as

$$m\frac{d^2x}{dt^2} = mg$$

where g is the gravitational constant. Given some initial conditions, the action of a body falling under these conditions is easily simulated. However, the inclusion of only gravitational forces does not yield a realistic model. Another force that is normally included is the damping force due to air resistance. If it is assumed that this force is proportional to the velocity, the model yields

$$m\frac{d^2x}{dt^2} = -c\frac{dx}{dt} + mg$$

where c is known as the damping constant. Note that the sign convention defines the positive direction as downward, in the direction of motion.

A different model is derived if it is assumed that the body is falling from a great height (the expression mg for the gravitational force is no longer valid) and if other forces such as the perturbing forces due to the nonspherical nature of the earth are assumed. These models will not be considered here.

   Example 8.4   Another common problem is that of the familiar spring-mass system illustrated in figure 8.1. In this system a mass m is

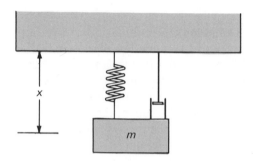

Figure 8.1
A harmonic oscillator

suspended from a fixed surface by a spring with spring constant k. Also attached is a dashpot, or shock absorber, which supplies a resisting or damping force. The mass is displaced from its equilibrium point and then released, oscillating about the position of equilibrium.
   A model for this system is

$$m\frac{d^2x}{dt^2} + D\frac{dx}{dt} + kx = f(t)$$

where m is the mass, D is the damping constant, k is the spring constant, and f(t) is an external applied force. The form of the applied force f basically determines the characteristics of the motion. This system is represented in the real world by such things as the suspension of automobiles.

   Example 8.5   The last model of a physical system that we shall consider is that of the simple pendulum illustrated in figure 8.2. In this system a mass m is attached to the end of a massless rod of length L. The other end of the rod is attached to a fixed surface by a frictionless pivot. The assumptions of a massless rod and frictionless pivot greatly simplify the model; one additional assumption is that air resistance is negligible.

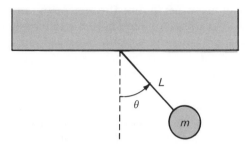

Figure 8.2
A simple pendulum

The mass is displaced from its equilibrium point, and allowed to swing back and forth. Under these three assumptions a model for this system is

$$\frac{d^2\theta}{dt^2} + \frac{g}{L} \sin \theta = 0$$

In this case, the quantity of interest is the angular position of the mass with respect to the equilibrium point.

Note the similarity in the development of the models just discussed. The models for physical systems were developed by considering all the forces that had an influence on the quantity of interest (response variable), as well as the forces included by the analyst. Newton's second law of motion was then applied to produce the desired model. Note also that the models were developed under a number of assumptions. In the model of the simple pendulum, it was assumed that the rod was massless, the pivot frictionless, and the resistance of the air negligible. The validity of these assumptions should be questioned, since these simplifications are not expected in a real system. Assumptions like these are usually made to simplify the model and thus make it amenable to analytical solutions. If the mathematical model is tractable, it is economically advantageous over any simulation model.

If a realistic formulation of the model is desired, the system can be simulated without any simplifying assumptions, although it will not be mathematically tractable. The analyst must be aware of the impact that simplifying assumptions have on the obtained results, whether the results are obtained from a simulation model or an analytical model.

A continuous system was defined as one in which changes in the system state occur in a smooth, continuous manner. Yet in example 8.2 changes in the system state occur discretely, but the system was modeled as a continuous system. In the population growth problem, the system state is the number present at some given point in time. Changes to this state occur at discrete points in time through births and deaths. This system could therefore also be modeled as a discrete system. Problems of this type, however, are sometimes more easily solved as continuous systems. The treatment of discrete systems as continuous systems can lead to unrealistic results in some cases. For example, the population may turn out to contain fractional units.

The analyst must determine whether to use the discrete or the continuous approach based on considerations such as the specific problem, the state of the system being simulated, the representation of the state of the system, and the resulting output. The results of the simulation should therefore be interpreted with this determination in mind.

Solution of linear differential equations

8.2   The previously presented models are similar in form. They all involve combinations of some dependent variable and one or more of the associated derivatives with respect to some independent variable. In fact, with the exception of example 8.5, the models all involve linear combinations of the dependent variable and associated derivatives. The dependent variable and corresponding derivatives, if they appear, are raised only to the first power and do not appear as the argument of some nonlinear function such as $\sin x$, $\cos x$, or e^x. Equations of this form are called *linear differential equations* and are defined as follows.

DEFINITION 8.1   *An equation of the form*

$$a_0(t)\, x^{(n)} + a_1(t)\, x^{(n-1)} + \cdots + a_{n-1}(t)\, x^{(1)} + a_n(t)\, x = F(t)$$

where $x^{(k)}$ denotes k successive differentiations of x with respect to t, is called an nth-order linear differential equation.

Linear differential equations, particularly those with constant coefficients (the coefficient functions $a_0, a_1, \ldots, a_n$ are constant), are of considerable interest in the modeling of continuous systems. First, the equations are generally easy to solve. Second, many systems existing in the real world can be satisfactorily modeled by using mathematical models of this form.

The use of a linear differential equation to describe a system influences the analyst in a number of ways. First, if the system can be described satisfactorily using linear differential equations, it may be advantageous to solve the model analytically rather than expending the required time and money to develop a simulation model. Second, even if simulation is desired, one way to validate the simulator would be to solve the problem analytically and compare the results from the two approaches. For these reasons an analyst involved in the simulation of a continuous system must be familiar with linear differential equations. To illustrate the solution approach, we briefly survey the techniques for solving linear differential equations, restricting our discussions to equations with constant coefficients.

The first step to solving a linear differential equation of the form

$$a_0 x^{(n)} + a_1 x^{(n-1)} + \cdots + a_{n-1} x^{(1)} + a_n x = F$$

is to solve the corresponding *homogeneous* equation, that is, the equation with F set equal to zero. If the model is actually homogeneous, this will complete the solution process, otherwise another step is necessary.

The general technique for solving an nth-order linear homogeneous equation with constant coefficients will be illustrated with a second-order equation.

$$a_0 \frac{d^2 x}{dt^2} + a_1 \frac{dx}{dt} + a_2 x = 0$$

where a_0, a_1, and a_2 are constants. Now with the usual convention of representing dx/dt by $\dot{x}$ and d^2x/dt^2 as $\ddot{x}$, the equation can be rewritten as

$$a_0 \ddot{x} + a_1 \dot{x} + a_2 x = 0 \tag{8.1}$$

To solve this equation means to find a function of x that when added to a linear combination of its derivatives yields 0. One class of functions that has this property is the exponential function of the form

$$x = e^{rt}$$

where r is a suitably chosen constant.

Suppose then that we guess at a solution of the form $x = e^{rt}$, where r is to be determined. If $x = e^{rt}$, then $\dot{x} = re^{rt}$ and $\ddot{x} = r^2 e^{rt}$. Substituting these functions for $\dot{x}$, $\ddot{x}$, and x in equation 8.1 yields

$$a_0 r^2 e^{rt} + a_1 r e^{rt} + a_2 e^{rt} = 0$$

Then dividing both sides of the equation by e^{rt} results in

$$a_0 r^2 + a_1 r + a_2 = 0$$

This equation, known as the *characteristic equation*, is an ordinary second-degree linear algebraic equation and can be solved by using the quadratic formula.

$$r = \frac{-a_1 \pm (a_1^2 - 4a_0a_2)^{1/2}}{2a_0}$$

Two values of r for which $x = e^{rt}$ satisfies equation 8.1 have thus been determined. The resulting two solutions of equation 8.1 are

$$x_1 = e^{r_1 t} \quad \text{and} \quad x_2 = e^{r_2 t}$$

where

$$r_1 = \frac{-a_1 + (a_1^2 - 4a_0a_2)^{1/2}}{2a_0} \quad \text{and} \quad r_2 = \frac{-a_1 - (a_1^2 - 4a_0a_2)^{1/2}}{2a_0}$$

Example 8.6   Consider the second-order equation

$$\ddot{x} - \dot{x} - 2x = 0$$

Letting $x = e^{rt}$, we get $\dot{x} = re^{rt}$ and $\ddot{x} = r^2 e^{rt}$. Substituting into the second-order equation results in

$$r^2 e^{rt} - re^{rt} - 2e^{rt} = 0$$

Now dividing by e^{rt} gives the characteristic equation

$$r^2 - r - 2 = 0$$

which has roots

$$r = \frac{1 \pm [(-1)^2 - (4)(1)(-2)]^{1/2}}{2} = \frac{1 \pm 9^{1/2}}{2} = \frac{1 \pm 3}{2}$$

Thus two solutions to the given differential equation are

$$x_1 = e^{-t} \quad \text{and} \quad x_2 = e^{2t}$$

The reader should verify that these functions are actually solutions.

This technique will provide a solution to the differential equation. It is sometimes of interest to find all solutions, since in most cases an entire family of functions will satisfy the given equation. This is easily done using the procedure given by the following theorem, stated without proof.

THEOREM 8.1   *Consider the second-order homogeneous linear differential equation with constant coefficients given by*

$$a_0\ddot{x} + a_1\dot{x} + a_2 x = 0$$

Suppose x_1 *and* x_2 *are two linearly independent solutions. Then the general solution is given by*

$$x = c_1 x_1 + c_2 x_2$$

where c_1 *and* c_2 *are arbitrary constants.*

This theorem can be easily generalized to an nth-order equation. We have yet to define linearly independent solutions. Essentially two solutions x_1 and x_2 are linearly independent if one is not a constant multiple of the another.

The equation solved in example 8.6 had roots to the characteristic equation that were real and distinct. Thus two linearly independent, real-valued solutions were immediately obtained. This is not always the case. In general the three cases that need to be considered are summarized in the following theorem.

THEOREM 8.2   *Consider the second-order homogeneous linear differential equation with constant coefficients given by*

$$a_0\ddot{x} + a_1\dot{x} + a_2 x = 0$$

The characteristic equation is $a_0 r^2 + a_1 r + a_2 = 0$, *which has roots* r_1 *and* r_2.

CASE 1   *If* r_1 *and* r_2 *are real and distinct, the general solution to the given differential equation is*

$$x = c_1 e^{r_1 t} + c_2 e^{r_2 t}$$

where c_1 *and* c_2 *are arbitrary constants.*

CASE 2   *If* r_1 *and* r_2 *are real repeated roots, the general solution to the given differential equation is*

$$x = c_1 e^{r_1 t} + c_2 t\, e^{r_1 t}$$

where c_1 *and* c_2 *are arbitrary constants.*

CASE 3 If r_1 and r_2 are complex roots, where $r_1 = \alpha + \beta i$ and $r_2 = \alpha - \beta i, i = \sqrt{-1}$, then the general solution to the given differential equation is

$$x = c_1 e^{\alpha t} \cos \beta t + c_2 e^{\alpha t} \sin \beta t$$

where c_1 and c_2 are arbitrary constants.

This theorem is easily generalized to the nth-order homogeneous linear differential equations. Some examples demonstrate this solution process.

Example 8.7 Consider the differential equation

$$\ddot{x} - \dot{x} - 6x = 0$$

The characteristic equation $r^2 - r - 6 = 0$ has roots

$$r = \frac{1 \pm [1 - (4)(1)(-6)]^{1/2}}{2} = \frac{1 \pm 5}{2}$$

Thus $r_1 = 3, r_2 = -2$. The general solution to the differential equation is

$$x = c_1 e^{3t} + c_2 e^{-2t}$$

Example 8.8 Consider the differential equation

$$\ddot{x} - 4\dot{x} + 4x = 0$$

The characteristic equation $r^2 - 4r + 4 = 0$ has roots

$$r = \frac{4 \pm [16 - (4)(1)(4)]^{1/2}}{2} = \frac{4 \pm 0}{2}$$

Thus $r_1 = 2, r_2 = 2$. The general solution to the differential equation is

$$x = c_1 e^{2t} + c_2 t e^{2t}$$

Example 8.9 Consider the differential equation

$$\ddot{x} - 2\dot{x} + 5x = 0$$

The characteristic equation $r^2 - 2r + 5 = 0$ has roots

$$r = \frac{2 \pm [4 - (4)(1)(5)]^{1/2}}{2} = \frac{2 \pm [-16]^{1/2}}{2} = \frac{2 \pm 4 [-1]^{1/2}}{2} = \frac{2 \pm 4i}{2}$$

Thus $r_1 = 1 + 2i$, $r_2 = 1 - 2i$. The general solution to the differential equation is

$$x = c_1 e^t \cos 2t + c_2 e^t \sin 2t$$

Now that we can find the general solution to a linear homogeneous differential equation with constant coefficients, it is time to consider a specific physical case. Physical systems generally provide a deterministic output from a given set of initial conditions. Consider the harmonic oscillator problem in example 8.4. If the mass is displaced some distance from equilibrium and released, it will move in some fixed manner. If the experiment is repeated after it is in equilibrium again, the mass should move in precisely the same manner as before. This solution process produces an infinite family of functions that satisfy the given differential equation. To produce the single function that describes the behavior of that system, *initial conditions* must be specified. For the harmonic oscillator, we might specify $x(0) = 1$, $\dot{x}(0) = 0$. These conditions mean that at the beginning of the experiment, the mass is displaced one unit away from equilibrium in the positive direction and is at rest (the initial velocity $\dot{x}$ is 0). In general, for an nth-order equation, we must specify n initial conditions. By constraining the general solution with these initial conditions, a single function can be produced that describes the behavior of the system. This process of constraining the general solution is illustrated by the following example.

Example 8.10   Consider the differential equation $\ddot{x} - \dot{x} - 6x = 0$ subject to the initial conditions $x(0) = 1$, $\dot{x}(0) = 0$. From example 8.7 the general solution to this equation is given by

$$x = c_1 e^{3t} + c_2 e^{-2t}$$

If $x = c_1 e^{3t} + c_2 e^{-2t}$, then $\dot{x} = 3c_1 e^{3t} - 2c_2 e^{-2t}$. The initial conditions specify that $x(0) = 1$ and $\dot{x}(0) = 0$. Evaluating the expressions for x and $\ddot{x}$ at $t = 0$ and equating them to the specified initial conditions results in

$$x(0) = c_1 + c_2 = 1$$
$$\dot{x}(0) = 3c_1 - 2c_2 = 0$$

We thus obtain a set of linear algebraic equations which, once solved, yield

$$c_1 = 2/5, \qquad c_2 = 3/5$$

Then substituting these values into the general solution gives

$$x = (2/5)e^{3t} + (3/5)e^{-2t}$$

This function describes the behavior of the system under the listed initial conditions.

A differential equation along with an appropriate number of initial values is called an *initial value problem*, commonly abbreviated IVP.

By way of review, an nth-order linear differential equation with constant coefficients is defined as an equation of the form

$$a_0 x^{(n)} + a_1 x^{(n-1)} + \cdots + a_{n-1} x^{(1)} + a_n x = f(t)$$

If $f(t) = 0$ (the equation is homogeneous), we can find the general solution to the equation using a procedure similar to that outlined before. We can then apply initial conditions to constrain the general solution to the particular case of interest. We now consider the case in which $f(t)$ is not identically 0. That is, we will now outline a solution process for the nonhomogeneous equation. Again, for convenience, we restrict the discussion to a second-order equation.

To solve the nonhomogeneous equation, we must first solve the homogeneous equation, as pointed out in the following theorem.

THEOREM 8.3   *Consider the second-order nonhomogeneous linear differential equation with constant coefficients given by*

$$a_0 \ddot{x} + a_1 \dot{x} + a_2 x = f(t)$$

The general solution to this equation is

$$x = x_h + x_p$$

where x_h is the general solution to the corresponding homogeneous equation and x_p is any solution to the nonhomogeneous equation.

Since we know how to find a general solution to the nonhomogeneous equation, all we need is a technique for obtaining any solution to the nonhomogeneous equation. This sounds simple enough, but it is sometimes difficult. The technique illustrated here involves guessing the form of the particular equation. This technique, commonly referred to as the *method of undetermined coefficients*, is illustrated with examples. The details of this method, as well as other techniques for solving linear differential equations, can be found in the many excellent texts on differential equations.

Example 8.11   Consider the differential equation

$$\ddot{x} - 3\dot{x} - 4x = 2e^{2t}$$

The characteristic equation $r^2 - 3r - 4 = 0$ has roots $r_1 = -1, r_2 = 4$. Thus the general solution to the associated homogeneous equation is

$$x_h = c_1 e^{-t} + c_2 e^{4t}$$

To find a particular solution to the nonhomogeneous equation, we guess a solution of the form of the right-hand side. In this case we guess that a particular solution is of the form

$$x_p = A e^{2t}$$

where A is some constant that must be determined. If $x_p = A e^{2t}$, then $\dot{x} = 2A e^{2t}$, and $\ddot{x} = 4A e^{2t}$. Substituting these quantities into the original equation gives

$$4A e^{2t} - 3(2A e^{2t}) - 4(A e^{2t}) = 2e^{2t}$$

Collecting terms and dividing by e^{2t} gives $-6A = 2$, or $A = -1/3$. A solution to the nonhomogeneous equation then becomes

$$x_p = -(1/3)e^{2t}$$

Combining this with the general solution of the homogeneous equation as outlined by theorem 8.3, we see that the general solution to the non-homogeneous equation is

$$x = c_1 e^{-t} + c_2 e^{4t} - 1/3 \, e^{2t}$$

Initial conditions can then be applied to this general solution to obtain a single function.

Example 8.12 Consider the differential equation

$$\ddot{x} + 2\dot{x} + x = \cos t$$

The characteristic equation $r^2 + 2r + 1 = 0$ has two repeated roots of $r = -1$. Thus the general solution to the homogeneous equation is

$$x_h = c_1 e^{-t} + c_2 t e^{-t}$$

To find a solution to the nonhomogeneous equation, we assume a solution of the form of the right-hand side as before. In this case we assume a solution of the form $x_p = A \sin t + B \cos t$. Note that we must include both the sin and cos terms in this case. If $X_p = A \sin T + B \cos t$, then

$\dot{x}_p = A \cos T - B \sin t$ and $\ddot{x}_p = -A \sin t - B \cos t$. Substituting into the original equation gives

$$(-A \sin t - B \cos t) + 2(A \cos t - B \sin t) + (A \sin t + \cos t) = \cos t$$

Collecting terms, we get

$$(-2B) \sin t + (2A) \cos t = \cos t$$

Then equating coefficients yields $-2B = 0$, $2A = 1$. So a solution to the nonhomogeneous equation is

$$x_p = (1/2) \sin t$$

Thus the general solution to the nonhomogeneous equation is

$$x = c_1 e^{-t} + c_2 t e^{-t} + (1/2) \sin t$$

The method of undetermined coefficients does not yield a particular solution to the nonhomogeneous equation in all cases. In fact, it is limited to equations in which $f(t)$ is a function of one of the following types: t^j, $t^j e^{ct}$, $t^j e^{at} \cos bt$, and $t^j e^{at} \sin bt$. The analyst who encounters an equation of another type must resort to some other means to obtain the particular solution. This section concludes with a comprehensive example of the techniques surveyed.

Example 8.13   Consider the harmonic oscillator as given in example 8.4 with $m = 1$, $D = -2$, and $k = 13/4$. Suppose a time-varying force is applied to the system with $f(t) = \cos 2t$ and that the mass is displaced one unit in the positive direction and then released. This problem can be modeled by

$$\ddot{x} - 2\dot{x} + (13/4)x = \cos 2t; \qquad x(0) = 1, \dot{x}(0) = 0$$

The characteristic equation $r^2 - 2r + 13/4 = 0$ has roots $r_1 = 1 + (3/2)i$ and $r_2 = 1 - (3/2)i$. Thus the general solution to the homogeneous equation is

$$x_h = c_1 e^t \cos (3/2)t + c_2 e^t \sin (3/2)t$$

Since f is in trigonometric form, a particular solution to the nonhomogeneous equation is assumed to be of the form $x_p = A \cos 2t + B \sin 2t$. Thus $\dot{x}_p = -2A \sin 2t + 2B \cos 2t$, and $\ddot{x}_p = -4A \cos 2t - 4B \sin 2t$.

Substituting these equations results in

$$(-4A \cos 2t - 4B \sin 2t) - 2(-2A \sin 2t + 2B \cos 2t)$$

$$+ \frac{13}{4}(A \cos 2t + B \sin 2t) = \cos 2t$$

or

$$(-3/4A - 4B) \cos 2t + (4A - 3/4B) \sin 2t = \cos 2t$$

Equating coefficients yields $A = 12/265$ and $B = 64/265$. Thus the general solution to the nonhomogeneous equation is

$$x = c_1 e^t \cos \frac{3}{2}t + c_2 e^t \sin \frac{3}{2}t + \frac{12}{265} \cos 2t + \frac{64}{265} \sin 2t$$

Now

$$x(0) = c_1 + \frac{12}{265} = 1 \quad \text{and} \quad \dot{x}(0) = \frac{3}{2}c_2 + \frac{128}{265} = 0$$

so

$$c_1 = 253/265 \quad \text{and} \quad c_2 = 256/795$$

Thus the solution to the initial value problem is

$$x = \frac{253}{265} e^t \cos \frac{3}{2}t + \frac{256}{795} e^t \sin \frac{3}{2}t + \frac{12}{265} \cos 2t + \frac{64}{265} \sin 2t$$

Analog computing

8.3   Although the concepts of modeling have been in use for many years, the development of the electronic computer renewed interest in these ideas. At first, analysts investigating systems that lent themselves to continuous simulation turned to the use of the analog computer. The high cost and the limited availability of digital computers at that time were reasons for this orientation. Recall that models for continuous systems usually involve differential equations. The solving of such equations is readily accomplished by analog devices, since they are extremely efficient integrators.

According to Vichnevetsky (8.4), the idea of solving a differential equation with a computer dates back to Lord Kelvin in 1876. Kelvin's ideas were implemented in the 1930s at the Massachusetts Institute of Technology when Bush developed a mechanical differential analyzer. In the years following World War II an electronic differential analyzer was developed by Lovell and Philbrick. This analyzer operated by implementing a simple or elementary mathematical operation with a combination of direct-current amplifiers and passive electronic circuits. More recent developments in analog computers have combined logical computation components with the older analog computers.

The simple analog computer has five basic elements. The first element is a *summer*, which accepts a number of input signals and outputs the sum of the inputs. The standard block symbol for such a summer is

Operation: $x_3 = (x_0 + 10x_1 + x_2)$

The second component is the *attenuator*, which accepts an input, multiplies it by some constant, and outputs the product. The standard symbol for this element is

Operation: $x_1 = \alpha x_0$

The third element is the *multiplier*, which accepts two inputs and produces the product of these inputs as an output. The block symbol for the multiplier is

Operation: $x_2 = x_0 \cdot x_1$

The next component is a *function generator*, which accepts some input, performs some specified operation on it, and outputs the result. The block symbol for this component is

Operation: $x_1 = f(x_0)$

The fifth component is the *integrator*, which is represented by the following diagram

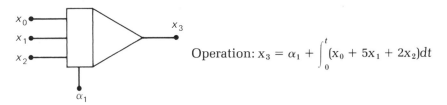

Operation: $x_3 = \alpha_1 + \int_0^t (x_0 + 5x_1 + 2x_2)dt$

With these elements in mind, we can now discuss how an analog computer is used in simulation. First, just as with a discrete system, a mathematical model representing the system is constructed. We assume in this case that the model is in the form of differential equations. Next, individual computing elements are assigned to accomplish each necessary operation. The output voltages of the components are scaled to represent actual physical conditions. The next step is to establish interconnections between the elements by using patch cords to link the appropriate elements. Then the initial conditions are set up and the simulation begun. If the model has been constructed properly, the output of the analog computer should represent the behavior of the real system.

To illustrate these ideas, we shall see how the harmonic oscillator discussed in example 8.13 can be simulated using an analog computer. Recall that the model constructed for the system was

$$\ddot{x} - 2\dot{x} + (13/4)x = \cos 2t$$

We can rewrite this equation as

$$\ddot{x} = \cos 2t + 2\dot{x} - (13/4)x$$

If we had values for $\cos 2t$, $\dot{x}$, and x at every value of t, we could solve the system quite easily by linking two integrators in series. All we have in this case is x and $\dot{x}$ evaluated at a particular value of t, namely $t = 0$, so we must construct circuitry that will provide the remaining quantities. A block diagram of an analog computer simulator for this problem is illustrated in figure 8.3. The initial conditions are used to start the simulator. Study this diagram carefully for a clear understanding of the process.

Note that the speed of an analog computer is almost independent of the number of equations involved. Furthermore, it should be apparent that the solution of differential equations using analog computers is not restricted to the solution of linear equations. This is noteworthy, since the analytic solution of nonlinear differential equations is at best an arduous process.

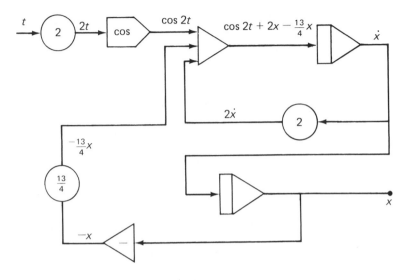

Figure 8.3
Analog simulation of the harmonic oscillator

Digital simulation of continuous systems

8.4 The present widespread availability of digital computers in conjunction with some severe drawbacks in the use of analog computers to simulate continuous systems has increased interest in modeling continuous systems by using digital computers. Digital computers are capable of performing arithmetic and logical operations at very high speeds, storing large amounts of data, and maintaining a high degree of accuracy. These highly desirable attributes are not present in analog computers. In this section we survey some aspects of simulating the operation of a continuous system by using a digital computer.

Recall that the mathematical model of a continuous system generally involves one or more differential equations. To simulate the operation of a continuous system, then, generally requires the solution of these differential equations. In an analog computer simulation, voltages represent values. The values (voltages) are operated on by high-gain, direct-current amplifiers and circuit arrangements. These scaled voltages represent the coefficients of the equations of the model. When these voltages are passed through a special circuit called an integrator, the output value represents the integral with respect to time of a single input voltage, or the sum of several input voltages. Digital computers perform the integration of differential equations by a process of numerical approximations. Whenever differential equations are involved, simulation of continuous systems on a digital computer becomes slow because of the iterative process necessary to solve such equations. According to Ord-Smith and Stephenson (8.1) this speed difference between digital and analog solutions of differential equations can be at least a factor of 100 even for small problems. The speed of an analog computer is nearly independent of the size of the problem. This is not the case with digital computers. As the problem grows, so does the time necessary to solve it, and the speed differential between the analog and the digital solutions becomes even greater.

The digital computer performs integration as a series of approximations. The literature provides a large number of numerical schemes for obtaining an approximate solution to an initial value problem. The methods are generally restricted to solving systems of first-order equations because an arbitrary nth-order differential equation can be represented by an equivalent set of n first-order equations. Equivalence in this sense means that if the n first-order equations are solved simultaneously, a solution to the original nth-order equation is obtained. This reduction of order is done by the introduction of a suitable number of state variables. Consider the nth-order equation given by

$$a_0(t)x^{(n)} + a_1(t)x^{(n-1)} + \ldots + a_{n-1}(t)x^{(1)} + a_n(t)x = f(t)$$

This equation can be rewritten

$$x^{(n)} = \frac{1}{a_0(t)} [f(t) - a_1(t)x^{(n-1)} - \ldots - a_{n-1}(t)x^{(1)} - a_n(t)x]$$

$$= g(t, x, x^{(1)}, \ldots, x^{(n-1)})$$

Now introducing the state variables $Y_1, Y_2, \ldots, Y_n$ to represent x and its first $n - 1$ derivatives results in the system of equations

$$\dot{Y}_1 = Y_2$$
$$\dot{Y}_2 = Y_3$$

$$\cdot$$
$$\cdot$$
$$\cdot$$

$$\dot{Y}_n = g(t, Y_1, Y_2, \ldots, Y_n)$$

This process is best illustrated by an example.

Example 8.14   Consider the harmonic oscillator described in Example 8.4. The model for this system was given by

$$m\ddot{x} + D\dot{x} + kx = f(t)$$

Solving this equation for $\ddot{x}$ yields

$$\ddot{x} = \frac{1}{m}[f(t) - D\dot{x} - kx]$$

Now let $x = Y_1$ and $\dot{x} = Y_2$. Then

$$\dot{Y}_1 = Y_2 \quad \text{and} \quad \dot{Y}_2 = \frac{1}{m}[f(t) - DY_2 - kY_1]$$

These equations are of first order and, when coupled with suitable initial conditions, are amenable to solution using any of the standard initial value integrators.

All the initial value integrators involve some approximation of the derivative. We state the problem more succinctly, and then survey some of the more common integrators. The first-order initial value problem may be stated as $\dot{x} = g(x, t); x(t_0) = x_0$. We are given an equation relating the first derivative of the dependent variable x to some function of x and the independent variable t. We generally know the value of the variable x at some initial point and wish to determine its value on some interval $[t_0, T]$. The interval of interest is divided into k subintervals whose left boundaries are represented by $t_0, t_1, \ldots, t_k$, where $t_k = T$. The value of the variable x at these points is represented by $x(t_i)$, $i = 0, 1, \ldots, k$. We may find it more convenient to use the notation $x(t_i) = x_i$.

Finite difference schemes. Finite difference schemes involve approximating the derivative with a first-order difference equation. The most common of these schemes is probably the *forward difference* scheme. In the forward difference scheme the derivative is approximated by

$$\dot{x}(t_i) \approx \frac{x(t_{i+1}) - x(t_i)}{h}$$

where h is the subinterval width. Substituting this approximation gives

$$\frac{x(t_{i+1}) - x(t_i)}{h} = g(x(t_i), t_i)$$

or $x(t_{i+1}) = x(t_i) + h\, g(x(t_i), t_i)$

or $x_{i+1} = x_i + h\, g(x_i, t_i)$

Example 8.15   Consider the first-order initial value problem given by $\dot{x} = x; x(0) = 1$. Suppose we desire the value of x on the interval $[0, 1]$. Subdivide the interval into ten subintervals, so that $h = 0.1$. Then the forward difference recursion relation becomes

$$x_{i+1} = x_i + 0.1x_i = 1.1x_i$$

resulting in $x_0 = 1$

$$x_1 = 1.1\, x_0 = 1.1$$
$$x_2 = 1.1\, x_1 = 1.21$$
$$x_3 = 1.1\, x_2 = 1.331$$
$$x_4 = 1.1\, x_3 = 1.464$$
$$x_5 = 1.1\, x_4 = 1.610$$
$$x_6 = 1.1\, x_5 = 1.771$$
$$x_7 = 1.1\, x_6 = 1.948$$
$$x_8 = 1.1\, x_7 = 2.143$$
$$x_9 = 1.1\, x_8 = 2.357$$
$$x_{10} = 1.1\, x_9 = 2.593$$

Two other finite difference schemes that are sometimes used are the central difference scheme and the backward difference scheme. The recurrence relations that result from these schemes are as follows.

Central difference

$$x_{i+1} = 2h\, g(x_i, t_i) + x_{i-1}$$

Backward difference

$$x_{i+1} - h\, g(x_{i+1}, t_{i+1}) = x_i$$

Runge-Kutta schemes. The finite difference schemes are somewhat limited in accuracy. The error incurred is approximately proportional to h^2. To obtain the required accuracy, one would have to use an extremely small step size (subinterval width), which increases the run time. A class of methods that circumvents this problem is known as Runge-Kutta methods. These techniques involve an averaging process to obtain a better approximation of the derivative.

First order. The first-order Runge-Kutta scheme, also referred to as Euler's method, is identical to the forward difference scheme, that is,

$$x_{i+1} = x_i + h \, g(x_i, t_i)$$

Second order. The second-order Runge-Kutta scheme, also referred to as the modified Euler method, results in the recurrence relationship

$$x_{i+2} = x_i + 2h \, g(x_{i+1}, t_{i+1})$$

Higher-order Runge-Kutta schemes are available. Use of the second-order method results in an error approximately equal to h^3. Runge-Kutta methods of order four and five are commonly used to further decrease the truncation error.

Example 8.16   Consider the problem defined in example 8.15. To use the second-order Runge-Kutta formula, we need the value of x_1 as well as x_0.

$$x_{i+2} = x_i + 0.2x_{i+1}$$

We can use the value of x_1 obtained using the forward difference scheme. Thus

$$x_0 = 1$$

$$x_1 = 1.1$$

$$x_2 = x_0 + 0.2x_1 = 1.22$$

$$x_3 = x_1 + 0.2x_2 = 1.344$$

$$x_4 = x_2 + 0.2x_3 = 1.489$$

$$x_5 = x_3 + 0.2x_4 = 1.642$$

$$x_6 = x_4 + 0.2x_5 = 1.817$$

$$x_7 = x_5 + 0.2x_6 = 2.005$$

$$x_8 = x_6 + 0.2x_7 = 2.218$$

$$x_9 = x_7 + 0.2x_8 = 2.449$$

$$x_{10} = x_8 + 0.2x_9 = 2.708$$

The true value of x_{10} [$x(1.0)$], correct to three decimal places, is 2.718. Thus the second-order Runge-Kutta method offers a significant improvement in accuracy at no additional effort.

There are a multitude of initial value integrators in the literature, but most are similar in form to the two methods surveyed; the major difference is the way that the derivative is approximated. The purpose of surveying these two methods was to illustrate how differential equations can be solved on a digital computer. For more detail see any of the standard numerical analysis texts.

The major disadvantage to using a digital computer in lieu of an analog computer to simulate a continuous system is that solving differential equations is relatively slow (8.1). On the other hand, digital computers offer a number of significant advantages. Among these are greater accuracy, the availability of storage facilities, ease of debugging, greater reliability, and the general-purpose nature of the digital computer. Analog computers are special-purpose devices, capable of efficiently performing only those tasks for which they were designed. A digital computer, on the other hand, can be used for many applications other than the simulation study.

Because the analog computer possesses a distinct speed advantage in the solution of differential equations, while the digital computer offers advantages in other areas, a reasonable compromise might be to combine the two. With the space program of the 1960s providing the impetus, digital-analog computers were built. This combination of computer systems was termed a *hybrid* computer. The specific goals of the hybrid computer were to gain the large memory, precision, and logic capabilities of the digital computer while retaining the integration capability of the analog computer. This hybrid approach had some limited success, because the actual programming of the hybrid computer was difficult. Programmers had to be able to perform analog programming in addition to programming the digital portions of the computer. Furthermore, the hardware cost for the interface between the two computers was quite expensive. These drawbacks in the hybrid computer motivated yet another approach.

Special-purpose, continuous-system simulation languages were designed to simplify programming as well as to replace the analog portion of the hybrid computer with special digital simulation programs. These continuous-system simulation languages are the subject of the next section. With the development of these special-purpose languages and the return to pure digital simulation of continuous systems, proponents of the special-purpose languages seemed willing to concede the speed advantage of the analog computer in order to obtain the numerous advantages of the digital computer.

Continuous-system simulation languages

8.5   Special-purpose, continuous-system simulation languages were developed for the same reasons that discrete-system simulation languages were. Researchers involved in the simulation of continuous systems realized that a number of common functions were being performed: the representation of time, the handling of delays, the input of initial conditions, the formatting and printing of output, and the calculation of numerous functions, such as integration. Most of the continuous system simulation languages that have been widely accepted are based on FORTRAN, because of its widespread availability as well as the features offered in most implementations.In this section we briefly survey two such continuous system simulation languages, CSMP III and DYNAMO. These two languages, in addition to GASP IV, are probably the most commonly used of the continuous-system simulation languages. However, just as with discrete systems, many continuous-system simulation models are implemented directly in FORTRAN. Before we consider CSMP III and DYNAMO specifically, let us consider some of the general characteristics of continuous-system simulation languages.

There are two types of continuous-system simulation languages. The first is the block-form language. In this type of language the model is first constructed in a block diagram similar to that illustrated for an analog computer representation. The model is then implemented through a set of connection statements. The common functions accomplished by particular blocks are specified, and the user is not concerned with the details of their development. This approach to continuous system simulation is similar to the approach used by GPSS for discrete system simulation. Neither example language is of this form, and we are not aware of any widely accepted language of this type, so we will not discuss block-form languages any further. The second form of a continuous-system simulation language is the expression-based language. In this type of language the model is implemented in equation form, similar to that used by FORTRAN or by any of the other procedural languages. As an example, consider the model of example 8.13. This model can be implemented in an equation-based language using equations similar to

XDOT = V
VDOT = COS(2*T) + 2*V − (13/4)*X

Expression-based languages are popular because programming in these languages is similar to programming in the procedure-oriented languages such as FORTRAN. Throughout the remainder of this chapter we restrict our discussion to this type of language.

A continuous-system simulation program generally consists of three parts. The first part is the initialization section. In this section the initial values of the state variables (the initial conditions of the problem) are specified, the values of the constants of the model are assigned, and the parameters of the model such as the solution interval and time increment are established. The second section is the main program. In this section the equations of the model are specified and used to generate a solution. A number of standard functions or user-defined subprograms may be invoked in this section. The third section is the termination routine. In this section housekeeping chores such as the printing or the plotting of the output and reinitialization for a second run are accomplished. This organization is not unique to a continuous-system simulation program. It is mentioned here only because many simulation languages classify statements based on their utility in each phrase. For particular examples, let us now examine CSMP III and DYNAMO briefly.

The Continuous System Model Program, Version III, abbreviated CSMP III, is an equation-based programming language designed to facilitate the construction of continuous-system simulation models. There are a number of data-type statements for use in the initialization phase of the model. These include the CONST statement to assign particular values to constants in the model. This statement functions in much the same manner as the DATA statement in FORTRAN. The model specification in the main program section of the model is facilitated by the availability of a number of standard functions. These include functions to compute the integral of a variable between specified limits, the exponentiation of a specified variable, the natural logarithm of a quantity, as well as the standard trigonometric functions. See Speckhart and Green (8.3), for example, for a complete list of functions provided. The means of invoking these functions are similar to FORTRAN, as will be shown by an example.

Simulation time is specified by the use of a control statement TIMER. This statement is used to specify the length of the simulation time, the subinterval width used in integration, and the interval widths for the printing and plotting of output. This statement is also illustrated by an example.

Two types of output are possible in CSMP, standard printed output and plotted output. The first routine is invoked by using the PRINT statement. If plotted output is desired, the statement PRTPLT is used. Title and header information can be printed using the TITLE and LABEL statements respectively.

Example 8.17 Consider the harmonic oscillator described in example 8.13. The mathematical model for this system was

$$\ddot{x} - 2\dot{x} + (13/4)x = \cos 2t; \qquad x(0) = 1, \dot{x}(0) = 0$$

Suppose that we wish to simulate the operation of this system from $t = 0$ to $t = 10$ and want output printed every 0.5 time units. This could be accomplished with the following CSMP III program.

```
 1   TITLE=  HARMONIC OSCILLATOR
     *
 2   ACCEL= FUNCT + D*VEL − K*X
 3   VEL=    INTEGRL (0.0, ACCEL)
 4   X=      INTGRL (0.0, VEL)
 5   FUNCT=COS (2.0*TIME)
     *
 6   CONST  D=2.0, K=3.25
 7   TIMER  DELT=0.01, FINTIM=10.0, PRDEL=0.5
 8   PRINT  TIME, X, VEL, ACCEL
 9   END
10   STOP
```

In this example line 1 specifies the heading that will be printed at the beginning of the output. Lines 2–5 are a specification of the model. Line 2 is the mathematical model, line 3 defines the first derivative VEL as $\int_0^T$ ACCEL dt, and line 4 defines the displacement x as $\int_0^T$ VEL dt. Line 5 defines the forcing function. The variable TIME is a CSMP variable representing the current simulation time. Line 6 assigns values to the damping coefficient D and the spring constant K. Line 7 specifies the integration subinterval width (DELT), the end of the simulation run (FINTIM), and the print interval width (PRDEL). Line 9 indicates the variables to be printed. A line of output would be produced every 0.5 units of simulation time, resulting in 20 lines of output.

The second example language is DYNAMO, an acronym for Dynamic Model. It was developed at the Massachusetts Institute of Technology by Pugh (8.2). DYNAMO, like CSMP III is an equation-based language. The form of the language is much like FORTRAN. The allowable equation forms in DYNAMO are specified through prototypes. The prototype or equation forms are numbered. To use a particular equation form, the user lists its number and then the particular information required by that form. Like CSMP III, DYNAMO supplies a number of standard functions. These include exponential, logarithmic, trigonometric, square root, random number generators, and maximum and minimum functions. Although no integration function is provided, a summing function through which integration is accomplished is provided. DYNAMO provides PRINT and PLOT functions much as CSMP III.

Too much detail is required to understand how a system such as the harmonic oscillator could be simulated using DYNAMO, so no example will be given. See Pugh (8.2) for details and illustrative examples.

Summary

In this chapter we have introduced some of the aspects of continuous system simulation. The problem that requires special consideration in continuous system modeling as opposed to discrete system modeling is the solution of differential equations. Analog computers are effective integrators, but they have drawbacks in other areas of the simulation process. The trend has been to use either hybrid computers, which encompass the best of both worlds (digital and analog) but are expensive and difficult to program, or digital simulation aided by special-purpose, continuous-system simulation languages. Two of the more common of these languages are CSMP III and DYNAMO. Both are equation-based languages, similar to FORTRAN in program structure.

Exercises

8.1   Find the solution to the model of example 8.2 if $k = 2$, and $x(0) = 20$. What would the population be at the end of ten time units?

8.2   An approximate solution to the model of example 8.5 can be obtained by "linearizing" the model. That is, if small oscillations are assumed, $\sin \theta \approx \theta$. In this case the model becomes

$$\ddot{\theta} + \frac{g}{L}\theta = 0$$

Solve this linearized model for a system with $L = 2$ feet. Note that $g \approx 32$ ft/sec². If initial conditions $\theta(0) = 0, \dot{\theta}(0) = 1$ are applied, find the particular solution.

8.3   Verify that the function obtained in example 8.10 actually satisfies the differential equation.

8.4   Draw a block-diagram representation of how the system described in example 8.2 could be simulated using an analog computer.

8.5   Given the initial value problem $\dot{x} + x = 0$, $x(0) = 1$, solve the problem analytically, and evaluate the solution at the point $t = 2$.

8.6   Determine an approximate solution for the initial value problem of exercise 8.5 using the forward difference scheme with $h = 0.1$.

8.7   Determine an approximate solution for the initial value problem of exercise 8.6 using the modified Euler scheme with $h = 0.1$.

8.8   Compare the results of exercises 8.5–8.7.

8.9   Write a FORTRAN function subprogram RUNG2 to implement the modified Euler scheme. Parameters should include the initial value X0, the stop size h, and the number of subintervals n.

8.10   Use the subprogram developed in exercise 8.9 to approximate the solution of the initial value problem of exercise 8.6 with $h = 0.01$.

8.11   Repeat exercise 8.10 with $h = 0.001$. Does it yield improved results?

8.12   Using the function developed in exercise 8.9, write a FORTRAN simulation program for the harmonic oscillator described in example 8.13.

8.13   If CSMP III is supported at your installation, develop a CSMP III simulation program for the harmonic oscillator described in example 8.13.

8.14   Compare the results of exercises 8.12 and 8.13. Explain, if possible, any differences noted.

References

8.1   ORD-SMITH, R. J., and STEPHENSON, J. *Computer Simulation of Continuous Systems*. Cambridge: Cambridge University Press, 1975.

8.2   PUGH, ALEXANDER, III. *Dynamo II User's Manual*. Cambridge, Mass.: MIT Press, 1973.

8.3   SPECKHART, H., and GREEN, W. H. *A Guide to Using CSMP*. Englewood Cliffs, N.J.: Prentice-Hall, 1976.

8.4   VICHNEVETSKY, R. *Simulation in Research and Development*. AMA Management Bulletin, no. 125, New York: American Management Association, 1969.

9

The design of simulation experiments

One of the most difficult problems encountered in a simulation study is validating the simulation model. The validation of a simulator refers to the proof that the simulator accurately reflects the behavior of the system being modeled when confronted with identical conditions. One approach used in validation is to observe the system being modeled under a set of controlled or measurable conditions. The simulator is then run under identical conditions, and its output is compared to the results obtained from the system being modeled. When the compared results agree within some given level of tolerance, the simulator is considered to be validated.

Whether this validation procedure actually proves the validity of the simulation model is open to question. The degree of confidence attached to such a validation decision is tempered by the number of experiments on which it is based, as well as by the range of parameter settings (conditions) considered in each experiment. To measure the degree of confidence that one might attach to the validation decision, as well as to reduce the number of experiments required to achieve some preselected minimum level of confidence, the well-known technique for the statistical design and analysis of experiments can be applied.

Statistical experimental design methodology is also useful in the execution phase. Once the simulator has been validated, the behavior of the system being modeled can be studied under a variety of conditions by exercising (running) the simulator. Experimental design methodology is useful in this phase to indicate the significance of simulated effects through the tests of various hypotheses and to minimize the number of simulation runs necessary to measure given effects.

For the purposes of this chapter the simulation model can be visualized as a black box. The input to the model can be specified in terms of parameters set at various levels. The simulator is run under these input conditions, and a measure of the system's performance under these conditions is produced. This black-box approach is shown in figure 9.1.

Figure 9.1
Simplified view of a simulator

The parameters that are set before any simulation run correspond to the factors that have an influence on the aspect of the system's performance being studied. As mentioned by Ferrari (9.2), the identification of the factors that influence a given performance measure is in general a very difficult task. The analyst has to rely on past experience, knowledge of the system, and in some cases intuition. Once the factors affecting a certain aspect of system performance have been determined, the allowable levels of each factor must be determined. In some cases the allowable levels are apparent, such as for an on-off type of parameter. In other cases the allowable levels must be determined carefully, so that the fewest possible parameter settings are used to explain the total range of variability in the performance measure.

The statistical design of experiments is a collection of principles that provide a procedure for designing experiments that maximize the information gained from each run of the simulator. This procedure also permits valid inferences about the effect on the performance variables of varying input parameters. The fundamental concepts of this methodology were formalized by R. A. Fisher (9.3). Most of this methodology was developed for agricultural and laboratory experiments, so the terminology that has evolved reflects those applications. The system variables that affect the measure of the system performance of interest are known as *factors*. The allowable settings of those factors are known as *levels*. A combination of a specific factor and level is called a *treatment*. The measure of system performance, stated as a function of the factors, is called the *response variable*. If the simulator is run repeatedly with the same treatment, the experiment has been *replicated*. We will use this

terminology in this chapter when we review some of the common experimental designs.

Completely randomized design

9.1   The completely randomized design is applicable when the response variable is affected by a single factor that may be set at various levels. The
order in which these levels are set for successive runs of the simulator is
completely random, hence the name *completely randomized design*.
The number of simulation runs (observations) for each level is determined by economic considerations (how many runs one can afford) and
by the degree of confidence desired in the inferences. With this design
the same number of observations is not required for each level. The key
to this design is that the treatments (factor levels) are assigned at random. This randomization tends to average out the effect of factors that
are not being considered or controlled in a given experiment.

Once a simulation experiment has been run, the data must be analyzed. To this end a mathematical model is developed to describe the
experiment. The validity of the model is then tested. The model for the
completely randomized design can be stated as

$$Y_{ij} = \mu + T_j + \epsilon_{ij},$$

where Y_{ij} is the ith observation of the jth treatment, μ is the common
"average" effect for all treatments, T_j is the additional effect due to the
particular treatment, and ϵ_{ij} is the random error associated with the ith
observation of the jth treatment. These error terms are usually considered independent, identically distributed normal random variables with
mean 0 and variance σ_ϵ^2. Furthermore, it is usually assumed that

$$\sum_{j=1}^{n} T_j = 0.$$

Example 9.1   Suppose that the system to be simulated is a single-
channel queueing system in which arrivals occur according to a Poisson
process with rate λ and service times are exponentially distributed with
service rate μ. Suppose further that it is desired to test the effect that
various queueing disciplines (FIFO, SIRO, LIFO) have on the number of
customers in the system at the end of one hour. The response variable
then is the number of customers in the system after one hour; the single
factor influencing this variable is the queueing discipline, and this factor
can assume three levels. To collect data using a completely randomized

design, it is necessary to randomly assign one of the queueing disciplines, run the simulation to simulate one hour of operation, and then count the number in the system. Then one of the two remaining disciplines is selected, and the experiment repeated. Finally, the third discipline is assigned and the experiment repeated. If multiple replications of the experiment are desired, the whole process is repeated as often as necessary. Care must be taken to randomize the treatment for each replication.

This example illustrates that the factors influencing a response variable need not be quantitative. The response variable, however, does have to be quantifiable.

To analyze the data obtained from a completely randomized design, one normally performs a one-way analysis of variance. This analysis involves partitioning the variability of the recorded data into components due to the treatments and due to random error. In particular, suppose that there are k levels of the factor, and that n_j replications were obtained on the jth treatment, giving a total of $\sum_{j=1}^{k} n_j = N$ observations. Then we have the following.

Total sum of squares

$$SS_{TOT} = \sum_{j=1}^{k} \sum_{i=1}^{n_j} Y_{ij}^2$$

Treatment sum of squares

$$SS_{TRT} = \sum_{j=1}^{k} n_j(\bar{Y}_{\cdot j} - \bar{Y}_{\cdot\cdot})^2$$

where

$$\bar{Y}_{\cdot j} = \sum_{i=1}^{n_j} \frac{Y_{ij}}{n_j} \quad \text{and} \quad \bar{Y}_{\cdot\cdot} = \sum_{j=1}^{k} \sum_{i=1}^{n_j} \frac{Y_{ij}}{N}$$

Error sum of squares

$$SS_{ERR} = \sum_{j=1}^{k} \sum_{i=1}^{n_j} (Y_{ij} - \bar{Y}_{\cdot j})^2$$

Mean sum of squares

$$SS_{MEAN} = N \bar{Y}_{\cdot\cdot}^2$$

The dot subscript indicates that the response variable is summed over the entire range of that subscript. One can readily verify that

$$SS_{TOT} = SS_{MEAN} + SS_{TRT} + SS_{ERR}$$

Each of these sums of squares is divided by the appropriate degrees of freedom to produce sample variances. The sample variance corresponding to the treatment effect is compared with the sample variance of the error using an F-test to assess the statistical significance of the difference in treatment effect. The particular hypothesis that is normally tested is

$$H_0 : T_j = 0, \qquad j = 1, \ldots, k$$

That is, all treatment effects are the same. The test statistic is $F = (SS_{TRT/(k-1)})/(SS_{ERR/(N-k)})$, and the hypothesis is rejected if

$$F > F_{\alpha,(k-1,N-k)}$$

Rejection of such a hypothesis indicates that there is a significant difference in the effects of one or more of the treatments. It does not tell which of the effects is different or how much it is different. Other tests are available to determine this difference. See for example, Hicks (9.4) for these tests.

Example 9.2 Suppose that in the experiment described in example 9.1, the simulator was run four times for each of the queueing disciplines and that the following observations for the response variable were noted.

| | | j | |
i	FIFO	SIRO	LIFO
1	50	32	80
2	48	18	73
3	61	64	54
4	58	72	63

Test the hypothesis that the queueing discipline has no effect on the number of customers in the system after one hour. From these data, it can be determined that

$$\bar{Y}_{.1} = 54.25$$

$$\bar{Y}_{.2} = 46.50$$

$$\bar{Y}_{.3} = 67.50$$

$$\bar{Y}_{..} = 56.08 \sum_{i=1}^{4} \sum_{j=1}^{3} Y_{ij}^2 = 41,131$$

And

$$SS_{TOT} = 41,131$$

$$SS_{MEAN} = 37,739.6$$

$$SS_{TRT} = 902.17$$

$$SS_{ERR} = 2489.23$$

with the result that $F = (902.17/2)/(2489.23/9) = 451.08/276.58 = 1.63$. If $\alpha = 0.05$, then $F_{0.05,(2, 9)} = 4.26$, and the hypothesis that the queueing discipline has no effect cannot be rejected.

Randomized complete block design

9.2   There are sometimes additional factors that cannot be controlled or whose effect on the response variable is of no interest to the analyst. If the effects of these secondary factors cannot be assumed to be constant or negligible, it is sometimes convenient to subtract these effects from consideration by using a randomized complete block design. This design accounts for the effect of a secondary factor by including a block effect in the model. For data collection a simulation run must be made for each level of the primary factor and for each level of the secondary factor, or block variable. The order in which the various levels of the primary factor are set is again random.

Example 9.3 Suppose that in the simulation experiment described in example 9.1 there are four different service rates, corresponding to shift changes in the real system. That is, one rate is in effect when the period between midnight and 6 a.m. is being simulated; a second rate for the period between 6 a.m. and noon; a third rate between noon and 6 p.m., and the fourth rate between 6 p.m. and midnight. This difference in service rates will affect the number of customers in the system after one hour of elapsed simulation time. However, if we are interested only in assessing the effect of queueing discipline, a randomized complete block design, with four blocks corresponding to the different servers might be appropriate. In this case three simulation runs for each of the four blocks would be required, with the order of the setting of the queueing discipline made at random for each of the blocks.

The mathematical model for the randomized complete block experiment is

$$Y_{ij} = \mu + B_i + T_j + \epsilon_{ij}$$

The B_i term accounts for the block effect, and the other terms are defined in the previous section. Analysis of the data obtained from a design of this type is usually accomplished by using a two-way analysis of variance. In addition to the components of variation listed in the previous section for the completely randomized design, a component due to the block effect can be isolated. If there are n blocks and k levels of the primary factor, the appropriate sums of squares can be calculated from

$$SS_{TOT} = \sum_{i=1}^{n} \sum_{j=1}^{k} Y_{ij}^2$$

$$SS_{MEAN} = nkY..^2$$

$$SS_{TRT} = \sum_{j=1}^{n} nY_{.j}^2 - nkY..^2$$

$$SS_{BLOCK} = \sum_{i=1}^{n} kY_{i.}^2 - nkY...^2$$

$$SS_{ERR} = SS_{TOT} - SS_{MEAN} - SS_{TRT} - SS_{BLK}$$

Thus the hypothesis that there is no difference in treatment effect is tested using the test statistic

$$F = SS_{TRT}/(k - 1)/SS_{ERR}/(n - 1)(k - 1)$$

and the hypothesis is rejected whenever

$$F > F_{1-\alpha,(k-1),(n-1)(k-1))}$$

The hypothesis can also be used to test that there is no difference in the effect of the blocks. This is generally not done, because it is frequently either of no interest or meaningless to the analyst.

Example 9.4   Consider the experiment described in example 9.3, and assume that the data listed in example 9.2 were collected for this experiment. That is, each row of the data listed as a replication in example 9.2 should be considered a block. Then

$$\overline{Y}_{.1} = 54.25 \qquad \overline{Y}_{1.} = 54.0$$

$$\overline{Y}_{.2} = 46.50 \qquad \overline{Y}_{2.} = 46.33$$

$$\overline{Y}_{.3} = 67.50 \qquad \overline{Y}_{3.} = 59.67$$

$$\overline{Y}_{4.} = 64.33$$

$$\overline{Y}.. = 56.08 \qquad \sum_{i=1}^{4} \sum_{j=1}^{3} Y_{ij}^2 = 41,131$$

and

$$SS_{TOT} = 41,131$$

$$SS_{MEAN} = 37,739.6$$

$$SS_{TRT} = 902.17$$

$$SS_{BLOCK} = 544.38$$

$$SS_{ERR} = 1944.85$$

with the results that

$$F = (902.17/2)/(1944.85/6)$$

$$= 451.08/324.14$$

$$= 1.39$$

But $F_{0.05,(2,\,6)} = 5.14$, and we are still not able to reject the hypothesis that the treatment effects are the same.

It may not be possible to apply each treatment to each block because of time or money constraints. When this is the case, a randomized incomplete design should be used. This design is described in the work by Hicks (9.4).

Factorial design

9.3 The two previous experimental designs concerned the effect of a single factor on the response variable. In most simulation experiments we must consider the effect of multiple factors on a given response variable. An experimental design known as the factorial design is then applicable. Consider an experiment in which a response variable Y is affected by two factors, A and B. For purposes of illustration, assume that factor A can assume three levels while factor B can assume two levels. Now the effect that factor A has on the response variable can be tested by holding factor B constant and making, say, n runs of the simulator at each of the three levels of factor A. The model used to test this effect then would be

$$Y_{ij} = \mu + A_j + \epsilon_{ij}$$

where i would vary from 1 to n and j would vary from 1 to 3. Similarly, the effect of factor β on the response variable could be tested by holding factor A constant and making n runs at each level of factor B. The model used to test this effect would be

$$Y_{ij} = \mu + B_j + \epsilon_{ij}$$

where again i would vary from 1 to n and j would vary from 1 to 2. Thus to test the main effects of factors A and B for this example would require $5n$ runs of the simulator.

In many cases the effect of multiple factors on a response variable is characterized not only by the effects of the individual factors but also by a synergistic or interaction effect caused by the simultaneous application of the factors. This means that we should test the effect of factor A, the effect of factor B, and the effect of the interaction of the two, AB. Unfortunately the one-at-a-time design does not allow testing of this interaction effect. This drawback, along with the inordinate number of runs required in one-at-a-time testing is the primary motivation for using the factorial design.

With the factorial design, $n/2$ simulation runs are made for each unique treatment combination, with the treatment combinations assigned in random order to each run. Therefore there are $3 \times 2 = 6$ unique treatment combinations, which require $3n$ simulation runs to acquire the same degree of precision as with the one-at-a-time design. As an illustration, assume that the levels of factor A are denoted 0, 1, and 2 while the levels of factor B are denoted 0 and 1. The unique treatment combinations are 00, 01, 10, 11, and 21, where the level of factor A is listed first in this notation. The $3n$ runs result in $3n/2$ observations of levels 0 and 1 for factor B, compared with n observations in each case with the one-at-a-time design. Thus we have achieved more information about the factors in fewer runs of the simulator. This simultaneous varying of the levels of the two factors allows us to isolate and to test for the effect of the interaction of the two factors.

Let us assume that the proper randomization has been done, and the data collected for $m = n/2$ replications of the experiment. The data can then be analyzed using the mathematical model

$$Y_{ijk} = \mu + A_i + B_j + (AB)_{ij} + \epsilon_{ijk}$$

where $i = 1, 2, 3; j = 1, 2;$ and $k = 1, 2, \ldots, m$. In this case A_i represents the effect of the ith level of factor A; B_j represents the effect of the jth level of factor B; $(AB)_{ij}$ represents the interaction effect of the ith level of factor A and the jth level of factor B, μ is the "mean" effect; and ϵ_{ijk} is the random error term.

In general, if factor A can assume a levels while B can assume b

levels, the appropriate sums of squares to test for the significance of the effects are

$$SS_{TOT} = \sum_{i=1}^{a} \sum_{j=1}^{b} \sum_{k=1}^{m} Y_{ijk}^2$$

$$SS_{MEAN} = mab \, \bar{Y}_{...}^2$$

$$SS_A = \sum_{i=1}^{a} mb\bar{Y}_{i..}^2 - mab\bar{Y}_{...}^2$$

$$SS_B = \sum_{j=1}^{b} ma\bar{Y}_{.j.}^2 - mab\bar{Y}_{...}^2$$

$$SS_{AB} = \sum_{i=1}^{a} \sum_{j=1}^{b} m\bar{Y}_{ij.}^2 - \sum_{i=1}^{a} mb\bar{Y}_{i..}^2 - \sum_{j=1}^{b} ma\bar{Y}_{.j.}^2 + mab\bar{Y}_{...}^2$$

$$SS_E = SS_{TOT} - SS_{MEAN} - SS_A - SS_B - SS_{AB}$$

where just as before, a quantity such as $\bar{Y}_{.j.}$ means to average over the dotted subscripts.

Now to test for the various effects, we need to determine an estimate for the variances and form the F-ratios as before.

To test A

$$F = \frac{SS_A/(a-1)}{SS_E/ab(m-1)}, \quad \text{reject if } F > F_{1-\alpha,(a-1,ab(m-1))}$$

To test B

$$F = \frac{SS_B/(b-1)}{SS_E/ab(m-1)}, \quad \text{reject if } F > F_{1-\alpha,(b-1,ab(m-1))}$$

To test AB

$$F = \frac{SS_{AB}/(a-1)(b-1)}{SS_E/ab(m-1)}, \quad \text{reject if } F > F_{1-\alpha,((a-1)(b-1),ab(m-1))}$$

These results are readily extended to more than two factors. As the number of factors grow, so do the ineraction effects that can be tested. Unfortunately, three- and four-way interactions have very little meaning and are rarely tested.

Example 9.5 Consider again a queueing system in which arrivals occur according to a Poisson process and service times are exponentially distributed. Suppose that the manager of the system is investigating the feasibility of hiring a second server and simultaneously wants to compare the relative efficiency of two queueing disciplines, FIFO and SIRO. The quantity of interest is the number of customers in the system at the end of one hour of simulated time.

This experiment could be readily handled using a factorial design. Call the factor "number of servers" S, with levels 1 and 2, and the factor "queueing discipline" Q, with levels FIFO and SIRO. There are four treatment combinations to consider.

Suppose that two replications of the experiment were obtained and the data in the following table were recorded.

Factor S	Factor Q	
	FIFO	*SIRO*
1	62	48
	71	47
2	32	28
	22	28

Then

$$SS_{TOT} = 16531.0$$

$$SS_{MEAN} = 14{,}365.125$$

$$SS_Q = 153.125$$

$$SS_S = 1711.25$$

$$SS_{SQ} = 210.125$$

$$SS_{ERR} = 91.501$$

To test the various effects, we use the following.

To test Q

$$F = \frac{(153.125/1)}{(91.501/4)} = 6.69$$

To test S

$$F = \frac{(1711.125/1)}{(91.501/4)} = 74.8$$

To test SQ

$$F = \frac{(210.125/1)}{(91.501/4)} = 9.18$$

Then if $\alpha = 0.05$, $F_{0.05,(1,4)} = 7.71$, and we would conclude that the number of servers has an effect on the response variable, as does the interaction of the number of servers and the queueing discipline. There are insufficient data to prove that the queueing discipline alone has an effect.

Many simulation experiments involve a relatively large number of factors. Experiments of this type require a simulation run for each unique treatment combination to be considered one replication of the experiment. For example, suppose we are conducting a simulation experiment to investigate the effect of three factors, A, B, and C, on a response variable. Suppose further that factor A can assume three levels, factor B two levels, and factor C four levels. Then a total of $2 \times 3 \times 4 = 24$ simulation runs are required to be considered one replication. The effects to be tested include the main factors A, B, and C; the two-way interactions AB, AC, and BC; and the three-way interaction ABC. As the number of factors and levels per factor increase, the number of simulation runs required to be considered a complete replication can become intolerably large. This has led to the development and use of fractional replications.

The feature that allows the satisfactory use of fractional replications in factorial experiments is that in many applications, the higher-order (greater than two) interaction terms have little or no meaning to the analyst. These higher-order interaction terms can be omitted from the model, and their contribution can be lumped into the random error term. This confounding of the interaction effects with the random error term descreases the number of simulation runs necessary to test for the desired effects. The analyst must decide before the experiment which of the interaction effects to combine with the error term and design the experiment accordingly. The details behind the design of a fractional replication of a factorial experiment are too lengthy to include here. Hicks gives an excellent treatment using fractional replications (9.4).

Optimization of response surfaces

9.4   A response variable is a quantification of the aspect of the system's performance of interest in a simulation experiment and can be thought of as the output of the simulation experiment Alternatively, it can be visualized as a function of the input parameters (factors). It is of interest in some simulation experiments to determine which input parameter settings optimize (either maximize or minimize) the response variable. We will survey some of the more common techniques that have been employed in this optimization process. Farrell, McCall, and Russell (9.1) list a total of 11 such optimization techniques and compare them with regard to convergence, nearness to optimum, and running time. This work should be consulted for more details, because we will only survey some of the more common techniques.

If the response variable Y is expressed as a function of n factors, call them $X_1, X_2, \ldots, X_n$, represented as $Y = f(S_1, X_2, \ldots, X_n)$, then the plot of the response variable over the range of the input parameters can be thought of as a surface (hyperplane) in an $(n + 1)$-dimensional space. Such a surface is called a *response surface*. The optimization problem then consists of finding the highest (lowest) point on this surface. This idea of a response surface can be readily interpreted for $n = 2$ [$Y = f(X_1, X_2)$], illustrated in figure 9.2. Of course, visualization in higher than three dimensions becomes more difficult, but the idea is the same. We start from some initial point on the surface and through some algorithmic procedure move to the maximum (minimum) point on the surface.

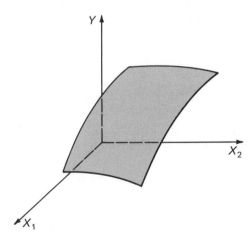

Figure 9.2
A three-dimensional response surface

Heuristic search

9.4.1   The heuristic search technique, according to Farrell, McCall, and Russell (9.1), is probably the most common of the techniques used in optimizing response surfaces. It also is the least sophisticated mathematically and can be thought of as a "seat of the pants" approach. The starting and stopping points are determined by the analyst based on previous experience with the system being simulated. The input parameters (factors) are set at levels that appear reasonable to the analyst, a simulation run is made with the factors set at those levels, and the value of the response variable is noted. If it appears to be maximum (minimum) to the analyst, the experiment is stopped. Otherwise the parameter settings are changed, and another run is made. This process continues until the analyst is satisfied that the output has been optimized. Suffice it to say that if the analyst is not intimately familiar with the process being simulated, this procedure can turn into a blind search and can expend an inordinate amount of time and computer resources without producing corresponding results.

Complete enumeration

9.4.2   The complete enumeration technique, although not applicable to all cases, does yield the optimal value of the response variable. All the factors must assume a finite number of values for this technique to be applicable. For such a system a complete factorial experiment is run, and the value of the response variable at each of the treatment combinations is noted. Normally a number of replications of the basic experiment are made, and the output values averaged over these replications at each of the treatment combinations. The analyst can attach some degree of confidence to the determined optimal point when using this procedure. Although this technique yields the optimal point, it has a serious drawback. If the number of factors or levels per factor is very large, the number of simulation runs required to find the optimal point can be exceedingly large. For example, suppose that an experiment is conducted with three factors; one can assume three levels, the second can assume four levels, and the third can assume five levels. Suppose further that five replications are desired to provide the proper degree of confidence. Then a total of $5(3 \times 4 \times 5) = 300$ runs of the simulator would be required to isolate the optimal point. If, on the other hand, there are ten factors, each of which can assume only two levels, a total of $5(2^{10}) = 5(1024) = 5120$ simulation runs would be necessary for the five replications. Thus this technique should be used only when the number of unique treatment combinations is relatively small.

Random search

9.4.3   The random search technique is similar to the complete enumeration technique except that a simulation run is not made at every unique treatment combination. Instead a set of treatment combinations is selected at random, and simulation runs are made at these points. The treatment combination of this set that yields the maximum (minimum) value of the response variable is taken to be the optimal point. This procedure reduces the number of simulation runs required to yield an "optimal" result; however, there is no guarantee that the point found is actually the optimal point. Of course, the more points selected, the more likely one is to achieve the true optimal point. Thus there is a trade-off between the number of runs one is willing to make and the likelihood that the value found is the true optimum. Note that the requirement that each factor assume only a finite number of values, inherent in the complete enumeration scheme, is not a requirement in the random search scheme. Just as with the complete enumeration scheme, replications can be made on those treatment combinations selected to increase the confidence in the optimal point. The trade-off is that it may be better to devote the simulation runs used in replicating to examining more points. The question which is the better strategy, replicating a few points or looking at a single observation on more points, has not been answered.

Steepest ascent (descent)

9.4.4   The steepest ascent (descent) method uses a fundamental result from calculus — that the gradient (vector of first partial derivatives) points in the direction of the maximum increase of a function — to determine how the initial settings of the parameters should be changed to yield an optimal value of the response variable. To visualize this method, consider a response surface in three dimensions, $Y = f(X_1, X_2)$, as illustrated in figure 9.3.

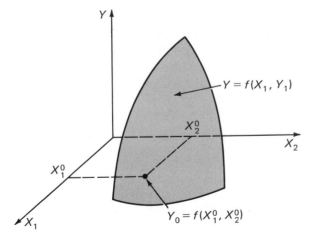

Figure 9.3
The method of steepest ascent (descent)

Suppose that some initial starting values for the two parameters have been determined. By running the simulator with parameter settings in the "neighborhood" of the initial values X_1^0 and X_2^0, it is possible to obtain an estimate of the shape of the response surface in that vicinity using the method of least squares. For example, assume that in the simple two-factor model, the vicinity of the initial point on the response surface can be postulated to be $Y = B_0 + B_1X_1 + B_2X_2$. To estimate the values of the coefficients B_0, B_1, and B_2, one needs at least three points. Thus the simulator would be run using at least three points in the vicinity of (X_1^0, X_2^0). Using the output values from these points and applying least squares, one can obtain an estimate of the shape of the response surface, $\hat{Y} = \beta_0 + \beta_1X_1 + \beta_2X_2$. The gradient to this surface at the point (X_1^0, X_2^0) is grad $\hat{Y} = (\partial\hat{Y}/\partial X_1, \partial\hat{Y}/\partial X_2) = (\beta_1, \beta_2)$. The direction in which the values for X_1 and X_2 should be changed is along a line given by

$$(X_2^1 - X_2^0) = \frac{\beta_1}{\beta_2}(X_1^1 - X_1^0)$$

The magnitude of the change is up to the analyst; the gradient gives only the direction. A similar procedure is followed for the vicinity of the point (X_1^1, X_2^1) to determine the direction by which the parameters should be changed for the next step. The process is then continued until no further change is indicated.

This description of the steepest ascent (descent) method is admittedly very brief, and many important factors have been omitted. For example, the goodness of fit of the model should be tested at each step, and a higher-order model used if the fit is not good enough. A procedure for the selection of starting values and the selection of points in the vicinity of the initial estimates has been studied. Other factors of interest for this method are the design of the experiment to collect the data in the vicinity of each of the points and the magnitude of the change required in the parameters at each step. These factors, although largely ignored in this survey of the method, must be considered before it is used. See Hicks (9.4) and Farrell, McCall, and Russell (9.1) for details.

Note that the method of steepest ascent (descent) is guaranteed to find the maximum (minimum) not of the entire response surface but a local maximum (minimum). Whether the two points coincide depends on the application and the incrementing values that are used. This may be a matter of some concern and should be kept in mind.

Coordinate or single-variable search

9.4.5   The single-variable search technique is similar to the steepest ascent technique in that some initial point on the response surface is chosen, and movement toward the optimal point is made through interative adjustments of the parameter levels. In the steepest ascent method the parameters are adjusted simultaneously in the direction of the gradient to an estimate of the response surface at the initial point; in this method, on the other hand, a single parameter is adjusted at each step. For example, consider the simple two-factor model $Y = f(X_1, X_2)$. With the coordinate search method an initial point (X_1^0, X_2^0) would be chosen, and a simulation run made with these parameter settings. Two additional runs would be made with values of $(X_1^0 + \epsilon, X_2^0)$ and $(X_1^0 - \epsilon, X_2^0)$. The values of the response variable would be compared. If neither $(f(X_1^0 + \epsilon, X_2^0)$ nor $f(X_1^0 - \epsilon, X_2^0)$ is greater than $f(X_1^0, X_2^0)$, the process would be stopped in the X_1 direction and a similar procedure followed for X_2. Otherwise the parameter setting for X_1 would be adjusted in the direction of increasing response until no further increase is possible by varying only X_1. This would yield a point (X_1^1, X_2^0). A similar procedure is then followed for X_2. That is, it is varied in the direction of increasing response until no further response is possible.

This technique, according to Farrell, McCall, and Russell (9.1), is useful only when the response surface is unimodal, and even then it is not always successful. Since the shape of a given response surface is not known beforehand, it does not appear to have much applicability. In fact, for the same effort expended, one could use the gradient search scheme.

Summary

In this chapter we have surveyed some of the more common experimental designs that seem to have application to simulation studies, both in the validation and the execution phases of the process. Many alternate designs have been omitted, since an in-depth coverage of all designs that have been proposed would require a complete and rather voluminous textbook by itself. Certain statistical experimental designs were mentioned to indicate their utility in simulation studies rather than to provide the analyst with the level of expertise to design an experiment.

In the last section we surveyed some of the approaches used in optimizing response surfaces. Five alternate techniques were viewed. The work by Farrell, McCall, and Russell (9.1) contains an excellent description of these five techniques as well as six additional techniques. The work by Hicks (9.4) contains an illustrative example of the method of steepest descent. Many other excellent treatments of response surface optimization exist in the literature.

Exercises

9.1   A simulation experiment to test the effect on a response variable by a single factor was conducted using a completely randomized design. Two replications at each of three levels of the factor were obtained, and the following data recorded.

Level	Response
0	19.5, 20.6
1	28.1, 31.6
2	37.4, 41.8

Test the significance of the effect of the treatments.

9.2   Two factors are believed to have an effect on a given response variable. The two factors can each assume two levels. Discuss the design of a simulation experiment that could be used to test the effects. Include in your discussion the model used to test the data, the effects to be tested, and the assignment of treatment combinations to the simulation runs. What advantage would be gained through replication of the experiment?

9.3   Describe a system for which the randomized complete block design might be useful. Why could one not use the factorial arrangement to analyze the system in lieu of the block arrangement?

9.4   Discuss the five optimization techniques described in section 9.5 in terms of
  a. Relative efficiency (number of simulation runs required)
  b. Optimality of the result obtained
  c. Ease of use

9.5   Suppose you were involved in a simulation project that required optimization of a response variable. Which technique would you use? List some of the factors that led to your decision.

9.6   Paging is a common technique for implementing virtual memory. In paging the physical memory of a computer system is subdivided into fixed-size page frames. A program submitted to the system is likewise subdivided into pages of like size. The illusion of unlimited memory is then created by requiring only those pages of a program that are likely to be referenced soon to actually reside in memory. Other pages are retained on auxiliary storage and loaded only when referenced. A measure of the efficiency of a paging system is the page fault rate — the relative frequency with which references are made to a page not in memory. Investigate this idea of paging, and determine some factors that may affect the page fault rate.

9.7   Using the factors determined in exercise 9.6, describe a simulation experiment by which you could test those effects.

9.8   Consider the response surface given by $f(x,y) = \sin(x + y); 0 \le x \le 5, 0 \le y \le 5$. Use the random search technique with 10 sample values of (x,y) drawn at random from the 36 integral pair values to find the maximum of $f(x,y)$.

9.9   Use the complete enumeration technique (x and y can take only integer values) to find the maximum of the response surface given in exercise 9.8. Does the value agree with that obtained in exercise 9.8? Should it agree?

9.10   Use the method of steepest ascent to find the maximum of the response surface given in exercise 9.8. Start with $x = 2, y = 2$.

9.11.   Use the coordinate search technique to find the maximum of the response surface given in exercise 9.8. Start with $x = 2, y = 2$.

9.12   Compare the techniques used in exercises 9.8–9.11 in terms of computation efficiency and results obtained.

References

9.1   FARRELL, W., McCALL, C. H., and RUSSELL, E. C. *Optimization Techniques for Computerized Simulation Models.* Technical Report 1200-4-75. Los Angeles: CACI, June 1975.

9.2   FERRARI, D. *Computer Systems Performance Evaluation.* Englewood Cliffs, N.J.: Prentice-Hall, 1978.

9.3   FISHER, R. A. *The Design of Experiments.* Edinburgh: Oliver and Boyd, 1935.

9.4   HICKS, C. R. *Fundamental Concepts in the Design of Experiments.* New York: Holt, Rinehart and Winston, 1973.

Appendix tables

$$F(x;\lambda) = \sum_{k=0}^{x} e^{-\lambda} \frac{\lambda^k}{k!}$$

λ \ x	0	1	2	3	4	5	6	7	8	9
0.02	0.980	1.000								
0.04	0.961	0.999	1.000							
0.06	0.942	0.998	1.000							
0.08	0.923	0.997	1.000							
0.10	0.905	0.995	1.000							
0.15	0.861	0.990	0.999	1.000						
0.20	0.819	0.982	0.999	1.000						
0.25	0.779	0.974	0.998	1.000						
0.30	0.741	0.963	0.996	1.000						
0.35	0.705	0.951	0.994	1.000						
0.40	0.670	0.938	0.992	0.999	1.000					
0.45	0.638	0.925	0.989	0.999	1.000					
0.50	0.607	0.910	0.986	0.998	1.000					
0.55	0.577	0.894	0.982	0.998	1.000					
0.60	0.549	0.878	0.977	0.997	1.000					
0.65	0.522	0.861	0.972	0.996	0.999	1.000				
0.70	0.497	0.844	0.966	0.994	0.999	1.000				
0.75	0.472	0.827	0.959	0.993	0.999	1.000				
0.80	0.449	0.809	0.953	0.991	0.999	1.000				
0.85	0.427	0.791	0.945	0.989	0.998	1.000				
0.90	0.407	0.772	0.937	0.987	0.998	1.000				
0.95	0.387	0.754	0.929	0.984	0.997	1.000				
1.00	0.368	0.736	0.920	0.981	0.996	0.999	1.000			
1.1	0.333	0.699	0.900	0.974	0.995	0.999	1.000			
1.2	0.301	0.663	0.879	0.966	0.992	0.998	1.000			
1.3	0.273	0.627	0.857	0.957	0.989	0.998	1.000			
1.4	0.247	0.592	0.833	0.946	0.986	0.997	0.999	1.000		
1.5	0.223	0.558	0.809	0.934	0.981	0.996	0.999	1.000		
1.6	0.202	0.525	0.783	0.921	0.976	0.994	0.999	1.000		
1.7	0.183	0.493	0.757	0.907	0.970	0.992	0.998	1.000		
1.8	0.165	0.463	0.731	0.891	0.964	0.990	0.997	0.999	1.000	
1.9	0.150	0.434	0.704	0.875	0.956	0.987	0.997	0.999	1.000	
2.0	0.135	0.406	0.677	0.857	0.947	0.983	0.995	0.999	1.000	

Table 1

Poisson distribution function

λ \ x	0	1	2	3	4	5	6	7	8	9
2.2	0.111	0.355	0.623	0.819	0.928	0.975	0.993	0.998	1.000	
2.4	0.091	0.308	0.570	0.779	0.904	0.964	0.988	0.997	0.999	1.000
2.6	0.074	0.267	0.518	0.736	0.877	0.951	0.983	0.995	0.999	1.000
2.8	0.061	0.231	0.469	0.692	0.848	0.935	0.976	0.992	0.998	0.999
3.0	0.050	0.199	0.423	0.647	0.815	0.916	0.966	0.988	0.996	0.999
3.2	0.041	0.171	0.380	0.603	0.781	0.895	0.955	0.983	0.994	0.998
3.4	0.033	0.147	0.340	0.558	0.744	0.871	0.942	0.977	0.992	0.997
3.6	0.027	0.126	0.303	0.515	0.706	0.844	0.927	0.969	0.988	0.996
3.8	0.022	0.107	0.269	0.473	0.668	0.816	0.909	0.960	0.984	0.994
4.0	0.018	0.092	0.238	0.433	0.629	0.785	0.889	0.949	0.979	0.992
4.2	0.015	0.078	0.210	0.395	0.590	0.753	0.867	0.936	0.972	0.989
4.4	0.012	0.066	0.185	0.359	0.551	0.720	0.844	0.921	0.964	0.985
4.6	0.010	0.056	0.163	0.326	0.513	0.686	0.818	0.905	0.955	0.980
4.8	0.008	0.048	0.143	0.294	0.476	0.651	0.791	0.887	0.944	0.975
5.0	0.007	0.040	0.125	0.265	0.440	0.616	0.762	0.867	0.932	0.968
5.2	0.006	0.034	0.109	0.238	0.406	0.581	0.732	0.845	0.918	0.960
5.4	0.005	0.029	0.095	0.213	0.373	0.546	0.702	0.822	0.903	0.951
5.6	0.004	0.024	0.082	0.191	0.342	0.512	0.670	0.797	0.886	0.941
5.8	0.003	0.021	0.072	0.170	0.313	0.478	0.638	0.771	0.867	0.929
6.0	0.002	0.017	0.062	0.151	0.285	0.446	0.606	0.744	0.847	0.916

λ	10	11	12	13	14	15	16
2.8	1.000						
3.0	1.000						
3.2	1.000						
3.4	0.999	1.000					
3.6	0.999	1.000					
3.8	0.998	0.999	1.000				
4.0	0.997	0.999	1.000				
4.2	0.996	0.999	1.000				
4.4	0.994	0.998	0.999	1.000			
4.6	0.992	0.997	0.999	1.000			
4.8	0.990	0.996	0.999	1.000			
5.0	0.986	0.995	0.998	0.999	1.000		
5.2	0.982	0.993	0.997	0.999	1.000		
5.4	0.977	0.990	0.996	0.999	1.000		
5.6	0.972	0.988	0.995	0.998	0.999	1.000	
5.8	0.965	0.984	0.993	0.997	0.999	1.000	
6.0	0.957	0.980	0.991	0.996	0.999	0.999	1.000

Table 1 — *Continued*
Poisson distribution function

x λ	0	1	2	3	4	5	6	7	8	9
6.2	0.002	0.015	0.054	0.134	0.259	0.414	0.574	0.716	0.826	0.902
6.4	0.002	0.012	0.046	0.119	0.235	0.384	0.542	0.687	0.803	0.886
6.6	0.001	0.010	0.040	0.105	0.213	0.355	0.511	0.658	0.780	0.869
6.8	0.001	0.009	0.034	0.093	0.192	0.327	0.480	0.628	0.755	0.850
7.0	0.001	0.007	0.030	0.082	0.173	0.301	0.450	0.599	0.729	0.830
7.2	0.001	0.006	0.025	0.072	0.156	0.276	0.420	0.569	0.703	0.810
7.4	0.001	0.005	0.022	0.063	0.140	0.253	0.392	0.539	0.676	0.788
7.6	0.001	0.004	0.019	0.055	0.125	0.231	0.365	0.510	0.648	0.765
7.8	0.000	0.004	0.016	0.048	0.112	0.210	0.338	0.481	0.620	0.741
8.0	0.000	0.003	0.014	0.042	0.100	0.191	0.313	0.453	0.593	0.717
8.5	0.000	0.002	0.009	0.030	0.074	0.150	0.256	0.386	0.523	0.653
9.0	0.000	0.001	0.006	0.021	0.055	0.116	0.207	0.324	0.456	0.587
9.5	0.000	0.001	0.004	0.015	0.040	0.089	0.165	0.269	0.392	0.522
10.0	0.000	0.000	0.003	0.010	0.029	0.067	0.130	0.220	0.333	0.458

	10	11	12	13	14	15	16	17	18	19
6.2	0.949	0.975	0.989	0.995	0.998	0.999	1.000			
6.4	0.939	0.969	0.986	0.994	0.997	0.999	1.000			
6.6	0.927	0.963	0.982	0.992	0.997	0.999	0.999	1.000		
6.8	0.915	0.955	0.978	0.990	0.996	0.998	0.999	1.000		
7.0	0.901	0.947	0.973	0.987	0.994	0.998	0.999	1.000		
7.2	0.887	0.937	0.967	0.984	0.993	0.997	0.999	0.999	1.000	
7.4	0.871	0.926	0.961	0.980	0.991	0.996	0.998	0.999	1.000	
7.6	0.854	0.915	0.954	0.976	0.989	0.995	0.998	0.999	1.000	
7.8	0.835	0.902	0.945	0.971	0.986	0.993	0.997	0.999	1.000	
8.0	0.816	0.888	0.936	0.966	0.983	0.992	0.996	0.998	0.999	1.000
8.5	0.763	0.849	0.909	0.949	0.973	0.986	0.993	0.997	0.999	0.999
9.0	0.706	0.803	0.876	0.926	0.959	0.978	0.989	0.995	0.998	0.999
9.5	0.645	0.752	0.836	0.898	0.940	0.967	0.982	0.991	0.996	0.998
10.0	0.583	0.697	0.792	0.864	0.917	0.951	0.973	0.986	0.993	0.997

	20	21	22
8.5	1.000		
9.0	1.000		
9.5	0.999	1.000	
10.0	0.998	0.999	1.000

Table 1 — *Continued*
Poisson distribution function

λ \ x	0	1	2	3	4	5	6	7	8	9
10.5	0.000	0.000	0.002	0.007	0.021	0.050	0.102	0.179	0.279	0.397
11.0	0.000	0.000	0.001	0.005	0.015	0.038	0.079	0.143	0.232	0.341
11.5	0.000	0.000	0.001	0.003	0.011	0.028	0.060	0.114	0.191	0.289
12.0	0.000	0.000	0.001	0.002	0.008	0.020	0.046	0.090	0.155	0.242
12.5	0.000	0.000	0.000	0.002	0.005	0.015	0.035	0.070	0.125	0.201
13.0	0.000	0.000	0.000	0.001	0.004	0.011	0.026	0.054	0.100	0.166
13.5	0.000	0.000	0.000	0.001	0.003	0.008	0.019	0.041	0.079	0.135
14.0	0.000	0.000	0.000	0.000	0.002	0.006	0.014	0.032	0.062	0.109
14.5	0.000	0.000	0.000	0.000	0.001	0.004	0.010	0.024	0.048	0.088
15.0	0.000	0.000	0.000	0.000	0.001	0.003	0.008	0.018	0.037	0.070

λ \ x	10	11	12	13	14	15	16	17	18	19
10.5	0.521	0.639	0.742	0.825	0.888	0.932	0.960	0.978	0.988	0.994
11.0	0.460	0.579	0.689	0.781	0.854	0.907	0.944	0.968	0.982	0.991
11.5	0.402	0.520	0.633	0.733	0.815	0.878	0.924	0.954	0.974	0.986
12.0	0.347	0.462	0.576	0.682	0.772	0.844	0.899	0.937	0.963	0.979
12.5	0.297	0.406	0.519	0.628	0.725	0.806	0.869	0.916	0.948	0.969
13.0	0.252	0.353	0.463	0.573	0.675	0.764	0.835	0.890	0.930	0.957
13.5	0.211	0.304	0.409	0.518	0.623	0.718	0.798	0.861	0.908	0.942
14.0	0.176	0.260	0.358	0.464	0.570	0.669	0.756	0.827	0.883	0.923
14.5	0.145	0.220	0.311	0.413	0.518	0.619	0.711	0.790	0.853	0.901
15.0	0.118	0.185	0.268	0.363	0.466	0.568	0.664	0.749	0.819	0.875

λ \ x	20	21	22	23	24	25	26	27	28	29
10.5	0.997	0.999	0.999	1.000						
11.0	0.995	0.998	0.999	1.000						
11.5	0.992	0.996	0.998	0.999	1.000					
12.0	0.988	0.994	0.997	0.999	0.999	1.000				
12.5	0.983	0.991	0.995	0.998	0.999	0.999	1.000			
13.0	0.975	0.986	0.992	0.996	0.998	0.999	1.000			
13.5	0.965	0.980	0.989	0.994	0.997	0.998	0.999	1.000		
14.0	0.952	0.971	0.983	0.991	0.995	0.997	0.999	0.999	1.000	
14.5	0.936	0.960	0.976	0.986	0.992	0.996	0.998	0.999	0.999	1.000
15.0	0.917	0.947	0.967	0.981	0.989	0.994	0.997	0.998	0.999	1.000

Table 1 — Continued
Poisson distribution function

λ \ x	4	5	6	7	8	9	10	11	12	13
16	0.000	0.001	0.004	0.010	0.022	0.043	0.077	0.127	0.193	0.275
17	0.000	0.001	0.002	0.005	0.013	0.026	0.049	0.085	0.135	0.201
18	0.000	0.000	0.001	0.003	0.007	0.015	0.030	0.055	0.092	0.143
19	0.000	0.000	0.001	0.002	0.004	0.009	0.018	0.035	0.061	0.098
20	0.000	0.000	0.000	0.001	0.002	0.005	0.011	0.021	0.039	0.066
21	0.000	0.000	0.000	0.000	0.001	0.003	0.006	0.013	0.025	0.043
22	0.000	0.000	0.000	0.000	0.001	0.002	0.004	0.008	0.015	0.028
23	0.000	0.000	0.000	0.000	0.000	0.001	0.002	0.004	0.009	0.017
24	0.000	0.000	0.000	0.000	0.000	0.000	0.001	0.003	0.005	0.011
25	0.000	0.000	0.000	0.000	0.000	0.000	0.001	0.001	0.003	0.006

	14	15	16	17	18	19	20	21	22	23
16	0.368	0.467	0.566	0.659	0.742	0.812	0.868	0.911	0.942	0.963
17	0.281	0.371	0.468	0.564	0.655	0.736	0.805	0.861	0.905	0.937
18	0.208	0.287	0.375	0.469	0.562	0.651	0.731	0.799	0.855	0.899
19	0.150	0.215	0.292	0.378	0.469	0.561	0.647	0.725	0.793	0.849
20	0.105	0.157	0.221	0.297	0.381	0.470	0.559	0.644	0.721	0.787
21	0.072	0.111	0.163	0.227	0.302	0.384	0.471	0.558	0.640	0.716
22	0.048	0.077	0.117	0.169	0.232	0.306	0.387	0.472	0.556	0.637
23	0.031	0.052	0.082	0.123	0.175	0.238	0.310	0.389	0.472	0.555
24	0.020	0.034	0.056	0.087	0.128	0.180	0.243	0.314	0.392	0.473
25	0.012	0.022	0.038	0.060	0.092	0.134	0.185	0.247	0.318	0.394

	24	25	26	27	28	29	30	31	32	33
16	0.978	0.987	0.993	0.996	0.998	0.999	0.999	1.000		
17	0.959	0.975	0.985	0.991	0.995	0.997	0.999	0.999	1.000	
18	0.932	0.955	0.972	0.983	0.990	0.994	0.997	0.998	0.999	1.000
19	0.893	0.927	0.951	0.969	0.980	0.988	0.993	0.996	0.998	0.999
20	0.843	0.888	0.922	0.948	0.966	0.978	0.987	0.992	0.995	0.997
21	0.782	0.838	0.883	0.917	0.944	0.963	0.976	0.985	0.991	0.994
22	0.712	0.777	0.832	0.877	0.913	0.940	0.959	0.973	0.983	0.989
23	0.635	0.708	0.772	0.827	0.873	0.908	0.936	0.956	0.971	0.981
24	0.554	0.632	0.704	0.768	0.823	0.868	0.904	0.932	0.953	0.969
25	0.473	0.553	0.629	0.700	0.763	0.818	0.863	0.900	0.929	0.950

	34	35	36	37	38	39	40	41	42	43
19	0.999	1.000								
20	0.999	0.999	1.000							
21	0.997	0.998	0.999	0.999	1.000					
22	0.994	0.996	0.998	0.999	0.999	1.000				
23	0.998	0.993	0.996	0.997	0.999	0.999	1.000			
24	0.979	0.987	0.992	0.995	0.997	0.998	0.999	0.999		
25	0.966	0.978	0.985	0.991	0.994	0.997	0.998	0.999	1.000	

Table 1 — *Continued*
Poisson distribution function

z	0.00	0.01	0.02	0.03	0.04	0.05	0.06	0.07	0.08	0.09
0.0	0.5000	0.5040	0.5080	0.5120	0.5160	0.5199	0.5239	0.5279	0.5319	0.5359
0.1	0.5398	0.5438	0.5478	0.5517	0.5557	0.5596	0.5636	0.5675	0.5714	0.5753
0.2	0.5793	0.5832	0.5871	0.5910	0.5948	0.5987	0.6026	0.6064	0.6103	0.6141
0.3	0.6179	0.6217	0.6255	0.6293	0.6331	0.6368	0.6406	0.6443	0.6480	0.6517
0.4	0.6554	0.6591	0.6628	0.6664	0.6700	0.6736	0.6772	0.6808	0.6844	0.6879
0.5	0.6915	0.6950	0.6985	0.7019	0.7054	0.7088	0.7123	0.7157	0.7190	0.7224
0.6	0.7257	0.7291	0.7324	0.7357	0.7389	0.7422	0.7454	0.7486	0.7517	0.7549
0.7	0.7580	0.7611	0.7642	0.7673	0.7704	0.7734	0.7764	0.7794	0.7823	0.7852
0.8	0.7881	0.7910	0.7939	0.7967	0.7995	0.8023	0.8051	0.8078	0.8106	0.8133
0.9	0.8159	0.8186	0.8212	0.8238	0.8264	0.8289	0.8315	0.8340	0.8365	0.8389
1.0	0.8413	0.8438	0.8461	0.8485	0.8508	0.8531	0.8554	0.8577	0.8599	0.8621
1.1	0.8643	0.8665	0.8686	0.8708	0.8729	0.8749	0.8770	0.8790	0.8810	0.8830
1.2	0.8849	0.8869	0.8888	0.8907	0.8925	0.8944	0.8962	0.8980	0.8997	0.9015
1.3	0.9032	0.9049	0.9066	0.9082	0.9099	0.9115	0.9131	0.9147	0.9162	0.9177
1.4	0.9192	0.9207	0.9222	0.9236	0.9251	0.9265	0.9279	0.9292	0.9306	0.9319
1.5	0.9332	0.9345	0.9357	0.9370	0.9382	0.9394	0.9406	0.9418	0.9429	0.9441
1.6	0.9452	0.9463	0.9474	0.9484	0.9495	0.9505	0.9515	0.9525	0.9535	0.9545
1.7	0.9554	0.9564	0.9573	0.9582	0.9591	0.9599	0.9608	0.9616	0.9625	0.9633
1.8	0.9641	0.9649	0.9656	0.9664	0.9671	0.9678	0.9686	0.9693	0.9699	0.9706
1.9	0.9713	0.9719	0.9726	0.9732	0.9738	0.9744	0.9750	0.9756	0.9761	0.9767
2.0	0.9772	0.9778	0.9783	0.9788	0.9793	0.9798	0.9803	0.9808	0.9812	0.9817
2.1	0.9821	0.9826	0.9830	0.9834	0.9838	0.9842	0.9846	0.9850	0.9854	0.9857
2.2	0.9861	0.9864	0.9868	0.9871	0.9875	0.9878	0.9881	0.9884	0.9887	0.9890
2.3	0.9893	0.9896	0.9898	0.9901	0.9904	0.9906	0.9909	0.9911	0.9913	0.9916
2.4	0.9918	0.9920	0.9922	0.9925	0.9927	0.9929	0.9931	0.9932	0.9934	0.9936
2.5	0.9938	0.9940	0.9941	0.9943	0.9945	0.9946	0.9948	0.9949	0.9951	0.9952
2.6	0.9953	0.9955	9.9956	0.9957	0.9959	0.9960	0.9961	0.9962	0.9963	0.9964
2.7	0.9965	0.9966	0.9967	0.9968	0.9969	0.9970	0.9971	0.9972	0.9973	0.9974
2.8	0.9974	0.9975	0.9976	0.9977	0.9977	0.9978	0.9979	0.9979	0.9980	0.9981
2.9	0.9981	0.9982	0.9982	0.9983	0.9984	0.9984	0.9985	0.9985	0.9986	0.9986
3.0	0.9987	0.9987	0.9987	0.9988	0.9988	0.9989	0.9989	0.9989	0.9990	0.9990
3.1	0.9990	0.9991	0.9991	0.9991	0.9992	0.9992	0.9992	0.9992	0.9993	0.9993
3.2	0.9993	0.9993	0.9994	0.9994	0.9994	0.9994	0.9994	0.9995	0.9995	0.9995
3.3	0.9995	0.9995	0.9995	0.9996	0.9996	0.9996	0.9996	0.9996	0.9996	0.9997
3.4	0.9997	0.9997	0.9997	0.9997	0.9997	0.9997	0.9997	0.9997	0.9997	0.9998

Table 2
Normal distribution

From Irwin Miller and John E. Freund, *Probability and Statistics for Engineers*, 2nd ed., © 1977, p. 487. Reprinted by permission of Prentice-Hall, Inc., Englewood Cliffs, N.J.

ν	$\alpha = 0.995$	$\alpha = 0.99$	$\alpha = 0.975$	$\alpha = 0.95$	$\alpha = 0.05$	$\alpha = 0.025$	$\alpha = 0.01$	$\alpha = 0.005$	ν
1	0.0000393	0.000157	0.000982	0.00393	3.841	5.024	6.635	7.879	1
2	0.0100	0.0201	0.0506	0.103	5.991	7.378	9.210	10.597	2
3	0.0717	0.115	0.216	0.352	7.815	9.348	11.345	12.838	3
4	0.207	0.297	0.484	0.711	9.488	11.143	13.277	14.860	4
5	0.412	0.554	0.831	1.145	11.070	12.832	13.086	16.750	5
6	0.676	0.872	1.237	1.635	12.592	14.449	16.812	18.548	6
7	0.989	1.239	1.690	2.167	14.067	16.013	18.475	20.278	7
8	1.344	1.646	2.180	2.733	15.507	17.535	20.090	21.955	8
9	1.735	2.088	2.700	3.325	16.919	19.023	21.666	23.589	9
10	2.156	2.558	3.247	3.940	18.307	20.483	23.209	25.188	10
11	2.603	3.053	3.816	4.575	19.675.	21.920	24.725	26.757	11
12	3.074	3.571	4.404	5.226	21.026	23.337	26.217	28.300	12
13	3.565	4.107	5.009	5.892	22.362	24.736	27.688	29.819	13
14	4.075	4.660	5.629	6.571	23.685	26.119	29.141	31.319	14
15	4.601	5.229	6.262	7.261	24.996	27.488	30.578	32.801	15
16	5.142	5.812	6.908	7.962	26.296	28.845	32.000	34.267	16
17	5.697	6.408	7.564	8.672	27.587	30.191	33.409	35.718	17
18	6.265	7.015	8.231	9.390	28.869	31.526	34.805	37.156	18
19	6.844	7.633	8.907	10.117	30.144	32.852	36.191	38.582	19
20	7.434	8.260	9.591	10.851	31.410	34.170	37.566	39.997	20
21	8.034	8.897	10.283	11.591	32.671	35.479	38.932	41.401	21
22	8.643	9.542	10.982	12.338	33.924	36.781	40.289	42.796	22
23	9.260	10.196	11.689	13.091	35.172	38.076	41.638	44.181	23
24	9.886	10.856	12.401	13.484	36.415	39.364	42.980	45.558	24
25	10.520	11.524	13.120	14.611	37.652	40.646	44.314	46.928	25
26	11.160	12.198	13.844	15.379	38.885	41.923	45.642	48.290	26
27	11.808	12.879	14.573	16.151	40.113	43.194	46.963	49.645	27
28	12.461	13.565	15.308	16.928	41.337	44.461	48.278	50.993	28
29	13.121	14.256	16.047	17.708	42.557	45.772	49.588	52.336	29
30	13.787	14.953	16.791	18.493	43.773	46.979	50.892	53.672	30

Table 3
Chi-square distribution

This table is based on Table 8 of *Biometrika Tables for Statisticians,*
vol. 1, 3rd edition (1966), by permission of the *Biometrika* trustees.

ν	$\alpha = 0.20$	$\alpha = 0.10$	$\alpha = 0.05$	$\alpha = 0.02$	$\alpha = 0.01$	ν
1	3.078	6.314	12.706	31.821	63.657	1
2	1.886	2.920	4.303	6.965	9.925	2
3	1.638	2.353	3.182	4.541	5.841	3
4	1.533	2.132	2.776	3.474	4.604	4
5	1.476	2.015	2.571	3.365	4.032	5
6	1.440	1.943	2.447	3.143	3.707	6
7	1.415	1.895	2.365	2.998	3.499	7
8	1.397	1.860	2.306	2.896	3.355	8
9	1.383	1.833	2.262	2.821	3.250	9
10	1.372	1.812	2.228	2.764	3.169	10
11	1.363	1.796	2.201	2.718	3.106	11
12	1.356	1.782	2.179	2.681	3.055	12
13	1.350	1.771	2.160	2.650	3.012	13
14	1.345	1.761	2.145	2.624	2.977	14
15	1.341	1.753	2.131	2.602	2.947	15
16	1.337	1.746	2.120	2.583	2.921	16
17	1.333	1.740	2.110	2.567	2.898	17
18	1.330	1.734	2.101	2.552	2.878	18
19	1.328	1.729	2.093	2.539	2.861	19
20	1.325	1.725	2.086	2.528	2.845	20
21	1.323	1.721	2.080	2.518	2.831	21
22	1.321	1.717	2.074	2.508	2.819	22
23	1.319	1.714	2.069	2.500	2.807	23
24	1.318	1.711	2.064	2.492	2.797	24
25	1.316	1.708	2.060	2.485	2.787	25
26	1.315	1.706	2.056	2.479	2.779	26
27	1.314	1.703	2.052	2.473	2.771	27
28	1.313	1.701	2.048	2.467	2.763	28
29	1.311	1.699	2.045	2.462	2.756	29
inf	1.282	1.645	1.960	2.326	2.576	inf.

Table 4
Student t-distribution

Adapted from Table IV of R. A. Fisher, *Statistical Methods for Research Workers*, 14th edition, (copyright© 1970, University of Adelaide), by permission of Macmillan Publishing Co., Inc., Hafner Press.

ν_2 = Degrees of freedom for denominator	ν_1 = Degrees of freedom for numerator																		
	1	2	3	4	5	6	7	8	9	10	12	15	20	24	30	40	60	120	∞
1	161	200	216	225	230	234	237	239	241	242	244	246	248	249	250	251	252	253	254
2	18.50	19.00	19.20	19.20	19.30	19.30	19.40	19.40	19.40	19.40	19.40	19.40	19.40	19.50	19.50	19.50	19.50	19.50	19.50
3	10.10	9.55	9.28	9.12	9.01	8.94	8.89	8.85	8.81	8.79	8.74	8.70	8.66	8.64	8.62	8.59	8.57	8.55	8.53
4	7.71	6.94	6.59	6.39	6.26	6.16	6.09	6.04	6.00	5.96	5.91	5.86	5.80	5.77	5.75	5.72	5.69	5.66	5.63
5	6.61	5.79	5.41	5.19	5.05	4.95	4.88	4.82	4.77	4.74	4.68	4.62	4.56	4.53	4.50	4.46	4.43	4.40	4.37
6	5.99	5.14	4.76	4.53	4.39	4.28	4.21	4.15	4.10	4.06	4.00	3.94	3.87	3.84	3.81	3.77	3.74	3.70	3.67
7	5.59	4.74	4.35	4.12	3.97	3.87	3.79	3.73	3.68	3.64	3.57	3.51	3.44	3.41	3.38	3.34	3.30	3.27	3.23
8	5.32	4.46	4.07	3.84	3.69	3.58	3.50	3.44	3.39	3.35	3.28	3.22	3.15	3.12	3.08	3.04	3.01	2.97	2.93
9	5.12	4.26	3.86	3.63	3.48	3.37	3.29	3.23	3.18	3.14	3.07	3.01	2.94	2.90	2.86	2.83	2.79	2.75	2.71
10	4.96	4.10	3.71	3.48	3.33	3.22	3.14	3.07	3.02	2.98	2.91	2.85	2.77	2.74	2.70	2.66	2.62	2.58	2.54
11	4.84	3.98	3.59	3.36	3.20	3.09	3.01	2.95	2.90	2.85	2.79	2.72	2.65	2.61	2.57	2.53	2.49	2.45	2.40
12	4.75	3.89	3.49	3.26	3.11	3.00	2.91	2.85	2.80	2.75	2.69	2.62	2.54	2.51	2.47	2.38	2.38	2.30	2.30
13	4.67	3.81	3.41	3.18	3.03	2.92	2.83	2.77	2.71	2.67	2.60	2.53	2.46	2.42	2.38	2.34	2.30	2.25	2.21
14	4.60	3.74	3.34	3.11	2.96	2.85	2.76	2.70	2.65	2.60	2.53	2.46	2.39	2.35	2.31	2.27	2.22	2.18	2.13
15	4.54	3.68	3.29	3.06	2.90	2.79	2.71	2.64	2.59	2.54	2.48	2.40	2.33	2.29	2.25	2.20	2.16	2.11	2.07
16	4.49	3.63	3.24	3.01	2.85	2.74	2.66	2.59	2.54	2.49	2.42	2.35	2.28	2.24	2.19	2.15	2.11	2.06	2.01
17	4.45	3.59	3.20	2.96	2.81	2.70	2.61	2.55	2.49	2.45	2.38	2.31	2.23	2.19	2.15	2.10	2.06	2.01	1.96
18	4.41	3.55	3.16	2.93	2.77	2.66	2.58	2.51	2.46	2.41	2.34	2.27	2.19	2.15	2.11	2.06	2.02	1.97	1.93
19	4.38	3.52	3.13	2.90	2.74	2.63	2.54	2.48	2.42	2.38	2.31	2.23	2.16	2.11	2.07	2.03	1.98	1.93	1.88
20	4.35	3.49	3.10	2.87	2.71	2.60	2.51	2.45	2.39	2.35	2.28	2.20	2.12	2.08	2.04	1.99	1.95	1.90	1.84
21	4.32	3.47	3.07	2.84	2.68	2.57	2.49	2.42	2.37	2.32	2.25	2.18	2.10	2.05	2.01	1.96	1.92	1.87	1.81
22	4.30	3.44	3.05	2.82	2.66	2.55	2.46	2.40	2.34	2.30	2.23	2.15	2.07	2.03	1.98	1.94	1.89	1.84	1.78
23	4.28	3.42	3.03	2.80	2.64	2.53	2.44	2.37	2.32	2.27	2.20	2.13	2.05	2.01	1.96	1.91	1.86	1.81	1.76
24	4.26	3.40	3.01	2.78	2.62	2.51	2.42	2.36	2.30	2.25	2.18	2.11	2.03	1.98	1.94	1.89	1.84	1.79	1.73
25	4.24	3.39	2.99	2.76	2.60	2.49	2.40	2.34	2.28	2.24	2.16	2.09	2.01	1.96	1.92	1.87	1.82	1.77	1.71
30	4.17	3.32	2.92	2.69	2.53	2.42	2.33	2.27	2.21	2.16	2.09	2.01	1.93	1.89	1.84	1.79	1.74	1.68	1.62
40	4.08	3.23	2.84	2.61	2.45	2.34	2.25	2.18	2.12	2.08	2.00	1.92	1.84	1.79	1.74	1.69	1.64	1.58	1.51
60	4.00	3.15	2.76	2.53	2.37	2.25	2.17	2.10	2.04	1.99	1.92	1.84	1.75	1.70	1.65	1.59	1.53	1.47	1.39
120	3.92	3.07	2.68	2.45	2.29	2.18	2.09	2.02	1.96	1.91	1.83	1.75	1.66	1.61	1.55	1.50	1.43	1.35	1.25
∞	3.84	3.00	2.60	2.37	2.21	2.10	2.01	1.94	1.88	1.83	1.75	1.67	1.57	1.52	1.46	1.39	1.32	1.22	1.00

Table 5(a)
F-distribution—values of $F_{0.05}$

This table is reproduced from M. Merrington and C. M. Thompson, "Tables of percentage points of the inverted beta (F) distribution," Biometrika, vol. 33 (1943) by permission of the Biometrika trustees.

ν_1 = Degrees of freedom for numerator

ν_2 = Degrees of freedom for denominator	1	2	3	4	5	6	7	8	9	10	12	15	20	24	30	40	60	120	∞
1	4,052	5,000	5,403	5,625	5,764	5,859	5,928	5,982	6,023	6,056	6,106	6,157	6,209	6,235	6,261	6,287	6,313	6,339	6,366
2	98.50	99.00	99.20	99.20	99.30	99.30	99.40	99.40	99.40	99.40	99.40	99.40	99.40	99.50	99.50	99.50	99.50	99.50	99.50
3	34.10	30.80	29.50	28.70	28.20	27.90	27.70	27.50	27.30	27.20	27.10	26.90	26.70	26.60	26.50	26.40	26.30	26.20	26.10
4	21.20	18.00	16.70	16.00	15.50	15.20	15.00	14.80	14.70	14.50	14.40	14.20	14.00	13.90	13.80	13.70	13.70	13.60	13.50
5	16.30	13.30	12.10	11.40	11.00	10.70	10.50	10.30	10.20	10.10	9.89	9.72	9.55	9.47	9.38	9.29	9.20	9.11	9.02
6	13.70	10.90	9.78	9.15	8.75	8.47	8.26	8.10	7.98	7.87	7.72	7.56	7.40	7.31	7.23	7.14	7.06	6.97	6.88
7	12.20	9.55	8.45	7.85	7.46	7.19	6.99	6.84	6.72	6.62	6.47	6.31	6.16	6.07	5.99	5.91	5.82	5.74	5.65
8	11.30	8.65	7.59	7.01	6.63	6.37	6.18	6.03	5.91	5.81	5.67	5.52	5.36	5.28	5.20	5.12	5.03	4.95	4.83
9	10.60	8.02	6.99	6.42	6.06	5.80	5.61	5.47	5.35	5.26	5.11	4.96	4.81	4.73	4.65	4.57	4.48	4.40	4.31
10	10.00	7.56	6.55	5.99	5.64	5.39	5.20	5.06	4.94	4.85	4.71	4.56	4.41	4.33	4.25	4.17	4.08	4.00	3.91
11	9.65	7.21	6.22	5.67	5.32	5.07	4.89	4.74	4.63	4.54	4.40	4.25	4.10	4.02	3.94	3.86	3.78	3.69	3.60
12	9.33	6.93	5.95	5.41	5.06	4.82	4.64	4.50	4.39	4.30	4.16	4.01	3.86	3.78	3.70	3.62	3.54	3.45	3.36
13	9.07	6.70	5.74	5.21	4.86	4.62	4.44	4.30	4.19	4.10	3.96	3.82	3.66	3.59	3.51	3.43	3.34	3.25	3.17
14	8.86	6.51	5.56	5.04	4.70	4.46	4.28	4.14	4.03	3.94	3.80	3.66	3.51	3.43	3.35	3.27	3.18	3.09	3.00
15	8.68	6.36	5.42	4.89	4.56	4.32	4.14	4.00	3.89	3.80	3.67	3.52	3.37	3.29	3.21	3.13	3.05	2.96	2.87
16	8.53	6.23	5.29	4.77	4.44	4.20	4.03	3.89	3.78	3.69	3.55	3.41	3.26	3.18	3.10	3.02	2.93	2.84	2.75
17	8.40	6.11	5.19	4.67	4.34	4.10	3.93	3.79	3.68	3.59	3.46	3.31	3.16	3.08	3.00	2.92	2.83	2.75	2.65
18	8.29	6.01	5.09	4.58	4.25	4.01	3.84	3.71	3.60	3.51	3.37	3.23	3.08	3.00	2.92	2.84	2.75	2.66	2.57
19	8.19	5.93	5.01	4.50	4.17	3.94	3.77	3.63	3.52	3.43	3.30	3.15	3.00	2.92	2.84	2.76	2.67	2.58	2.49
20	8.10	5.85	4.94	4.43	4.10	3.87	3.70	3.56	3.46	3.37	3.23	3.09	2.94	2.86	2.78	2.69	2.61	2.52	2.42
21	8.02	5.78	4.87	4.37	4.04	3.81	3.64	3.51	3.40	3.31	3.17	3.03	2.88	2.80	2.72	2.64	2.55	2.46	2.36
22	7.95	5.72	4.82	4.31	3.99	3.76	3.59	3.45	3.35	3.26	3.12	2.98	2.83	2.75	2.67	2.58	2.50	2.40	2.31
23	7.88	5.66	4.76	4.26	3.94	3.71	3.54	3.41	3.30	3.21	3.07	2.93	2.78	2.70	2.62	2.54	2.45	2.35	2.26
24	7.82	5.61	4.72	4.22	3.90	3.67	3.50	3.36	3.26	3.17	3.03	2.89	2.74	2.66	2.58	2.49	2.40	2.31	2.21
25	7.77	5.57	4.68	4.18	3.86	3.63	3.46	3.32	3.22	3.13	2.99	2.85	2.70	2.62	2.53	2.45	2.36	2.27	2.17
30	7.56	5.39	4.51	4.02	3.70	3.47	3.30	3.17	3.07	2.98	2.84	2.70	2.55	2.47	2.39	2.30	2.21	2.11	2.01
40	7.31	5.18	4.31	3.83	3.51	3.29	3.12	2.99	2.89	2.80	2.66	2.52	2.37	2.29	2.20	2.11	2.02	1.92	1.80
60	7.08	4.98	4.13	3.65	3.34	3.12	2.95	2.82	2.72	2.63	2.50	2.35	2.20	2.12	2.03	1.94	1.84	1.73	1.60
120	6.85	4.79	3.95	3.48	3.17	2.96	2.79	2.66	2.56	2.47	2.34	2.19	2.03	1.95	1.86	1.76	1.66	1.53	1.38
∞	6.63	4.61	3.78	3.32	3.02	2.80	2.64	2.51	2.41	2.32	2.18	2.04	1.88	1.79	1.70	1.59	1.47	1.32	1.00

Table 5(b)
F-distribution—values of $F_{0.01}$

This table is reproduced from M. Merrington and C. M. Thompson, "Tables of percentage points of the inverted beta (F) distribution," *Biometrika*, vol. 33 (1943), by permission of the *Biometrika* trustees.

Sample size n	$D_{.10}$	$D_{.05}$	$D_{.01}$
1	0.950	0.975	0.995
2	0.776	0.842	0.929
3	0.642	0.708	0.828
4	0.564	0.624	0.733
5	0.510	0.565	0.669
6	0.470	0.521	0.618
7	0.438	0.486	0.577
8	0.411	0.457	0.543
9	0.388	0.432	0.514
10	0.368	0.410	0.490
11	0.352	0.391	0.468
12	0.338	0.375	0.450
13	0.325	0.361	0.433
14	0.314	0.349	0.418
15	0.304	0.338	0.404
16	0.295	0.328	0.392
17	0.286	0.318	0.381
18	0.278	0.309	0.371
19	0.272	0.301	0.363
20	0.264	0.294	0.356
25	0.24	0.27	0.32
30	0.22	0.24	0.29

Table 6
Critical values of D

Adapted from F. J. Massey, Jr., "The Kolgomorov-Smirnov test for goodness of fit," *J. Amer. Stat. Assoc.*, vol. 46 (1951), p. 70, with the kind permission of the author and publisher.

1306	1189	5731	3968	5606	5084	8947	3897	1636	7810
0422	2431	0649	8085	5053	4722	6598	5044	9040	5121
6597	2022	6168	5060	8656	6733	6364	7649	1871	4328
7965	6541	5645	6243	7658	6903	9911	5740	7824	8520
7695	6937	0406	8894	0441	8135	9797	7285	5905	9539
5160	7851	8464	6789	3938	4197	6511	0407	9239	2232
2961	0551	0539	8288	7478	7565	5581	5771	5442	8761
1428	4183	4312	5445	4854	9157	9158	5218	1464	3634
3666	5642	4539	1561	7849	7520	2547	0756	1206	2033
6543	6799	7454	9052	6689	1946	2574	9386	0304	7945
9975	6080	7423	3175	9377	6951	6519	8287	8994	5532
4866	0956	7545	7723	8085	4948	2228	9583	4415	7065
8239	7068	6694	5168	3117	1568	0237	6160	9585	1133
8722	9191	3386	3443	0434	4586	4150	1224	6204	0937
1330	9120	8785	8382	2929	7089	3109	6742	2468	7025
2296	2952	4764	9070	6356	9192	4012	0618	2219	1109
3582	7052	3132	4519	9250	2486	0830	8472	2160	7046
5872	9207	7222	6494	8973	3545	6967	8490	5264	9821
1134	6324	6201	3792	5651	0538	4676	2064	0584	7996
1403	4497	7390	8503	8239	4236	8022	2914	4368	4529
3393	7025	3381	3553	2128	1021	8353	6413	5161	8583
1137	7896	3602	0060	7850	7626	0854	6565	4260	6220
7437	5198	8772	6927	8527	6851	2709	5992	7383	1071
8414	8820	3917	7238	9821	6073	6658	1280	9643	7761
8398	5224	2749	7311	5740	9771	7826	9533	3800	4553
0995	8935	2939	3092	2496	0359	0318	4697	7181	4035
6657	0755	9685	4017	6581	7292	5643	5064	1142	1297
8875	8369	7868	0190	9278	1709	4253	9346	4335	3769
8399	6702	0586	6428	7985	2979	4513	1970	1989	3105
6703	1024	2064	0393	6815	8502	1375	4171	6970	1201
4730	1653	9032	9855	0957	7366	0325	5178	7959	5371
8400	6834	3187	8688	1079	1480	6776	9888	7585	9998
3647	8002	6726	0877	4552	3238	7542	7804	3933	9475
6789	5197	8037	2354	9262	5497	0005	3986	1767	7981
2630	2721	2810	2185	6323	5679	4931	8336	6662	3566
1374	8625	1644	3342	1587	0762	6057	8011	2666	3759
1519	7625	9110	4409	0239	7059	3415	5537	2250	7292
9678	2877	7579	4935	0449	8119	6969	5383	1717	6719
0882	6781	3538	4090	3092	2365	6001	3446	9985	6007
0006	4205	2389	4365	1981	8158	7784	6256	3842	5603
4611	9861	7916	9305	2074	9462	0254	4827	9198	3974
1093	3784	4190	6332	1175	8599	9735	8584	6581	7194
3374	3545	6865	8819	3342	1676	2264	6014	5012	2458
3650	9676	1436	4374	4716	5548	8276	6235	6742	2154
7292	5749	7977	7602	9205	3599	3880	9537	4423	2330
2353	8319	2850	4026	3027	1708	3518	7034	7132	6903
1094	2009	8919	5676	7283	4982	9642	9235	8167	3366
0568	4002	0587	7165	1094	2006	7471	0940	4366	9554
5606	4070	5233	4339	6543	6695	5799	58``	3953	9458
8285	7537	1181	2300	5294	6892	1627	3372	1952	3028

Table 7
Random digits

From D. B. Owen, *Handbook of Statistical Tables*, pp. 530–33, Reading, Mass.: Addison-Wesley (1962). Reprinted with permission.

2444	9039	4803	8568	1590	2420	2547	2470	8179	4617
5748	7767	2800	6289	2814	8281	1549	9519	3341	1192
7761	8583	0852	5619	6864	8506	9643	7763	9611	1289
6838	9280	2654	0812	3988	2146	5095	0150	8043	9079
6440	2631	3033	9167	4998	7036	0133	7428	9702	1376
8829	0094	2887	3802	5497	0318	5168	6377	9216	2802
9845	4796	2951	4449	1999	2691	5328	7674	7004	6212
5072	9000	3887	5739	7920	6074	4715	3681	2721	2701
9035	0553	1272	2600	3828	8197	8852	9092	8027	6144
5562	1080	2222	0336	1411	0303	7424	3713	9278	1918
2757	2650	8727	3953	9579	2442	8041	9869	2887	3933
6397	1848	1476	0787	4990	4666	1208	2769	3922	1158
9208	7641	3575	4279	1282	1840	5999	1806	7809	5885
2418	9289	6120	8141	3908	5577	3590	2317	8975	4593
7300	9006	5659	8258	3662	0332	5369	3640	0563	7939
6870	2535	8916	3245	2256	4350	6064	2438	2002	1272
2914	7309	4045	7513	3195	4166	0878	5184	6680	2655
0868	8657	8118	6340	9452	7460	3291	5778	1167	0312
7994	6579	6461	2292	9554	8309	5036	0974	9517	8293
8587	0764	6687	9150	1642	2050	4934	0027	1376	5040
8016	8345	2257	5084	8004	7949	3205	3972	7640	3478
5581	5775	7517	9076	4699	8313	8401	7147	9416	7184
2015	3364	6688	2631	2152	2220	1637	8333	4838	5699
7327	8987	5741	0102	1173	7350	7080	7420	1847	0741
3589	1991	1764	8355	9684	9423	7101	1063	4151	4875
2188	6454	7319	1215	0473	6589	2355	9579	7004	6209
2924	0472	9878	7966	2491	5662	5635	2789	2564	1249
1961	1669	2219	1113	9175	0260	4046	8142	4432	2664
2393	9637	0410	7536	0972	5153	0708	1935	1143	1704
7585	4424	2648	6728	2233	3518	7267	1732	1926	3833
0197	4021	9207	7327	9212	7017	8060	6216	1942	6817
9719	5336	5532	8537	2980	8252	4971	0110	6209	1556
8866	4785	6007	8006	9043	4109	5570	9249	9905	2152
5744	3957	8786	9023	1472	7275	1014	1104	0832	7680
7149	5721	1389	6581	7196	7072	6360	3084	7009	0239
7710	8479	9345	7773	9086	1202	8845	3163	7937	6163
5246	5651	0432	8644	6341	9661	2361	8377	8673	6098
3576	0013	7381	0124	8559	9813	9080	6984	0926	2169
3026	1464	2671	4691	0353	5289	8754	2442	7799	8983
6591	4365	8717	2365	5686	8377	8675	9798	7745	6360
0402	3257	0480	5038	1998	2935	1306	1190	2406	2596
7105	7654	4745	4482	8471	1424	2031	7803	4367	6816
7181	4140	1046	0885	1264	7755	1653	8924	5822	4401
3655	3282	2178	8134	3291	7262	8229	2866	7065	4806
5121	6717	3117	1901	5184	6467	8954	3884	0279	8635
3618	3098	9208	7429	1578	1917	7927	2696	3704	0833
0166	3638	4947	1414	4799	9189	2459	5056	5982	6154
6187	9653	3658	4730	1652	8096	8288	9368	5531	7788
1234	1448	0276	7290	1667	2823	3755	5642	4854	8844
8949	8731	4875	5724	2962	1182	2930	7539	4526	7252

Table 7 — *Continued*
Random digits

1758	1489	2774	6033	9813	1052	1816	7484	1699	7350
6430	8803	0478	4157	5626	1603	1339	4666	1207	2135
4893	8857	1717	1533	6572	8408	2173	4754	0272	1305
1516	2733	7326	8674	9233	1799	5281	0797	0885	0947
4950	3171	5756	3036	9047	8719	8498	1312	7124	4787
0549	6775	9360	6639	0990	0037	7309	4702	0812	4195
1018	7027	7569	7549	2539	2315	8030	7663	3881	8264
2241	9965	9729	7092	4891	9239	0738	1804	3025	1030
1602	0708	2201	9848	6241	1084	8142	8555	7291	5016
5840	8381	1549	9902	6935	3681	6420	0214	8489	5911
1676	0367	7484	1595	5693	3008	9816	7311	6162	1024
6048	4175	8940	9029	8306	8892	4127	1709	4043	6591
5549	9621	2563	0515	0560	9021	0632	4309	4044	7010
5317	4584	9418	4600	0640	9668	6379	6515	6310	7916
2532	7784	6469	4793	5957	4123	6555	3237	6915	6960
2300	5412	3106	4877	6936	4109	8060	1896	6881	7028
1499	8699	4534	5367	7557	2701	2587	2521	2159	6991
6201	3791	2946	2863	5684	5517	7448	2227	8991	7505
6839	9736	8312	8068	7339	5395	9559	3416	6169	5484
0092	5537	1933	3186	8482	6680	2656	1864	4535	2193
1862	3253	6515	6299	2929	2219	9145	7511	2146	4962
9886	6744	3097	8894	0446	3494	8211	1723	6138	3181
5289	9071	1231	0651	9109	7448	2228	9700	0224	4595
2685	7104	7193	5506	2993	7028	4830	3866	8698	0277
6055	7092	4786	6847	4543	7448	2017	4114	8385	3625
4092	4995	0280	9371	3375	3503	4496	8642	5388	1831
5951	4937	3670	5797	5030	6524	2265	7748	7875	6976
7687	3849	4821	2373	1157	4208	3623	9399	7349	6663
9886	3463	2055	4872	2702	1807	9056	8576	4237	8757
3193	3011	8899	6721	0086	2623	7977	7578	4024	1997
9181	7365	9135	1669	2007	7784	6363	6913	6017	6588
9459	2175	5728	4933	0111	6703	1234	2410	1620	4859
9874	5278	2849	3163	6372	2600	9887	7060	3919	1111
7729	2099	7513	2774	6030	8260	9023	1368	9513	6122
4699	8102	3001	7947	1659	6571	1969	7152	7356	1062
1872	7244	3954	7422	2688	8649	0156	1965	5012	2461
9636	0123	2438	1757	4204	1650	2486	0002	4724	7412
6403	9054	7632	7469	8973	3332	0294	5062	0303	7315
4433	3293	2314	7431	2389	4094	5062	0118	0046	6070
2361	3933	8026	0431	8012	3214	8927	7355	0585	7638
4077	8463	6580	6983	0181	3327	6812	1755	3387	4569
6678	0006	3686	8478	9187	2291	9032	9852	1450	7940
6499	2582	5207	4627	0456	4245	3583	8996	1006	5839
6663	9021	0319	7908	1241	9977	7042	6923	2539	2103
9999	4503	6105	5525	1068	6272	7036	0200	6291	2841
9048	6982	3845	6865	9029	8700	0349	3416	8236	1129
5136	9653	3654	2863	5565	8923	5596	8389	9927	9092
9906	1070	5693	3012	1218	7309	4361	3041	4327	8423
4198	7035	8182	6270	6461	2079	2998	5507	9605	6734
2030	5878	8989	6789	4359	1820	5063	9199	7751	6337

Table 7 — *Continued*
Random digits

4357	4146	8353	9952	8004	7945	1530	5207	4730	1967
5339	7325	6862	7584	8634	3485	2278	5832	0612	8118
6583	8433	0717	0606	9284	2719	1888	2889	0285	2765
6564	3526	2171	3809	3428	5523	9078	0648	7768	3326
4811	1933	3763	6265	8931	0649	8085	6177	4450	2139
6931	7236	1230	0441	4013	1352	6563	1499	7332	3068
8755	3390	6120	7825	9005	7012	1643	9934	4044	7022
6742	2260	3443	0190	9278	1816	7697	7933	0067	2906
6655	3930	9014	6032	7574	1685	5258	3100	5358	1929
8514	4806	4124	9286	0449	5051	4772	4651	0038	1580
8135	5004	7299	8981	4689	1950	2271	2201	8344	3852
4414	6855	0127	5489	5157	6386	7492	3736	7164	0498
3727	7959	5056	5983	8021	0204	7616	4325	7454	5039
5434	7342	0314	7525	0067	2800	6292	4706	3454	6881
7195	8828	9869	2785	3186	8375	7414	7232	0401	2483
2705	8245	6251	9611	1077	0641	0195	7024	6202	3899
1547	8981	4972	1280	4286	5678	0338	8096	8284	7010
3424	1435	1354	7631	7260	7361	0151	8903	9056	8684
8969	7551	3695	4915	7921	2913	3840	9031	9747	9735
5225	8720	8898	2478	3342	9200	8836	7269	2992	6284
6432	9861	1516	2849	2539	2208	4595	8616	6170	5865
3085	5903	8319	2744	0814	7318	8619	7614	3265	5999
0264	1246	3687	9759	6995	6565	3949	1012	0179	0059
8710	2419	6065	0036	9650	2027	6042	5467	1839	5577
5736	9001	3132	4521	9973	5070	8078	4150	2276	5059
7529	1339	4802	5751	3785	7125	4922	8877	9530	6499
5133	7995	8030	7408	2186	0725	5554	5664	6791	9677
3170	9915	6960	2621	6718	4059	9919	1007	6469	5410
3024	0680	1127	8088	0200	5868	0084	6362	6808	3727
4398	3121	7749	8191	2087	8270	5233	3980	6774	8522
0082	5419	7659	2061	2506	7573	1157	3979	2309	0811
4351	6516	6814	5898	3973	8103	3616	2049	7843	0568
3268	0086	7580	1337	3884	5679	4830	4509	9587	2184
4391	8487	4884	1488	2249	6661	5774	7205	2717	7030
7328	0705	0652	9424	7082	8579	5647	5571	9667	8555
3835	2938	2671	4691	0559	8382	2825	4928	5379	8635
8731	4980	8674	4506	7262	8127	2022	2178	7463	4842
2995	7868	0683	3768	0625	9887	7060	0514	0034	8600
5597	9028	5660	5006	8325	9677	2169	3196	0357	7811
3081	5876	8150	1360	1868	9265	3277	8465	7502	6458
7406	4439	5683	6877	2920	9588	3002	2869	3746	3690
5969	9442	7696	7510	1620	4973	1911	1288	6160	9797
4765	9647	4364	1037	4975	1998	1359	1346	6125	5078
3219	2532	7577	2815	8696	9248	9410	9282	6572	3940
6906	8859	5044	8826	6218	3206	9034	0843	9832	2703
7993	3141	0103	4528	7988	4635	8478	9094	9077	5306
2549	3737	7686	0723	4505	6841	1379	6460	1869	5700
3672	7033	4844	0149	7412	6370	1884	0717	5740	8477
2217	0293	3978	5933	1032	5192	1732	2137	9357	5941
3162	9968	6369	1258	0416	4326	7840	6525	2608	5255

Table 7 — Continued
Random digits

Index

Activity:
   definition of, 11, 127
   endogenous, 12
   exogenous, 12
Additive congruential method, 82
Adkins, G., 10
ADVANCE block, 165
ALGOL, 156
Analog computer, 195
Analysis of simulation results, 144
Application phase, 10
Attribute, 11, 127, 133

Bernoulli distribution, 42
Binomial distribution, 43
Binomially distributed random numbers, 93
Blocking technique, 147
Bobillier, P., 164

Central limit theorem, 49, 92
Chain:
   current events, 135
   future events, 135
Characteristic equation, 188
Chi-square distribution, 50
Chi-square test, 9, 70
Complement, 19
Complete enumeration, 222
Completely randomized design, 211
Compound event, 18
Conditional probability, 21, 22
Confidence interval, 60

Consistent estimator, 60
Consolidated Analysis Centers, Inc. 172
Contingent event, 134
Continuous distributions, 28
Continuous system simulation, 181
Control variables, 144
Correlation, 41
Coordinate search, 224
Covariance, 40
Coveyou, R. R., 83
Critical region, 61
CSMP III, 204
Cumulative distribution function:
   definition, 39
   empirical, 55, 57
   properties of, 39
Curve:
   operating characteristic, 64
   power, 65

Degrees of freedom, 51, 56
Density function:
   marginal, 40
   probability; 29, 31, 39
DEPART block, 168
Design of experiments, 209
Designs:
   completely randomized, 211
   factorial, 216
   fractional factorial, 216, 220
   randomized complete block, 214
Difference equations, 105, 113

CONTENTS